ASSESSING WRITERS' KNOWLEDGE AND PROCESSES OF COMPOSING

Writing Research

Multidisciplinary Inquiries into the Nature of Writing

edited by Marcia Farr, University of Illinois at Chicago

Arthur N. Applebee, *Contexts for Learning to Write*

Lester Faigley, Roger Cherry, David Jolliffe, and Anna Skinner, *Assessing Writers' Knowledge and Processes of Composing*

Marcia Farr (ed.), *Advances in Writing Research, Volume One: Children's Early Writing Development*

Sarah W. Freedman (ed.), *The Acquisition of Written Language: Response and Revision*

IN PREPARATION

Carole Edelsky, *Writing in a Bilingual Program: Había Una Vez*

Robert Gundlach, *Children and Writing in American Education*

Martha L. King and Victor Rentel, *The Development of Meaning in Writing: Children 5–10*

Judith Langer, *Children Reading and Writing: Structures and Strategies*

Anthony Petrosky (ed.), *Reading and Writing: Theory and Research*

Leo Ruth and Sandra Murphy, *Designing Writing Tasks for the Assessment of Writing*

David Smith, *Explorations in the Culture of Literacy*

Jana Staton, *Interactive Writing in Dialogue Journals: Linguistic, Social, and Cognitive Views*

Elizabeth Sulzby, *A Longitudinal Study of Emergent Writing and Reading in 5–6 Year Olds*

William Teale and Elizabeth Sulzby (eds.), *Emergent Literacy: Writing and Reading*

Stephen Witte, Keith Walters, Mary Trachsel, Roger Cherry, and Paul Meyer, *Literacy and Writing Assessment: Issues, Traditions, Directions*

Assessing Writers' Knowledge and Processes of Composing

Lester Faigley
University of Texas at Austin

Roger D. Cherry
New Mexico State University

David A. Jolliffe
University of Illinois at Chicago

Anna M. Skinner
University of Texas at Austin

ABLEX PUBLISHING CORPORATION
NORWOOD, NEW JERSEY

Second Printing 1989

Printed in the United States of America.

Library of Congress Cataloging in Publication Data
Main entry under title:

Assessing writers' knowledge and processes of composing.

(Writing Research)
Bibliography: p.
Includes indexes.
1. English language—Rhetoric—Study and teaching—(Higher)—Evaluation. 2. English language—Rhetoric—Ability testing. I. Faigley, Lester, 1947–   .
PE1404.A85 1985   808'.042'071173   84-28428
ISBN 0-89391-226-3
ISBN 0-89391-320-0 (pbk.)

Ablex Publishing Corporation
355 Chestnut Street
Norwood, New Jersey 07648

Contents

v

Writing Research

Multidisciplinary Inquiries into the Nature of Writing

Marcia Farr, series editor
University of Illinois at Chicago

PREFACE

This series of volumes presents the results of recent scholarly inquiry into the nature of writing. The research presented comes from a mix of disciplines, those which have emerged as significant within the last decade or so in the burgeoning field of writing research. These primarily include English education, linguistics, psychology, anthropology, and rhetoric. A note here on the distinction between field and discipline might be useful: a field can be a multidisciplinary entity focused on a set of significant questions about a central concern (e.g., American Studies), while a discipline usually shares theoretical and methodological approaches which may have a substantial tradition behind them. Writing research, then, is a field, if not yet a discipline.

The history of this particular field is unique. Much of the recent work in this field, and much that is being reported in this series, has been conceptualized and funded by the National Institute of Education. Following a planning conference in June 1977, a program of basic research on the teaching and learning of writing was developed and funded annually. The initial research funded under this program is now coming to fruition, providing both implications for educational improvement and directions for future research. This series is intended as one important outlet for these results.

Preface

This book has three main purposes: to provide a thorough review of research on writers' knowledge and processes of composing, to argue the need for a theory of writing assessment, and to offer two detailed examples of theory-driven approaches to writing assessement. The work reported here was begun as part of a larger project aimed at developing new ways of evaluating writing instruction and writing abilities sponsored by the Fund for the Improvement of Postsecondary Education and the University of Texas at Austin.

Our work has benefited from the contributions of many people; consequently, our debts are many. First, we are grateful to those persons who made the FIPSE project possible. Without their support very little of the work reported in this book could have been accomplished. In particular, we thank Richard Hendrix, our Project Officer at FIPSE, Dean Robert King and Associate Deans Joseph Horn and John Weinstock of the College of Liberal Arts, and Joseph Moldenhauer, Chair, and Joseph Kruppa, Associate Chair, of the Department of English at the University of Texas. We also thank Barbara McFarland, Dorothy Rattey, and our project secretaries, Rebecca Francis and Susan Hackworth, for guiding us through the jungles of bureaucracy that accompany large academic projects. Clare Alesch helped us duplicate, collate, and staple—tasks we all had more than our fill of by the time we finished.

Much of the thinking represented in this book reflects our frequent discussions with the other members of the FIPSE project: John Daly, Jim Kinneavy, Paul Meyer, Tom Miller, Mary Trachsel, Keith Walters, and Steve Witte. Several other people read or heard parts of the book as it evolved. We appreciate the help of the consultants to the FIPSE project—Linda Flower, Sarah Freedman, Richard Larson, Richard Lloyd-Jones, and Ellen Nold—and the comments and suggestions of Andrew Cooper, Larry Johannessen, Betsy Kahn, Ann Matsuhashi, Greg Myers, Marty Nystrand, Lee Odell, and Mike Rose. Besides helping us to avoid numerous pitfalls and to understand better what we were doing, they encouraged us to finish when we were ready to quit. William Hayes and William Koch gave us advice on statistical analysis. Andrew Kerek and Maxine Hairston carefully read the entire manuscript in its penultimate version, and we profited greatly from their comments. Such friends are rare. We also thank the series editor, Marcia Farr, for her help in conceiving the form of the book and for her practical suggestions on other matters.

Finally, we are grateful to the numerous teachers and students who took time to contribute to our research efforts. To them this book is dedicated.

Austin, Texas
October 1983

Introduction

The purposes of higher education in the United States have changed radically since the turn of the century when composition courses were instituted in colleges and universities. At that time over 60% of the workforce consisted of unskilled laborers, and college-educated people formed an elite class. Writing was considered one of the "polite arts," and the ability to create a graceful written product was the mark of a tastefully educated person within this class. The idea that writing might be a useful tool in the workplace was just beginning to emerge (see Alred, Reep, & Limaye, 1981). Today unskilled laborers make up only 5% of the workforce, and over half of those who graduate from high school attend college. Writing is taught in high schools and colleges not only as a means of personal development and communication but also as a professional necessity. These changes raise several important questions regarding the nature and uses of writing: How have changes in the economy and in technology affected what and how we write? Do these changes fully explain why writing skills are now a chief focus of attention in educational programs at all levels? Are writing skills useful in private life? Will writing skills continue to be valued in the future?

Some information pertaining to these questions comes in a study conducted as part of the same project that produced the research described in this book. Faigley and Miller (1982) surveyed 200 people representing proportionately the kinds of occupations that college-trained people enter and the kinds of employers for whom college-trained people work. They found that writing is an important and frequently used skill across all major types of occupations and employers of college-trained people. Moreover, Faigley and Miller observed that the nature of writing in the workplace is in a period of change. Over a quarter of the people surveyed used computers for communicating in writing. Likewise, over a quarter of those sampled regularly dictated letters and reports.

There is also evidence to suggest that writing technologies are changing the workplace itself. In 1981, for example, there were approximately one million word processing installations in the United States (Gottschall, 1981). That number doubled by 1983. Strassman (1981) foresees over 20 million electronic workstations in 1990. Between 1972 and 1980, the number of computer and peripheral equipment operators tripled, while the number of stenographers dropped by half (Giuliano, 1982). Moreover, Giuliano anticipates the development of the "virtual office," an extension of the traditional workplace made possible by briefcase-size computers that can be linked to an organization's central computer.

Home computers are changing the way people write off the job as well. Computer networks now feature "bulletin boards" that allow users to discuss subjects of common interest. Hobbies (such as chess) and other recreational interests (such as science fiction) are prominent topics. Computer networks may result in the use of electronic mail at home as well as at the workplace, and people will likely discover as yet unforeseen uses of writing on their own. Secondary effects of technology, however, are much more difficult to anticipate than primary effects. It would have been easier, for example, to predict that Teflon could solve heat problems during spacecraft re-entry than to predict that Teflon skillets would replace standard frying pans.

The changes in writing brought about by widespread use of computers and other advanced communication systems are being compared to the changes brought about by the advent of literacy. Social historians such as Goody and Watt (1963), Havelock (1963, 1976), and McLuhan (1962) have pointed to several important effects of literacy. According to these historians, literacy changed what people remembered and thought was useful information, destroyed monopolies on knowledge by making certain kinds of knowledge widely available, brought uniformity and standardization, and altered how people classify and interpret the world. Some scientists and social historians claim that similar kinds of changes are occurring now. They believe that we are in the early stages of what Simon (1977) calls the "third information revolution." (The first according to Simon was the invention of written language, the second the invention of mechanical printing.)

One development that suggests our conceptions of literacy are changing is the current concern about a "literacy crisis." The term came to the public's attention following the publication of a *Newsweek* article titled "Why Johnny Can't Write," which concluded that "the U.S. eductional system is spawning a generation of semiliterates" (December 8, 1975, p. 58). Articles and broadcasts have continued to echo the same conclusion. For example, an article in *US News and World Report* on May 17, 1982, titled "Ahead: A Nation of Illiterates?" predicts that we are headed for "a new kind of dark age" (p. 53). Such pronouncements seem paradoxical in a nation that confers over 1 million bachelor's, master's, and doctor's degrees each year and enrolls over half of its high-school graduates in some form of postsecondary education (Grant & Eiden, 1982). In one respect, dire pronouncements of standards being broached and language abused are nothing new. Pattison (1982) calls these moans of despair "the same old whine." Nevertheless, complaints about the reading and writing skills of young Americans are coming from new sources. In particular, criticism of the literacy skills of college graduates is heard increasingly from those in the professions that hire these graduates. The popular media depict "illiteracy" in terms of falling test scores and deviance from standard usage, but Faigley and Miller (1982) found that employers are just as concerned with college graduates' abilities to write for different audiences and purposes.

Part of the confusion inherent in the "literacy crisis" is that more than one definition of literacy is operating. Pattison (1982) distinguishes two senses of literacy. The first assumes that literacy means being able to read and write. Literacy by this definition is monolithic and is based on some notion of a standard written dialect. By Pattison's second definition, literacy is "foremost [the] consciousness of the problems posed by language, and secondarily skill in the technologies, such as rhetoric and writing, by which this consciousness is expressed" (p. vi). This second sense of literacy defines it as the ability to use language in specific communities. It is what we mean when we say that most English teachers are illiterate in astrophysics. This second definition of literacy is necessarily pluralistic and suggests that definitions of literacy are always relative and always changing.

Changing conceptions of literacy have caused teachers of writing to reexamine how writing is understood and taught. First, teachers have had to question whether the writing instruction that students receive in school will necessarily be sufficient training for the type of writing they will have to do after they leave school. Sensing that current growth in knowledge and technology is changing the type of work people must do faster than traditional education can accommodate the change, educational planners have developed the concept of "lifelong learning." The influential UNESCO study, *Learning to Be* (Faure et al., 1972), maintains that every person must be in a position to keep learning throughout his life. Education must be carried on at all ages . . . according to each individual's needs and convenience. (p. 181)

Education should be dispensed and acquired through a multiplicity of means. All kinds of existing institutions, whether designed for teaching or not, and many forms of social and economic activity, must be used for educational purposes. The important thing is not the path an individual has followed, but what he has learned or acquired. (p. 185)

One result of the lifelong learning concept has been the development of teaching and research programs to improve written communication within business and government.

Changing conceptions of literacy have also raised the question of whether the writing instruction traditionally offered by English departments is the most useful training in composition for all students. Dissatisfaction with traditional composition instruction is in part responsible for the growth of writing-across-the-curriculum programs in American high schools, colleges, and universities. These programs assume that students should learn to write about different subject matters according to the conventions of particular disciplines.

A second and related development has been the concern with how people compose written texts. Numerous researchers have studied composing processes by examining how writers plan, draft, and revise. These studies have influenced classroom practice to the extent that many writing teachers, under the banner of "teach process, not product," now claim to follow a process-oriented curriculum. Hairston (1982) describes the movement toward a concern for process as a major paradigm shift in the teaching of composition. While advocates of "teaching writing as a process" may not agree on what that phrase means, it is clear that many college writing instructors believe that changing the ways students compose is one of the most important outcomes of their courses.

Changes in how writing is composed, used, understood, and taught have also called into question prevailing methods of evaluating writing. These methods typically assess written products according to some explicit or implicit standard of "goodness." But if we recognize the diversity and complexity of writing in our society by attempting to teach writing as a process, we must go beyond the relative "goodness" of students' texts to focus on their knowledge and strategies. Evaluation efforts driven by such a theoretical premise would have as their goal not merely the rank-ordering of individual student texts, but a thorough and detailed descriptive assessment of students' composing skills, knowledge, and strategies. Such a change in the theory of writing evaluation raises a number of difficult questions:

- How can a writing program that claims to emphasize "process" demonstrate that it is affecting the way its students compose?
- How does a teacher of writing diagnose deficiencies in the ways individual students compose?
- Do teachers know which aspects of a student's composing processes should be altered?
- What do writers at particular ability levels need to know about writing processes that they don't know?
- How does knowledge of particular aspects of writing such as the structure of arguments affect how students compose and what they produce?
- Can writing processes be facilitated by providing students with knowledge that experts possess?
- Do writers of differing abilities follow different paths of development?
- How does the writing that students must do in one academic discipline resemble the writing that students must do in other disciplines?
- Can students transfer the writing skills they learn in school to the types of writing they must do on the job?

Our changing understanding of writing and writing abilities requires us to reexamine the ways we evaluate writing. This book examines how writers' knowledge and processes of composing might be described for purposes of assessment, and it outlines two possible approaches to descriptive assessment. Part I moves toward a theoretical framework by reviewing studies of writers' strategies for composing, their knowledge of writing, and methodologies for studying both. We see this review as a necessary first step in identifying possible approaches to the assessment of writing abilities.

Parts II and III deal with the practical concerns of assessment. Part II describes a method for assessing text-production skills through performance on controlled writing tasks, a method that we call "Performative Assessment." Part III offers a more direct approach to describing changes in composing processes by focusing on writers' awareness of their composing strategies. Both Part II and Part III provide detailed explanations of the theory on which the instruments are based, the development and testing of the instruments, and the instruments themselves, along with practical suggestions for using them in writing classrooms. Part IV argues the need for a theory of writing assessment that takes into account writers' knowledge and processes.

Research on Writers' Knowledge and Processes of Composing

In Part I we survey theoretical and empirical research that considers how writers compose and what writers know about writing systems and contexts for writing. Because researchers have taken several approaches to each question, we distinguish in Chapter 1 three theoretical positions on composing and the primary assumptions of each position. In Chapters 2, 3, and 4, we review research on the strategies that writers use in producing a text. But writers must have more than a repertoire of strategies to be able to compose. In Chapter 5, we outline the kinds of knowledge writers possess about language in general, written texts, uses of writing, subjects for writing, and potential readers. We argue that examining a writer's knowledge is essential to understanding changes in composing. Finally, in Chapter 6, we look at the contexts in which students write and methodologies for examining changes in composing and knowledge of writing within those contexts.

Chapter 1

Theories of Composing

A prominent benchmark for research in writing is Braddock, Lloyd-Jones, and Schoer's survey of writing research published in 1963. Braddock et al. found nothing to suggest a discipline. Researchers typically were ignorant of past research in the field. Experiments almost exclusively tested pedagogical methods and curricula, ignoring questions of how writers compose or how writing skills develop. Contemporary researchers refer to the Braddock et al. survey to point out how much has happened since, and indeed, there have been major developments in writing research in the two decades that followed. Major rhetorical theories have been advanced, important applications of linguistics such as sentence combining have been tested, new methods of teaching writing such as peer tutoring have been formulated, and new approaches to incorporating writing into the overall curriculum have been instituted.

In terms of widespread impact—ranging from the elementary grades through college and adult writing instruction—no development has been more influential than the trend toward understanding and teaching writing as a process. Nearly every current article and book on writing claims to be concerned with "process" in one form or another. Old texts are refurbished with new titles, and old lessons are recast in new language. But in their eagerness to adopt process-oriented approaches to writing instruction, teachers frequently do not recognize crucial differences among the assumptions underlying these approaches. In this chapter we distinguish among approaches to studying and teaching writing as a process by first giving a brief history of recent research on composing and then by outlining major theoretical positions on composing.

THREE GENERATIONS OF RESEARCH ON COMPOSING

Recent research on composing can be divided into three generations. These divisions are not strictly chronological, but they do reflect changes in research methods and changes in how composing is understood.

First-Generation Research

First-generation studies of composing were similar to the studies described by Braddock, Lloyd-Jones, and Schoer in that they tested pedagogical methods intended to improve overall writing quality. First-generation studies typically employed a pretest–posttest research design that compared two groups of students (cf. Campbell & Stanley, 1963). One group was labelled the "experimental" group and was taught by the particular method under investigation. Another group was labelled the "control" group and was taught by some other method (often called "traditional" by the investigators). Very few studies included a true control group where students received no training in writing. At the beginning of instruction, both the "experimental" and "control" groups wrote an essay as a pretest. After receiving instruction, all students again wrote an essay as a posttest. The performance of the two groups was then compared, usually in terms of judgments of the overall quality of the posttest essays. Significant differences between the groups in these studies nearly always favored the "experimental" group. (For criticism of this design, see Witte & Faigley, 1983.)

In spite of the limitations of their research methods, first-generation studies raised issues that led to the identification of composing processes as a major focus of writing research. Research on the processes discussed in the following three chapters—planning, producing text, and revising—was to some extent initiated by pedagogical studies using a pretest–posttest design. Studies of methods of invention (e.g., Young & Koen, 1973; Odell, 1974) led to investigations of the nature of planning; sentence-combining studies (e.g., Mellon, 1969; Kerek, Daiker, & Morenberg, 1980) prompted questions about how texts are produced; and studies of revision (e.g., Buxton, 1958; Hansen, 1978) revealed some of the complexity of that process. One of the most influential of the pedagogical studies was Rohman and Wlecke's (1964) investigation of the effects of "prewriting" exercises (summarized in Rohman, 1965). "Experimental" students in Rohman and Wlecke's study kept a journal, did meditation exercises, and constructed analogies for the subjects of their essays while "control" students did none of these activities. As in other studies, Rohman and Wlecke found that "experimental" students wrote better essays at the end of instruction. But it was not so much the results of their study but the model of composing Rohman and Wlecke described that stimulated other research. Rohman and Wlecke posited a three-stage linear model of composing that consisted of *"Pre-Writing," "Writing,"* and *"Re-Writing."* This model became a popular representation of composing processes.

Second-Generation Research

Much of the research spurred by the Rohman and Wlecke model, however, came in reaction to it. As early as 1964, Emig argued against a linear model of composing and led a frontal assault against Rohman and Wlecke's notions of composing in a dissertation that was later published as an NCTE research monograph (1971). Emig concluded that planning goes on throughout composing and that stages of composing are not nearly so clear-cut as Rohman and Wlecke had suggested. Denunciations of Rohman and Wlecke came to be standard introductions for articles declaring that composing activities are "recursive" or "embedded" (e.g., Flower & Hayes, 1981a; Sommers, 1980). Even more important was Emig's shift from a pretest–posttest design relying on comparative judgments of written products to a research methodology that focused directly on writers' strategies for composing. Emig observed eight 12th graders as they wrote and asked them to voice their thoughts as they were writing, a technique that has come to be known as eliciting "thinking-aloud protocols." From evidence in the protocols, Emig arrived at a description of "the composing process," which included considerations of writing contexts, stimuli, prewriting, planning, starting, composing texts, reformulating, stopping, and teacher influence.

Emig's research was a forerunner of a second generation of studies in composing that moved away from comparisons of instructional methods to the strategies writers use in composing. The manifesto for second-generation research was issued in an edited volume published in 1978 titled *Research on Composing* (Cooper & Odell, 1978). Few of the essays in this book report research but instead argue for a new approach to the study of writing. This approach is summed up in the introduction to the book where the editors admonish researchers to cease pedagogical studies until more basic research has been conducted. Cooper and Odell write that:

comparison-group research may enable us to improve instruction in writing, but that research must be informed by . . . descriptions of written discourse and the processes by which that discourse comes into being. (p. xiv)

From the mid-1970s onward, researchers began to examine writers' strategies using several methodologies. Researchers inferred strategies from thinking-aloud protocols (e.g., Flower & Hayes, 1980b; Mischel, 1974; Perl, 1978), from *post-hoc* interviews (e.g., Pianko, 1977; Sommers, 1978; Stallard, 1974), from behavior during composing (e.g., Matsuhasi, 1981; Perl, 1978; Pianko, 1977), from text analysis (e.g., Bridwell, 1980; Faigley & Witte, 1981; Odell, 1977), and from theories of cognitive development (e.g., Barritt & Kroll, 1978; Lunsford, 1978, 1979).

A series of studies by Flower and Hayes (1980a, 1980b, 1981a; Hayes & Flower, 1980) helped to establish the study of composing strategies as a major line of research and gave that research a theoretical foundation. How Flower and Hayes extended first-generation research in composing is best understood by the model of composing they extrapolate from their studies. This model, represented in Figure 1.1, contains three sets of boxes.

One set labeled "Writing Processes" includes the three kinds of composing processes described in Rohman and Wlecke's model, but Flower and Hayes do not insist on a rigid sequence for these processes. It is easy to see what has been added. The notion of a "Monitor" comes from research in cognitive psychology, which in turn borrowed the concept from earlier work in cybernetics. The term *cybernetics* in its modern sense derives from Wiener (1948), who described the functioning mind using the Greek term for the pilot of a ship. Wiener suggested the precedent for his term was James Watt's use of the word "governor" to describe the mechanical regulator of the steam engine (discussed in Bell, 1982). Thus, the theory of cybernetics is based on the analogy of the mind as a control mechanism similar to those that keep machines self-adjusted or on course. A key principle is the "feedback loop" where the regulating device—for instance, an automatic pilot on an aircraft—receives data and makes adjustments. Cybernetic theory was adapted for cognitive psychology by Miller (1967), who saw the operations of human reasoning resembling those of computer programs. Miller theorized that much of human thinking is "recursive," with feedback loops and additional side operations called "subroutines." Miller's influence is clear in Flower and Hayes' model of composing depicted in Figure 1.1. The two added sets of boxes in Figure 1.1, "The Writer's Long-Term Memory" and the "Task Environment," operate on feedback loops to the monitor.

Flower and Hayes consider composing to begin when a writer is presented a "rhetorical problem," such as a school writing assignment. According to Flower and Hayes, rhetorical problems are quite

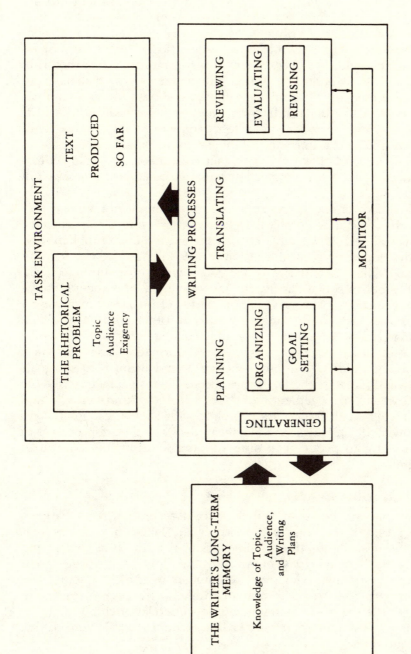

Figure 1.1. Flower and Hayes (1981a) Model of Composing (Reprinted with the permission of the National Council of Teachers of English)

complex, and writers simplify them by representing them in their own terms. From these representations writers create a hierarchical network of goals for writing. Flower and Hayes find the representation of the rhetorical problem to be a critical element in composing. Inexperienced writers are less able to conceptualize a rhetorical problem than experienced writers (Flower & Hayes, 1980a). Experienced writers spend more time thinking about how to accommodate potential readers and how to represent themselves in a text. In other words, experienced writers use more fully the concepts of *audience* and *persona* in rhetorical theory. Flower and Hayes' research not only supports key notions in rhetorical theory, but it also demonstrates how these notions can be applied to empirical research in composing.

While Flower and Hayes find that composing is not a linear process, they find it nevertheless to be an orderly one. The particulars of their model follow from a general theory of human problem solving developed by Newell and Simon (1972). Another major influence is Miller, Galanter, and Pribram's work on planning (1960). Most problem-solving research has examined how people solve mathematical problems and various kinds of puzzles. Since Flower and Hayes view composing as similar to other kinds of problem solving (Hayes & Flower, 1980), they theorize that a writer works in a "top-down" fashion, first taking information from the "task environment" and "long-term memory" and using it to set goals that will direct how the text is produced. They visually describe the subprocesses of "generating," "organizing," "translating," and "reviewing" with flowcharts complete with feedback loops (Hayes & Flower, 1980). Hayes and Flower understand the subprocesses of composing to proceed in step-by-step fashion like computer programs.

Third-Generation Research

Issues that will be at the center of third-generation research have been raised in reactions to the Flower and Hayes model. The first set of issues extends the cognitive science approach of Flower and Hayes. Beaugrande (1984) offers an agenda for this line of research. He adopts the methodology of researchers in artificial intelligence, whose goal is to *simulate* human thinking processes using computers. The design of a cognitive science model of composing, according to Beaugrande, must take into account the following criteria and questions:

1. the degree to which individuals vary in composing; [How general can a theory of composing be in its specifics?]

2. the degree to which writing is the reverse process of reading; [Are writing processes mirror images of reading processes? If not, how are they related?]
3. the scale of components in composing, the nature of these components, and the relationships among them; [What components are "chunked"? Which components dominate others?]
4. the depth of processing; [Descriptions of elaborate networks of goals represent "deep" processing as opposed to children's "shallow" concerns with letter formation and spelling.]
5. the nature of memory; [How is memory activated during composing?]
6. the available resources and the allotment of these resources; [Composing is characterized as placing high demands on mental resources, so that there are constant tradeoffs among competing demands. How, then, are resources allotted? What controls this distribution?]
7. how production processes are scheduled; [Which processes are simultaneous and which are sequential? Which are contingent on others?]
8. where "bottlenecks" occur in text production and what causes "blocks"; [Are "bottlenecks" inherent?]
9. the degree to which production is "automatic" versus "attentional"; [Automatic processes do not conflict with other processes; attentional processes do.]
10. how learning occurs; [How are strategies for writing acquired? Can instruction improve writing abilities?]

Beaugrande proposes a "parallel-stage interaction model," a model that allows component processes to occur simultaneously and to mutually influence each other. He claims that during attendant processes of text production—goal-setting, ideation, expression and phrase and word production—writers create a "text-world model," which Beaugrande defines as "the total configuration of knowledge activated for processing the text" (1984, p. 109). This view of an advancing conception of a text is "a view compatible with Gestalt theory" (p. 109). In this respect, Beaugrande's model is not radically different from that of Flower and Hayes. Where Beaugrande differs most is in his emphasis on what he calls "design criteria" for process models. These criteria are the writer's cognitive resources, including the limitations of those resources. Beaugrande outlines his design criteria as shown here in Figure 1.2.

Beaugrande defines the cognitive resources that will furnish design criteria as follows:

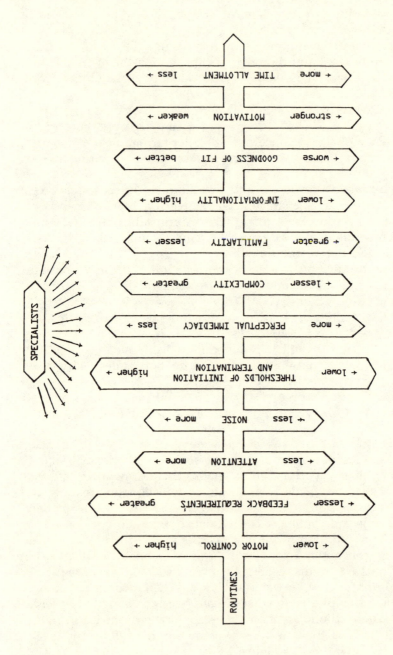

Figure 1.2. Design Criteria for Models of Processing. Reprinted from *Text Production: Toward a Science of Composition* by Robert de Beaugrande (1984), Norwood, NJ: Ablex, p. 123.

10

1. *motor control* refers to the formation of visual language;
2. *feedback* is response to the writer's actions;
3. *attention* is the degree to which a process interferes with another;
4. *noise* refers to extraneous distractions;
5. *thresholds of initiation and termination* are the stipulations that lead a writer to start and stop;
6. *perceptual immediacy* is the extent to which the text refers to immediate things and events;
7. *complexity* refers to the organization of components in a text;
8. *familiarity* is the extent to which the task is known in advance;
9. *informationality* is a technical term that refers to the novelty within a text;
10. *goodness of fit* is the degree to which the text matches intent;
11. *motivation* includes the reasons for writing;
12. *time allotment* refers to how long the writer has to finish the task.

Beaugrande's stage model allows for any single subprocess to be "dominant" at any point, thus controlling the writer's attention. A clear example of this phenomenon comes from music. Blues musician B. B. King has been performing 300 times per year for three decades. Yet King admits that he still cannot play the guitar and sing at the same time. Writers have a similar problem. They must allocate their attention during composing and at the same time monitor their progress toward fulfilling some overall plan. The thrust of Beaugrande's approach to teaching writing as a process is to enhance a writer's cognitive resources, not to reorder the strategies that a writer uses.

Another line of third-generation research is examining composing not from the perspective of the individual learner but from the perspective of how a society uses writing. This line of research borrows methodologies from several disciplines. An initial statement in this line of research is Bizzell's (1982) attack on the Flower and Hayes model for describing in the various subprocesses the *how* of composing but not the *why* of composing. In particular, Bizzell faults the separation of translating from planning. She points out that the Flower and Hayes model accommodates neither the generative force of language nor the dialectical relationship of thought and language. Bizzell offers an alternative view based on Soviet psycholinguistics following from Vygotsky ([1934] 1962). Vygotsky's basic argument is summarized as follows:

In order to explain the highly complex forms of human consciousness one must go beyond the human organism. One must seek the origins of conscious activity and "categorical" behavior not in the recesses of the human brain or in the depths of the spirit, but in the external conditions of life. Above all, this means that one must seek these origins in the external processes of social life, in the social and historical forms of human existence. (Luria, 1981, p. 25)

Furthermore, Vygotsky argues that language production is not a simple process of converting thoughts into words, but that thought evolves through several stages and is completed only when it emerges in language. Following these two lines of thought, Bizzell criticizes Flower and Hayes for neglecting the role of context and criticizes their conception of transcribing as oversimplified. "Producing text," according to Bizzell, "cannot take place unless the writer can define her goals in terms of the community's interpretative conventions" (p. 227).

Some researchers of writing have turned to other disciplines that describe "the community's interpretative conventions," including sociology, semiotics, sociolinguistics, and ethnography. For instance, Shaughnessy (1977) and others have tried to define the particular problems the academic discourse community poses for basic writers. This line of questioning has led some researchers to the sociology of knowledge (Bazerman, 1983). From this perspective, writing is viewed as a social act taking place in established contexts such as those of academic disciplines. For example, Bazerman's (1981) comparison of articles in biochemistry, sociology, and literary criticism illustrates differences in how each discipline uses previous literature and manages the expectations of readers. Moreover, Bazerman points to differences in the nature of inquiry among these disciplines and in the consequences of those inquiries.

Recent literary criticism has introduced writing teachers and researchers to the perspectives of semiotics and other interpretative systems that operate across traditional disciplinary lines. While composition theorists have not embraced the semiotics of Barthes (1968) and Eco (1976, 1979) or Foucault's description of language and power (1972), the tendency to read all sorts of social structures as "texts" may yet influence thinking about writing.

Many writing researchers encountered the field of sociolinguistics initially through the work of Labov (1966, 1973), who helped them understand the complexities of spoken dialects in the urban classroom. Other theoretical statements defining discourse communities (Hymes, 1974; Gumperz, 1971) have seemed to offer a basis for understanding the social constraints on writing and for criticizing the oversimplifications of the cognitive model. Ohmann (1982) is one of the many who try to adapt the work of Bernstein (1971) to apparent differences in writing that reflect divisions in social class. The main difficulty has been adapting theories describing variation in oral language for research in writing.

Finally, some writing researchers have recognized that the classroom is in itself a small community linked in important ways to the larger society. This point was first made by Dewey ([1899] 1915) who called classrooms "miniature communities" and saw the learning of literacy as a process of socialization. Clark et al. (1983) contend that the best way to study the process of becoming literate is by observing people write, listening to what they say about writing, and finding out what they accomplish in written communication. They report that the learning of writing in some ways resembles the learning of speech. In the classrooms they studied, children did not receive much direct instruction in writing unless they encountered some difficulty. Most writing skills were learned tacitly and in the context of the social life of the classroom.

CURRENT THEORETICAL POSITIONS ON COMPOSING

In the previous section we divided the past 20 years of research in composing into three generations. Each generation is characterized by different research methodologies. Nevertheless, we do not mean to imply by this retrospective view that recent ideas of composing have evolved in a single line of descent. Just the opposite is true. Current discussions of composing reflect an array of theoretical positions. We cannot describe each of these positions in this chapter. Instead, we attempt to identify three foci around which we group contemporary views of composing. The differences among these positions are most obvious in the way that each accounts for how a writer discovers what to write—the process referred to in classical rhetoric as *invention*.

Literary View of Composing

For many years writing researchers did not examine how writers discover ideas because they thought of invention as a process unavailable for study. If researchers consider the creative act inaccessible, then they must either study writers' observable behavior or draw inferences about invention from the texts writers produce. An interesting case in point is the Rohman and Wlecke study discussed above. While Rohman and Wlecke sought to facilitate the discovery of ideas, they still conceived the process of discovery to be beyond rational formulation. Rohman (1965) says that a writer must discover a "personal context," and that teachers must "use as the psychologists do in therapy, a person's desire to actualize himself" (p. 108). Rohman and Wlecke (1964) had students keep journals and engage in religious meditation to "unlock discovery" (p. 110). A similar view of invention comes from Murray (1978), who talks about revision as a process of discovery. Murray says that revision is a process whereby "the writer must try not to force the writing to what the writer hopes the text would say, but instead try to help the writing say what it intends to say" (1980, p. 5). Murray's metaphor of a text with a will of its own underscores his nonrational view of invention.

Because discovery has been viewed as a deeply mysterious process by many poets and novelists over the years, we refer to this perspective as the "literary view" of composing. (We note later, however, that much contemporary literary theory has moved away from this view of composing.) Young (1978) and others have attributed the persistence of the literary view to the continuing influence of Romanticism. Rohman's and Murray's conceptions of invention recall major statements of the Romantic period such as Wordsworth's *Preface to the Lyrical Ballads* and Coleridge's account of the writing of "Kubla Khan." Perhaps the most detailed comparison of rational and nonrational theories of invention among the romantics is Friedrich von Schiller's essay, "Naive and Sentimental Poetry" ([1795] trans. 1966). Schiller describes two major types of poets: the naive poet who is spontaneous, nonrational, and lacking in self-consciousness, and the sentimental poet who is intellectual, rational, and self-conscious. Schiller speaks of the naive poet composing in a "fine frenzy" while the sentimental poet composes with an internal critic looking over his shoulder. For Schiller, "true genius must be naive, or it is not genius" (p. 96). True genius is "unacquainted with the rules, those crutches for weakness and taskmasters of awkwardness" and "goes calmly and surely through all the snares of false taste" (p. 96).

The ultimate source of the nonrational view of composing is attributed to Plato. Whether Plato actually advocated the views assigned to him is difficult to determine because of the elusive nature of the *Dialogues* (trans. 1961). Many readers of the *Phaedrus* have decided that Plato's goal for discovery is not the communication of ideas but the discovery of truth. Socrates in the *Phaedrus* says, "A real art of speaking . . . which does not seize hold of truth, does not exist and never will" (1919, 260E). According to Plato truth is found not in particulars but in absolutes, and reason alone is incapable of finding and communicating truth because truth is not located in the material world. To reason must be added a kind of mystical intuition achieved through years of arduous training in dialectic at the hands of a benevolent (i.e., loving) master. From interpretations of Plato's notion of the mystical apprehension of truth, transmitted through Romanticism, come the main assumptions for the literary view of composing and the approaches to teaching writing based on that view. First, the purpose of invention is the discovery of truth. Second, truth can be learned but it cannot be explicitly taught. Berlin (1982) sees these assumptions as motivating "expressionist" methods of teaching writing such as those of Elbow (1973), Coles (1978), and Macrorie (1980). Macrorie thinks that the teacher's job is to "create a climate that encourages truthtelling" (1980, p. 283). Coles eschews the writing teacher's conventional role as an instructor of rhetoric and style and opts for that of a demanding reader who refuses to accept the bland, uncommitted content of most student essays. He uses Plato's method of the dialectic to probe the truth of ideas. Elbow proposes that teachers should be learners in their own classrooms.

Cognitive View of Composing

Much recent research in writing proceeds from a cognitive view of composing. Its primary assumptions are that the goal of composing is to communicate, that writing abilities follow a developmental sequence, that composing is an orderly process from which general principles can be abstracted, and that these general principles can be used to teach writing. We discussed above how work in cybernetics, cognitive psychology, and artificial intelligence led to Flower and Hayes' influential model of composing and to extensions of that model by Beaugrande and others. Less well understood, however, are affinities between the assumptions of the cognitive view and certain assumptions in classical rhetoric. A theory of invention that anticipates in many respects cognitive science theories of how ideas are discovered appears in Aristotle's *Rhetoric* (trans. 1954). The *Rhetoric* divides the art of persuasion into component parts such as the nature of the audience, the kinds of evidence involved, and stylistic choices to be made. The individual speaker analyzes each of the components to determine what content, arrangement, style, and delivery will be most effective for a particular subject, audience, and purpose. Aristotle does not leave invention to the muses but provides methods for generating content that are similar in several aspects to contemporary notions of schemata. Like contemporary theorists who use physical metaphors such as "knowledge structures," Aristotle calls these aids for invention *topoi* or "places." Aristotle distinguishes two kinds of *topoi*: "common" *topoi* similar in kind to the knowledge schemata described by R. Anderson (1978) and others, and "general" *topoi* similar to the organizational schemata such as comparison described by Meyer (1975, 1979, 1981) and others. Aristotle's first type, the "common" *topoi*, are encyclopedia-like parcels of knowledge on subject matter commonly used in oratory. The second type—the "general" *topoi*—are free of specific subject matter. Aristotle classifies 28 lines of argument (such as arguments from definition, division, induction, and consequence) that can serve as guides for a speaker in filling out an argument. Indeed, some of Aristotle's categories have carried through a 2,400-year-old tradition of teaching rhetoric to become useful for discourse linguists such as Pike (1954) and Grimes (1975) and rhetorical theorists such as D'Angelo (1979, 1981), who in turn have influenced psychologists such as Meyer.

Contemporary cognitive scientists represent how people find solutions to problems in ways similar to Aristotle's approach to finding arguments. One such line of research examines how people solve puzzles and mathematical problems. From these investigations, general theories are constructed. Newell (1980) theorizes a "problem space," which he defines as a "set of symbolic structures within which to move around, an arena wherein many specific problems can be posed and attempted" (p. 697). Similar to Aristotle's notion of *topoi* is Newell's characterization of "paths" toward solutions as "locations" in the problem space. A person "searches" the problem space for the strategy that can solve the problem at hand. People conduct searches using what Newell calls "search control knowledge," which leads them to new ideas. Newell's search control knowledge is another term for "heuristics," the strategies that writers use to discover ideas. Discussions of heuristics are prominent in both classical and contemporary rhetoric.

The current revival of interest in methods of discovery came in part as a reaction to the analysis of linguistic forms in texts (i.e., words and sentences) as the primary tool of writing research. Even before the turn of the century, words in texts were analyzed according to parts of speech (Kirkpatrick, 1891). In the 1920s and 1930s many researchers began looking at how syntax develops in children's writing as part of an expansive effort to study language development. By 1924, researchers had measured sentence length from grade 4 through college upper-classmen, finding a steady growth along the way (Stormzand & O'Shea, 1924), and by 1933, some of the problems of measuring children's written syntax had been identified (LaBrandt, 1933). For researchers committed to "scientific" approaches to education that employ quantitative methodologies, written texts appeared to be bountiful sources of observable data. They could be analyzed into parts, things could be counted, and conclusions drawn. Such approaches became pervasive in the 1960s and early 1970s when researchers began applying work in stylistics (e.g., Milic, 1965), generative grammar (e.g., Hunt, 1965), tagmemics (e.g., Becker, 1965), case grammar (Winterowd, 1970), and Prague-school text linguistics (e.g., Lybert & Cummings, 1969) to the study of student writing.

These new approaches, however, remained *post-hoc* analytic schemes. They did not explain how a writer's intentions are carried out in a written text, nor did they provide methods for generating ideas. Consequently, many teachers of writing turned to classical rhetoric (e.g., Corbett, 1971) for methods of invention, and they adapted linguistic approaches to meet this need (e.g., Young, Becker, & Pike, 1970). Because many teachers recognized that students have great difficulty in generating content, Flower and Hayes' application of cognitive science research in idea generation to the study of writing was enthusiastically received. The important point here is that a continuity of assumptions (if not always a direct influence) exists between classical rhetoric and much contemporary research in composing. In spite of often large fundamental differences among varying positions, most researchers of writing processes assume that writers use identifiable strategies for composing, that these strategies follow a developmental sequence, and that an understanding of these strategies can be directly applied to the teaching of writing.

Social View of Composing

A third view of composing emphasizes the social nature of writing. Bizzell (1982) and Nystrand (1982b) criticize the notion that a writer's competence can be explained in terms of strategies. Each argues that a writer's competence includes something much broader which can be explained only in terms of a community connected by written discourse. Whereas both literary and cognitive theorists focus on the writer as an individual, social theorists view the writer as a member of a larger literate community. Invention is understood not strictly as a process involving an individual's heuristic strategies, but as a socially determined action.

Much of the writing in the world of work must be viewed from this perspective. For example, a team of scientists and engineers who work for an engineering firm may write an environmental impact statement for a large construction project that their company has won by competitive bid. The content of such a report would be determined to a large extent by environmental law and expectations of regulatory agencies. As a result, the report might be largely formulaic. For example, the Environmental Protection Agency might expect to see a species checklist of birds present on the proposed site, including a specific description of how data were collected. The success of the report depends not so much on team members' skills in generating new ideas but in their understanding of an environmental impact statement as a social act occurring within certain strictly defined parameters.

No specific social model of composing has been advanced by researchers interested in a social view of writing, but written communication is considered in some larger theories of language that incorporate context. Some sociolinguists, for instance, maintain that "communication cannot be studied in isolation; it must be analyzed in terms of its effect on people's lives (Gumperz & Cook-Gumperz, 1982, p. 1). And the social view underlies the Vygotskian school of psycholinguistics in the Soviet Union, which insists that language systems cannot be studied apart from their use and history. The social view of composing is more encompassing than the traditional concern for audience in persuasion or even the study of conventions. The social view takes us ultimately into areas of social roles, individual and group purposes, and communal organization.

To understand the notion of a discourse community (and the basis for the social view of composing), we need first to look at how sociolinguists have characterized speech communities. Like the recent emphasis on invention in writing research, the thrust of contemporary sociolinguistics is in part a reaction to the research program for linguistics set out by Saussure (trans. 1959) and codified by Bloomfield (1933). That program limited research to the forms of language by excluding the functions and contexts of language. This tradition was carried on with the advent of transformational grammar. Chomsky's (1965) notion of a speech community as a group of speakers who share the same underlying language is similar to Bloomfield's notion of a language. Chomsky seeks to describe the linguistic competence of idealized speakers in idealized communities. From Chomsky's point of view, the important fact is that any healthy human has the potential to become a member of any speech community because human languages are structured in certain fundamentally similar ways. The goal of research based on this assumption is to identify language universals (Bach & Harms, 1968; Greenberg, 1963). From the sociolinguists' point of view, however, the important fact is that people maintain social identity through language. Sociolinguists see social organization reflected in language. Language is stratified and divided into social and occupational groups. The goal of research based on these premises is to identify speech communities and explain the relationships that hold within and among them (Gumperz, 1982b). Differences among communities are held responsible for the increasing legal disputes, communication breakdowns, and educational failures in technologically advanced nations (Gumperz, 1982a).

Sociolinguists have investigated speech communities for the past two decades. Hymes ([1964] 1972) introduced a series of articles on the ethnography of communication in *American Anthropologist* by setting out seven components of "communicative events": "(1) a code or codes, intelligible to (2) participants in (3) an event, characterized by (4) a channel or channels, (5) a setting or context, (6) a definite form or shape of the message, and (7) a topic or comment that says something about something" (p. 26). Hymes goes on to show how communicative events can be described in terms of the capacity of and the relationship among these components.

Gumperz (1971) describes a speech community as "any human aggregate characterized by regular and frequent interaction by means of a shared body of verbal signs and set off from similar aggregates by significant differences in language usage" (p. 114). Gumperz adds that speech communities may be composed of residents of a geographic region, members of occupational associations, or even compatriots in neighborhood gangs. He claims that before one can judge any speaker's intent, one must investigate the norms of appropriateness for the individual's speech community since these norms constrain an individual's language production. They determine who an individual talks to, what he talks about, how he forms his message, when he knows that the listener has understood his intent, and so on.

The concept of a community associated by written discourse must be different from the sociolinguist's speech community. To begin with, the linguistic variables that mark speech communities, such as phonology, often cannot be matched by similar properties in written language. Written language is actually a collection of media, composed in and coming to us through many forms—in newspapers, in notes to ourselves, in scripts read to us by newscasters on television, in books, in dictated business letters, on traffic signs. As many theorists have pointed out, written language is not restricted by time and space. It can transcend centuries and continents.

In societies where literacy is restricted to an elite, it is easy to identify communities connected by written discourse. For example, literacy in European medieval culture was restricted largely to an ecclesiastical discourse community. But in technologically advanced nations where most of the population is literate, discourse communities are formed by more than an emphasis on writing. Major corporations develop their own in-house language and conventions for discourse. For instance, the phone company refers to a telephone as a "station." Furthermore, advances in electronic technology make possible for oral language what was formerly only possible for written language. Electronically recorded oral texts can be stored and "reread." For these reasons we use the term *discourse community* instead of *written discourse community*. The key notion is that within a general language and discourse competence, there exist many specialized kinds of discourse competence that allow people to participate in a specialized group. Participants know what is worth communicating, how it can be communicated, what other members of the community are likely to know about that topic, how members of the community can be persuaded, and so on. The point here is that the strategies for composing described by cognitive researchers are part of the repertoire of the discourse community. Every plan and every decision the writer makes—including the decision to compose a text—reflect the broader community. We will elaborate this concept in Chapter 5. Some rhetorical theorists such as Kinneavy (1971) and Perelman and Olbrechts-Tyteca ([1958]1969) acknowledge the role of the writer's community, but cognitive researchers with few exceptions overlook this dimension of a writer's competence.

COMPOSING THEORIES AND COMPOSING RESEARCH

The three theoretical positions we have outlined are sometimes articulated in debates over the assumptions these positions represent. Proponents of the literary view criticize the cognitive view for denying the emotional element in writing. In particular, they are repelled by the analogy of the human mind as a computer with "workspace," "executive systems," "subroutines," "monitors," and the like. Besides objecting to the cognitivists' jargon, those who hold the literary view argue that these metaphors lead to an overly simplified view of human language and human communication. They criticize the social view for its failure to account for genius—the possibility of a Shakespeare or a Cervantes transcending his discourse community and his era. More broadly, they fault the social view for its failure to account for style—both in describing different kinds of style (e.g., "witty," "pompous") and in explaining how such styles can be persuasive. Applications of social research are feared to reify existing uses of writing and to reject what might be possible.

Proponents of the cognitive view accuse the literary view of presenting a mystical view of composing that has little value in the classroom. They criticize the prestige given to the study of literary texts, pointing out that the great bulk of written texts serve relatively mundane ends. They see the arguments of the literary view leading away from the possibility of improving writing instruction. For example, Scardamalia and Bereiter (in press) argue that most expressive writing tasks do not give students practice in goal-directed planning.

Proponents of the social view criticize the cognitive view for failing to make a key distinction between oral and written language. Luria (1981) theorizes that oral speech evolves naturally in the process of social interaction while writing is the result of specialized instruction. Social theorists fault both the literary and the cognitive views for misunderstanding the nature of written communication. In their view culture is not the board on which the game of writing is played, but the game itself.

Certain aspects of the three theoretical positions we have outlined have been argued since classical antiquity. It would seem likely, therefore, that assumptions of each of these positions would have been the focus of some of the research on composing. This has not been the case. The cognitive view has dominated much research on composing. Some of the assumptions of the literary view may not be testable, but the assumptions of the social view have largely been neglected in the United States.[1] Ochs (1979b) notes that "it is commonplace to say that language is a social behavior. But the social quality itself is not seriously examined" (p. 209).

To accommodate the implications of each position for composing, we have divided our review into sections on composing processes and writers' knowledge. We have divided composing into three chapters: *Planning, Producing Text,* and *Revising.* We use these terms because Rohman and Wlecke's "Pre-Writing," "Writing," and "Re-Writing," and Flower and Hayes' "Planning," "Translating," and "Reviewing" have established a tripartite division for composing

---

[1]British research has, however, been more attentive to the social view. See, for example, Halliday, 1978; Hoggart, 1957; Widdowson, 1978.

research. To be sure, these divisions have come under strong attack. Rose (1984) argues that if revising occurs throughout composing, then it makes little sense to call it a "recursive" process. Scardamalia and Bereiter (in press) insist that it makes little sense to treat changing a sentence after it is written as a different process from changing it before it is written. In Chapter 3 we will present arguments from both the cognitive and social positions that reject the distinction between planning and production. Nevertheless, we use these divisions simply because most studies of composing label themselves accordingly. These divisions do not represent our own theoretical view. We present in Chapter 5 an alternative view that takes into account what writers know about the discourse communities of which they are members.

Chapter 2

Research on Planning

Writing has been characterized as *planned* discourse. Ochs (1979a) places "formal expository writing" at one end of a continuum with spontaneous speech at the other end. She offers the following definitions:

1. UNPLANNED DISCOURSE is discourse that lacks forethought and organizational preparation.
2. PLANNED DISCOURSE is discourse that has been thought out and organized (designed) prior to its expression. (p. 55)

Ochs finds that in unplanned discourse, adult language takes on many of the characteristics of child language. Planned discourse, on the other hand, "draws upon knowledge transmitted through formal education" (p. 54). Ochs allows that some written discourse is relatively unplanned, discourse such as "stream-of-consciousness writing" and "casual letter-writing" (p. 53). Nonetheless, because most school writing is planned, it has been studied using methodologies developed for analyzing other kinds of planned activities. In particular, researchers have adapted methodologies and language from problem-solving research. Using the metaphor of a "problem space," Flower and Hayes (1981c) claim that in planning, "writers form an internal *representation* of the knowledge that will be used in writing" (p. 372). In this chapter we review studies that examine the timing of planning, the nature of planning, planning strategies, as well as studies of instruction in planning. We see these issues as being important for developing methods of assessing writer's processes of composing.

THE TIMING OF PLANNING

Early research on planning focused merely on the time that writers of varying ability spent on planning. More recent research, however, has tried to infer cognitive strategies and metacognitive knowledge from studies of the timing of planning.

Emig (1971) found that students did little prewriting planning, but that they did pause during writing, apparently to plan. Emig's call for more research on composing was heeded by a number of other researchers who also looked at the timing of planning. Young children typically begin writing as soon as they are given a writing topic (Scardamalia & Bereiter, in press). High school writers start writing almost as quickly. Mischel (1974) found that his one high school subject spent little time planning before writing began, but that this brief planning time varied. The student spent less than one minute engaged in pre-writing planning on autobiographical assignments but 20 minutes on a memoir-writing task. Stallard (1974) compared the writing behavior of 15 "good" high school senior writers (determined by STEP Essay Writing Test scores) with that of 15 randomly selected writers from the same senior class. He found that both groups quickly began to write when they received a writing task but that the good writers did wait longer (mean = 4.18 minutes) than the writers selected at random (mean = 1.20 minutes).

Another issue in research on the timing of planning has been the percentage of total writing time devoted to planning. Gould (1980) examined how much time writers spend planning in relation to the actual writing and dictating of a text. He conducted a series of experiments with eight college graduates who had never composed by dictating and eight business executives who were expert dictators. All 16 subjects composed by dictating, writing, and speaking. Gould distinguished speaking and dictating in the following way: "Speaking differs from dictating in that the author assumes the recipient will listen to rather than read what has been composed, and the author need not give typing instructions" (p. 97). In experiments where subjects wrote and spoke routine letters, complex letters, "competitive" letters, and messages, Gould found that planning time maintained a constant ratio of two-thirds total composition time— regardless of the type of letter being written or dictated. While this ratio differed for individual subjects (from 47% to 87%), the mean planning time for all subjects was 65%.

Other researchers have looked at the timing of planning in relation to cognitive issues. Matsuhashi (1981) studied time spent planning by videotaping four high school writers composing. The students wrote two reporting tasks, two generalizing tasks, and two persuading tasks. Matsuhashi found that mean pause time during writing ranged from 47% to 70% of total composing time. The substantial proportion of time spent pausing is especially interesting because students selected their topics for writing two days in advance. Although they were not allowed to bring notes to the writing sessions, they were "encouraged to rehearse and plan" their papers ahead of time (p. 117).

Matsuhashi's main concerns were to determine when in the text pauses occur and how long these pauses were in relation to type of discourse. She reached several conclusions. Students paused longer before "abstract" T-units than they did before T-units that added supporting details. Furthermore, students paused longer before abstract T-units when they were generalizing than when they were reporting some incident, a fact that Matsuhashi attributed to the additional need while generalizing to consider the organization of larger segments of text. Matsuhashi (1982) found additional support for these conclusions in a detailed analysis of one high school student's hand and eye movements during 10 long pauses.

THE NATURE OF PLANNING

Research on the nature of planning has led to discoveries about what strategies are involved in planning and how writers employ those strategies.

Creating Goals

Protocol research has been used to great advantage in studying the nature of planning. Flower and Hayes (1980a, 1981a) have found that experts' planning during composing is similar to other kinds of problem solving. Experts translate writing tasks into goals, which in turn are used to generate subgoals. For example, in an article on water quality, a writer might begin with the goal of getting the reader's attention and translate that into a specific strategy such as portraying what might happen in a major city if the water was not drinkable. Goals help writers to reduce the number of constraints they must work within (Flower & Hayes, 1980b). Although writers draw some goals and plans directly from long-term memory, most goals are created by the writer in response to a specific situation. Flower and Hayes have found evidence in protocols that the creation and revision of goals continues throughout composing. Goals are frequently tested and reevaluated in light of what has been written. Furthermore, Flower and Hayes have observed that good writers readily move back and forth between higher-level and lower-level goals. This finding is consistent with problem-solving research, where successful problem-solvers divide problems into subproblems and solve the subproblems one at a time (Newell & Simon, 1972).

But goals are not often present in the protocols of younger children. In 24 protocols collected from sixth graders, Scardamalia and Bereiter (in press) found that 17 contained no reference to goals and only one contained as many as two references. The children undoubtedly had goals for writing, but these goals apparently did not enter into planning. In another study (discussed in Scardamalia & Bereiter, in press) Burtis discovered no greater evidence of planning when children composed stories than when they composed arguments. Scardamalia & Bereiter surmise that students have more trouble in constructing goals than in executing them. They see the ability to create goals as an important aspect of mature writing competence.

Goals develop as the text advances, and in this sense, they interact with the text itself as well as with the situation surrounding the text. Children in the early grades use the sentence they have just written to prompt the next one—a kind of associative planning that takes the form of "I just said that, now I can say this." As early as the fourth grade (about age 10), children writing one sentence are planning what to say in the next sentence (Scardamalia, Bereiter, & Goelman, 1982). Older children and novice adults often rely on the topic to stimulate new goals in school-sponsored writing tasks. When they get stuck, they reread the topic for inspiration (Perl, 1980), arriving at such decisions as "Oh, yes, I can talk about that too." Experienced writers use both the text and the rhetorical situation to generate new goals. Flower and Hayes (1981b) describe four strategies that produce new operative goals from existing text: pursuing an interesting feature in extant text, looking for some contradiction in or objection to what has been written, discovering "what I really mean," and looking for a focus. Experienced writers frequently evaluate what they have written in light of their goals. They use these evaluations to generate additional goals and to refine existing ones. Scardamalia & Bereiter (in press) call this process "reflective planning." They conclude that it is virtually impossible to teach reflective planning to students who have not experienced it.

In another study, Flower and Hayes (1981c) examined the contents of planning pauses using thinking-aloud protocols. Three experts and one novice writer participated in their study. Their writing task was the following: "Write about your job for the readers of *Seventeen* magazine, 13- and 14-year-old girls." Specifically, Flower and Hayes sought to discover whether writers were thinking when they pause about what to say in the next sentence or about broader rhetorical considerations such as the intended audience. Flower and Hayes claimed that goal-directed psychological units can be discerned in writers' protocols. They called these units "composing episodes" and claimed they are made coherent by the writer's focusing on one particular goal. The four writers tended to pause at the boundaries of these episodes. Flower and Hayes found that "nearly 70% of the comments at episode beginnings [were] related to [rhetorical] goals and nearly 50% of them [were] devoted to actually setting goals" (1981c, p. 241). Neither paragraph beginnings nor shifts in topics were good predictors of shifts in episodes. "Goal-related activity," according to Flower and Hayes, was the best predictor. Finally, Flower and Hayes noted that the pauses of both the experts and the one novice were used for sentence-level planning and for setting more global rhetorical goals, but the experts were far more proficient at making a variety of plans than the one novice.

Rose (1984) takes issue with the hierarchical character of goals in the Flower and Hayes model. He contends that an alternative cognitive model of planning developed by B. Hayes-Roth and F. Hayes-Roth (1979) more accurately represents what occurs during composing. The Hayes-Roths' model of planning is based on the notion of *opportunism*. Their model does not so much stand in opposition to the problem-solving model of Flower and Hayes as it differs in emphasis. The Hayes-Roths consider planning to be at times an orderly, top-down sequence, but at other times a much less orderly process characterized by the planner's willingness to follow opportunities as they occur. When this model is extrapolated to composing, it suggest that writers' plans are not always in a hierarchical sequence. Rose thinks that both deductive, "top-down" planning and inductive, "bottom-up" planning go on during composing. Much anecdotal evidence supports the view that planning is not always hierarchically organized. For example, Guy Davenport observes "I do not know what the story means. I only know that I found a way to fit everything in" (1982, p. 30). What is fundamental to opportunistic planning during composing, according to Rose, "is a repertoire of strategies, rules, plans, frames, and, possibly, evaluative criteria, and the richer the repertoire the richer the opportunistic activity" (p. 83). He concludes that writers who have limited strategies for composing often are forced to use inappropriate strategies.

Two other studies look at the initial decisions students make when they are presented a writing assignment. Pianko (1977, 1979a, 1979b) videotaped 17 college freshmen (7 in regular classes and 10 in remedial classes) while they composed and questioned them immediately afterward about their thoughts during composing. She concluded that during prewriting planning students were making decisions about the following: (a) whether to write on the topic given them or to choose another topic, (b) what subject or incident to focus on in the essay, (c) how to begin, and, (d) for some students, how, generally, they might develop their essay. In a general study of how unskilled adults compose, Perl (1978, 1979) had five community college students write in four sessions on topics from an introductory social science course each student was taking. In each writing session, the students verbalized their thoughts during composing. Perl examined transcripts of the tape-recorded sessions of students composing aloud, looking particularly at what students said during their brief prewriting planning (mean = 4 minutes). She found that they (a) rephrased the topic until they thought of an appropriate experience to write about, (b) changed the "large conceptual issue in the topic" into "manageable pieces for writing," and (c) from a word in the topic, began free associations leading to the development of one or more of the associations in writing the essay (1979, p. 328).

Generating Content

Children and adults have little difficulty generating ideas in conversation because of the many external cues for memory retrieval. During writing, however, these cues are often absent, and teachers of writing at all levels often hear the same complaint: "I can't think of anything else to say." While expert writers often generate surplus content and have the luxury of pruning their texts, student writers have difficulty generating content and rarely throw away what they have written (Bereiter & Scardamalia, 1982). Part of the problem is that often students simply do not know much about their subject, but students also fail to draw on what knowledge they do have (Scardamalia & Bereiter, in press). Writing teachers have offered numerous methods of generating ideas—including the use of writing itself as a method of discovering ideas (e.g., Murray, 1978)—but very few studies have considered this subprocess in detail.

Scardamalia and Bereiter (in press) find that by age 12 most children have developed a "knowledge telling" strategy that allows them to sidestep many of the complex demands of planning. "Knowledge telling" consists of translating a writing assignment into a topic and then telling what is known about that topic. Scardamalia and Bereiter infer the knowledge telling strategy from several kinds of evidence, among them the fact that goal-setting is absent from the protocols of young writers (Burtis et al., 1983) and that novice writers return to the assignment for cues when they are stuck (Flower & Hayes, 1980a). Scardamalia and Bereiter claim that children can be taught to modify the knowledge telling strategy in ways that will produce better texts. Nevertheless, these researchers note that even with modifictions this strategy can never be developed into the sophisticated idea-generation searches that experts employ.

Flower and Hayes (1981b) have found that most ideas generated by experts are in response to goals, but Caccamise (1981) found that writers also use an associative, trial-and-error strategy for generating ideas (Anderson & Bower, 1973). Caccamise conducted two experiments that examine what hinders writers from retrieving ideas from long-term memory. In both, students were told that the ideas they generated were to appear in a "pamphlet which presented all facts on the topic" (p. 33). For the first experiment, students were asked to generate ideas orally for an adult audience on two different topics, one familiar to the writers and one unfamiliar to them. In the second, the topics were held constant, but the audience was varied, one specified as adults and the other as children. Caccamise then analyzed these verbal protocols for effects imposed by the writer's long-term memory, the writing task, the topic specificity, and the audience type. These effects were measured in terms of the number of ideas produced, repetition of ideas, and the time when new ideas were introduced during the idea-generation task.

In Caccamise's study, under the more-constrained conditions— the audience of children and the unfamiliar topic—students generated a smaller range of ideas (perhaps appropriately for an audience of children) and these ideas were less cohesive. Furthermore, in the more-constrained conditions, students were more likely to repeat ideas, a fact that Caccamise suggested might be due to editing processes. Students in these conditions made more comments evaluating previously expressed ideas. In terms of time, the rate of ideas generated slowed down across time and related ideas were also clustered in time, findings which replicate existing research in memory retrieval. Caccamise, however, observed that current models of information processing are inadequate for predicting how writers generate ideas because they are based on relatively small, fixed memory sets. Writing, on the other hand, uses a vast amount of memory.

Scardamalia and Bereiter (in press) theorized that skilled and unskilled writers use both goal-directed and spontaneously associated kinds of memory search in generating content. The difference between skilled and unskilled writers seems to be that unskilled writers rely more heavily on associative processes. They lack the ability to create an elaborate plan and carry out this plan. Experts, on the other hand, are better able to use their plans to generate content.

Organizing

When material is drawn from long-term memory, it must be organized in some sequence. Inexperienced writers often write down information in the order of retrieval, creating what Flower (1979) calls "writer-based" prose. More experienced writers attempt to find an order that will meet the needs of the subject matter and potential readers. Three kinds of knowledge help to shape the organization of a written text—knowledge of subject matter, knowledge of potential readers' expectations and beliefs, and knowledge of discourse structure. We will discuss the role of the first two kinds of knowledge in Chapter 5. Here we are concerned with structural knowledge.

One of the oldest tenets of rhetoric as a discipline is that structural paradigms shape discourse. Greek rhetoric (e.g., Aristotle, trans. 1954) contained structural formulas for arranging orations, and in Roman rhetoric, arrangement was established as a major department of rhetoric (e.g., Cicero, trans. 1942; Quintilian, trans. 1920–1922). Many 20th-century textbook discussions of organization derive from the structural paradigms of the 19th-century theorist Alexander Bain (1866). Bain's influence has been supplemented by a number of important models of basic organizational patterns from writing researchers (e.g., D'Angelo, 1975; Kinneavy, Cope, & Campbell, 1976) and from researchers in other disciplines (e.g., Grimes, 1975; Longacre, 1976).

Researchers in comprehension find organization a fruitful area for study. Differences in overt organization affect how well texts are remembered (e.g., Meyer, 1979; Meyer & Freedle, 1979). Olson, Mack, and Duffy (1981) have shown that readers make use of structural knowledge to predict what follows in a text. One implication of these studies for composing is that organization in some text types, such as simple stories, is easily achieved (Applebee, 1978), but the ability to organize other types, such as classificatory essays, develops much later (Stein & Trabasso, 1982).

A troublesome question for writing teachers and writing researchers alike is the extent to which writers make use of explicit structural knowledge while composing (cf. Bracewell, C. Frederiksen, & J. Frederiksen, 1982). Some rhetoricians assign a large role to structural knowledge. D'Angelo (1979, 1981) claims that organizational paradigms represent patterns of thought. He links organization skills and conceptual development, and he theorizes that the same organizational patterns underlie invention, arrangement, and style. Protocols gathered by Scardamalia and Bereiter (in press) suggest that some skilled writers do make use of explicit structural knowledge, but for other experts this knowledge remains tacit. Children, like adults, have some knowledge of discourse structure. Even at age 10, they can name structural elements characteristic of certain text types (Bereiter & Scardamalia, 1982). But again, the question remains as to how well children can access this knowledge. Scardamalia and Bereiter (in press) have found no evidence of children using structural knowledge in the thinking-aloud protocols they have analyzed. Children must have some awareness of structure in order to write stories, yet gaps in their narratives suggest that this knowledge is largely unconscious.

EMPLOYING PLANNING STRATEGIES

Rereading

While rereading is a major subprocess of revision, several researchers argue for the importance of rereading as a planning strategy. Whatever the impulse or pressure that causes a writer to begin a text, once that text is begun, the text itself exerts a strong influence over what follows since new ideas have to be meshed with existing ones. Four studies examine the effects of "blind" writing—denying writers the opportunity to reread what they have just written. Britton, Burgess, Martin, McLeod, and Rosen (1975) gave writers inkless pens to complete a writing task. A record of their writing appeared on a carbon copy below the paper they were writing on. Writers did not seem impeded when they were writing a narrative, but more complex tasks, such as persuasive tasks, proved to be very difficult. Britton and his colleagues attributed this difficulty to the fact that the writers could not reread what they had written to help plan what to say next. Gould (1980) had eight novice dictators and eight expert dictators write both routine and complex letters with a wooden stylus that made an impression on a carbon copy underneath. Gould found that the quality of the written products—in the judgment of independent raters—is not affected by the restraint of being unable to see what was written. The writers, however, felt uncomfortable with this method of composing.

Atwell (1981) and Hull, Arnowitz, and Smith (1981) conducted studies in which college students wrote essays in a normal, visible condition and in a blind condition. Atwell's subjects—ten students in traditional freshman composition classes and ten in basic skills classes—wrote narrative essays. Atwell analyzed the essays for coherence, and she found little difference in the products composed under blind and visible conditions. The basic writers, however, had a great deal more difficulty than the traditional freshmen students in producing texts under the blind condition. Hull et al. (1981) asked nine graduate students and nine basic skills students to write persuasive essays in both blind and visible conditions. For each of the two groups, Hull et al. compared several syntactic features in the essays produced under the two conditions. They noted few differences for most syntactic measures. The essays written under the blind condition, however, received lower ratings for quality when the essays were scored holistically.

Other researchers have investigated whether students do, in fact, reread the texts they are in the process of producing, and, if they do, why they reread. While observing his 17-year-old senior high school student, Mischel (1974) noted that he would often reread what he had written, seemingly "to keep the subject whole in his mind" (p. 309). Stallard (1974) reported that his 15 "good" 12th-grade writers reread what they had written much more often during composing than did his randomly selected group of 15 writers from the same grade. Pianko (1977, 1979a, 1979b) obtained similar results among her 10 community college writers in remedial classes and 7 community college writers in regular composition classes. The writers in the regular classes used the strategy of rescanning their texts, usually reading the last one or two sentences or the last paragraph as they were composing. Writers in remedial classes, on the other hand, rarely rescanned their texts.

In studies of 5 unskilled college writers (1978, 1979) and of writing teachers and college students of various skill levels (1980), Perl found that all writers reread while composing. All groups of writers paused to reread sections of their writing "until the act of rehearsal led to the creation of a new sentence" (1979, p. 330), or they referred to their topic, "particularly when they [were] stuck" (1980, p. 364), using it to think of something else to write. In verbal protocols gathered from novice and expert writers, Flower and Hayes (1981c) also noted the importance of rereading both the writing topic and sections of extant text during composing. Flower and Hayes speculated, however, that novice writers seem more tied to rereading in order to produce text than expert writers and that "*exclusive* dependence on sentence-level planning may . . . be one of the marks of a poor writer" (1981c, p. 231).

Concern for the Rhetorical Situation

Factors such as audience and purpose are often described as aspects of the *rhetorical situation*. Models of a rhetorical situation (e.g., Bitzer, 1968; Booth, 1963) usually include a *persona* (the image the writer wants to project), an *audience* (the readers), a *subject* (the information the writer wants to convey). In some models (e.g., Kinneavy, 1971; Britton et al., 1975), purpose is a configuration of writer, subject, and audience.

Stallard (1974) reported that 14 out of the 15 good 12th-grade writers he observed were concerned with purpose when planning, while only 8 of 15 randomly selected students claimed to be concerned with purpose. Sawkins (1971) found that the 5th-grade students in her "high" composition group—the more able writers—were concerned with ideas, organization, and, to some extent, purpose, while less able writers were primarily concerned about mechanics. Gould (1980) found that his adult subject was conscious of purpose, organization, and the audience.

Flower and Hayes suggest that inexperienced writers use a limited repertoire of planning strategies, while expert writers use diverse planning strategies, many of them generated by the rhetorical situation (1977, 1981c). Using thinking-aloud protocols, Flower and Hayes (1980a) explored how novice and expert writers represent the rhetorical situation. The researchers sought answers to the following questions: (a) "What aspects of a rhetorical problem do people actively represent to themselves?" (b) "If writers do spend time developing a full representation of the problem, does it help them generate new ideas?" (c) "Are there any significant differences in the way good and poor writers go about this task?" (1980a, p. 23). Flower and Hayes found that expert writers, when faced with a novel writing task, developed significantly more goals related to the rhetorical situation as they were writing than did poor writers. The expert writers whom Flower and Hayes observed generated the majority of their ideas (67%) by setting goals related to the rhetorical problem. Inexperienced writers, on the other hand, generated most ideas (83%) in response to the writing topic. Flower and Hayes concluded that "good writers are simply solving a different problem than poor writers" (1980a, p. 30). Furthermore, these researchers viewed their findings as strong evidence for the composition teacher's need to teach students new composing strategies (Flower, 1981).

In an extensive study of the writing done in several nonacademic settings, Odell and Goswami (1982) investigated writers' concerns for the rhetorical situation in ways different from Flower and Hayes. They developed research procedures for studying writing in nonacademic settings, and they explored rhetorical strategies that writers use in their on-the-job writing. Odell and Goswami analyzed cohesion and syntax in routine memos, formal memos, and business letters written on agency letterhead addressed to persons outside the agency. The researchers then wrote drafts of documents and asked workers to choose between alternative wordings these same workers had used at various times when composing documents themselves. Each worker was questioned about which alternative he or she would be willing to use in a specific situation and why a particular alternative would be preferable. Odell and Goswami found that nonacademic writers often adapted style and content to the demands of the rhetorical situation. These writers demonstrated a sense of purpose and audience for the documents they were writing and took great care to develop a persona appropriate to their purpose and audience.

Other evidence that people who write frequently on the job have a developed awareness of specific differences in writing for different audiences and purposes appears in a stratified survey of 200 college-trained people writing on and off the job. Faigley and Miller (1982) observed that while most college-trained people are not acquainted with rhetorical theory, many talk about the writing they do in terms of subject matter, audience, and the image they wish to project through their writing. For example, when a person in marketing was asked to explain her concept of clarity, she replied: "Planning and organization are most important in meeting the needs of the intended reader, whether he is a client, a potential client, a regulator, or some other person" (p. 563).

Classical Greek rhetorical theory stresses the role of audience in invention for persuasive oral discourse. Contemporary college writing textbooks have followed the classical tradition, dealing in emotional appeals and other legacies from classical rhetoric. These textbooks, however, have neglected to examine the differences between a writer's and a speaker's audience. Ong (1975) claims that composing is artificial because writers have no audience before them. Successful writers, according to Ong, are able to create a rhetorical situation by imagining their potential readers. Several studies of composing bear upon Ong's theory, and they illustrate that researchers have differing perceptions of what constitutes audience awareness. D. Graves observes that first-grade writers "are guarded from self-criticism and peer criticism by sheer egocentricity: they write invincibly with lofty indifference to the feelings of others, writing for their own sakes. But towards the end of first grade an uncomfortable awareness dawns—readers can be critical or scornful" (Walsche, 1981, p. 13). Calkins (1979, 1980) claims that concerns such as the desire to make compositions legible and mechanically "correct" in the first- through fourth-grade writers she observed marked the beginning of audience awareness. Other studies suggest that developing writers may take many years to extend their concerns about readers beyond correctness. For example, Mischel noted that his senior high school writer "appeared to have little conception of writing for an audience" (1974, p. 211). Neither the good high school senior writers nor the randomly selected seniors in Stallard's study (1974) were generally concerned with writing to a particular audience.

A common complaint about school-sponsored writing is that students do not learn to write for real audiences. Crowley (1977) reported that in the three semesters she studied the writing patterns of college composition students, they rarely wrote for anyone except their English teachers, whom they thought of as error hunters. Likewise, Britton et al. (1975) found that although the 500 British schoolchildren they studied showed a growing conception of audience between ages 11 and 18, the nature of school writing tasks tended to thwart this development. Most writing was done to demonstrate that the students knew certain facts from previous lessons. Although this writing is "informative" in purpose, students are not actually informing but instead proving tht they have learned something. Thus they are not learning how to present information to readers with varying levels of knowledge on that subject. Applebee (1981) reaches much the same conclusion about the nature of writing assignments in American schools.

A few experimental studies explore different aspects of audience awareness among writers planning texts. Atlas (1979) conducted a series of three experiments testing the abilities of community college students to adapt to a specific audience. He found that novice writers in general fail to address the concerns of their audiences. In one experiment Atlas gave subjects a questionnaire that elicited an evaluation of the reader's beliefs—in this case "Mr. Beyer," a leader of a group of handicapped persons who expressed reservations about a new transportation system. Atlas divided writers into high-, medium-, and low-ability groups. He found that writers in the low-ability group did not understand their audience's position as well as the other writers. Of the writers who clearly demonstrated an understanding of Mr. Beyer's position, however, very few were able to use their understanding to answer his complaints. When provided with a letter from Mr. Beyer specifically detailing his concerns about the new transportation system, these writers were much better able to address his concerns. Atlas concluded "that novice writers are not really insensitive to their audiences . . . but [rather] they are very context-dependent, relying on the most salient cues to tell them what points to address" (p. 37). Atlas further cautioned that crude methods of focusing attention on audience may have little effect upon how a student actually addresses an audience.

Other research on audience awareness stems from the cognitive-developmental tradition of Piaget. Kroll (1978) compared the audience responsiveness of 36 fourth graders in writing and speaking. He hypothesized that these young subjects' ability to decenter their perspective in writing is less developed than their ability to decenter it in their speaking. Kroll nonverbally taught each student a simple game and continued playing the game with each student until the student thoroughly understood the game. Afterwards, 18 students were asked to explain the game verbally, and the other 18 wrote explanations. The subjects were then asked to explain the game a second time in the medium they had not used before. All explanations were scored for content. The fourth graders showed limited ability to explain the game effectively regardless of the medium of communication. The spoken explanations during the first session, however, contained much more information than the written explanations, supporting Kroll's main hypothesis that children can decenter their perspective more readily when speaking than when writing.

Scardamalia, Bereiter, and McDonald (1977) explored the ability of writers in grades 4, 6, 9, and 11 to write adequate instructions as a measure of audience awareness. Students were taught a game through a televised demonstration of the game being played. Some writers at each grade level viewed another videotape of someone attempting—inadequately—to explain how the game was played. The second videotape was designed to sensitize writers by indirect means to the possible problems in communicating the game. All students were asked to write instructions for playing the game. Students who watched the second videotape included more of the essential ideas of the game, but their overall explanations were no clearer than those students who had watched only the first videotape. Viewing the second videotape produced certain specific effects among writers at different levels of development. For example, the youngest writers produced the most words. Scardamalia et al. concluded that writers develop their role-taking capacities in different ways at different stages.

The prose of unskilled adult writers tends to neglect the needs of potential readers in ways similar to the prose of younger children. Perl (1979) explained her five unskilled college writers' neglect of their readers' knowledge:

> The students in this study wrote from an egocentric point of view. While they occasionally indicated a concern for their readers, they more often took the reader's understanding for granted. They did not see the necessity of making their referents explicit, of making the connections among their ideas apparent, or carefully and explicitly relating one phenomenon to another, or of placing narratives or generalizations within an orienting, conceptual framework. (p. 332)

Berkenkotter (1981) considered how skilled adult writers conceive of audience. Her study examined whether adult skilled writers trained in rhetorical theory think of audience needs more actively than "expert" writers in other fields. As subjects she selected 5 professors of rhetoric and composition and 5 professors in other disciplines such as anthropology and metallurgy. All 10 had published in their fields. Using thinking-aloud protocols from these writers as her data source, she codified the types of audience-related statements these professionals made as they were writing about their career to an audience of high school seniors. Berkenkotter found that how the writer interpreted the writing task was more important in determining the number and kind of audience-related comments than professional background. The writers who wrote persuasive essays expressed the greatest number and most varied kinds of audience-related comments. The writers who chose informative discourse were second in both categories, making half as many audience-related comments as the writers of persuasive essays. Subjects who wrote narratives made still fewer comments. Nevertheless, Berkenkotter noted that what writers from the two groups shared was more important than the differences among them. She reported that all "formed a rich representation of the audience" (p. 395), which significantly affected what goals for writing these subjects set for themselves. Also, all of them created a specific rhetorical context for the task. Berkenkotter concluded that we need to teach students how to represent their audiences in the same ways that skilled academic writers in this study were able to do.

INSTRUCTION IN PLANNING

Researchers who have tested various methods of helping students generate content find that these methods produce better student essays. Scardamalia and Bereiter (in press) have summarized the results of several of their studies that provide students with aids for invention by noting that regardless of the kind of help, students will use it to generate content and will claim that the aid helped them to find what to say. Other researchers reach similar conclusions. In a study discussed in Chapter 1, for example, Rohman and Wlecke found that the essays of students who were taught "pre-writing" activities were better than those of students who were not exposed to these activities.

More systematic procedures for invention have also been tested. Young and Koen (1973) conducted an experimental class designed to determine whether teaching students tagmemic discovery procedures developed by Young, Becker, and Pike (1970) would result in improved invention skills. The 12 university engineering seniors who participated in the study were taught tagmemic discovery procedures as part of a required rhetoric course. Three kinds of data were collected from the subjects during the semester. Students kept a "reading log"—a journal expressing their feelings about the reading they were assigned to do in their courses—which faculty looked at three times during the semester. Students were also asked to do two writing tasks during the first and last weeks of the semester as a pre- and posttest. In one, students listed "problems that they were aware of in any domain of their experience," (Young & Koen, 1973, p. 17), and in the other, students wrote a list of "problems that came to mind about two short stories" (1973, p. 21). These lists were judged for the number and kinds of statements expressed, and judges found that students exhibited significantly "more systematic thinking in the posttest, more careful analysis and more precise statements, suggesting greater control of the process of inquiry" (1973, p. 22).

In another test of the tagmemic discovery procedures, Odell (1974) taught two of his classes of college freshmen to use the Young, Becker, and Pike heuristic. He collected essays from the students at the beginning of the semester and at the end, using the pre- and posttest essays to assess their improvement in writing. The posttest essays contained numbers of "conceptual gaps" similar to the pretest essays, but they did show evidence of an increase in the number of various kinds of intellectual operations—for example, "reference to contrast" and "reference to classification." There was also some evidence that students were able to "solve problems more adequately than they did in the pretest essays" (1974, p. 236).

Burns (1979) investigated the effects of three invention strategies on the qualitative and quantitative growth of ideas among college freshmen. The 69 subjects were distributed in four classes, each receiving different treatments. Three classes were taught to use a computer-assisted instruction module based on one of three heuristic systems: the Young, Becker, and Pike (1970) tagmemic matrix, Burke's (1969) dramatistic pentad, and Aristotle's (trans. 1954) topics. A fourth class receiving no instruction in heuristics served as a control group. The students receiving computer-assisted instruction were given 30 minutes to develop ideas about their paper topic by typing responses to open-ended questions such as "What could be considered a cause of [YOUR TOPIC]?" The control group was asked to spend 30 minutes during class writing down all of their ideas about their topic. All students were then asked to develop a plan for their paper, in no more than 2 hours, using either the computer printout of their ideas or the list of ideas written in class. Burns found that regardless of which computer-prompted heuristic students used, the quantity and quality of their ideas was significantly greater than the control group's. Furthermore, students using the computer-assisted instruction internalized their particular heuristic method well enough to list that strategy's questions when asked. They also responded favorably on an attitude questionnaire about computer-assisted instruction.

Two other studies examining computer-assisted composing have been conducted by Woodruff, Bereiter, and Scardamalia (1981–1982). In both studies students composed opinion essays with the assistance of computers. In the first, six male and six female sixth graders received help from a computer in response to requests for aid in developing ideas, developing the next sentence in a text, and changing words. Students wrote two essays on successive days on randomly assigned topics: one essay was written using the computer and one using pencil and paper. Students were interviewed concerning both writing experiences, and raters scored the essays holistically. Among other results, Woodruff, Bereiter, and Scardamalia reported that students were capable of composing on the computer. When using the computers, the children requested the most assistance with sentence openers. There was no difference in quality between the essays composed on the computer and the essays composed with pencil and paper. The researchers attributed this fact to the heavy reliance on the computer for help with sentence openers: "the students were . . . adopting [the] 'What next?' strategy of planning" which they used when producing texts with pencil and paper (p. 14).

In order to stimulate students to use the computer for help with "higher-level" composing strategies, Woodruff, Bereiter, and Scardamalia designed a second study in which 36 eighth graders participated—half males, half females. The students used two computer programs quite different from the one used in the first study. The questions in one of the new programs were "designed to foster more carefully considered and more fully developed essays" and had a "semi-rhetorical quality" (p. 142). The other computer program did not provide questions or prompts but was also designed to help students compose better essays. Students participating in the study were randomly assigned to one of three groups. Each group first wrote a theme using pencil and paper and then composed essays using the computer. Raters assessed all papers using a primary-trait scale. The researchers found that students participating in this study not only enjoyed composing on computers better than with pencil and paper, but also felt that using the computer to compose produced better themes. There was no significant difference, however, in the quality of essays as judged by the raters. The researchers speculated that the subjects in both studies might have produced better essays on the computer if they had had repeated practice doing so. But regardless of this possibility, the researchers emphasized the affective value of composing on the computer.

Another form of prewriting response popular in many writing programs is some kind of peer response, either in regular classroom settings or in writing labs. Many claims for the value of peer response have been made, and many suggestions have been offered for the training of peer tutors (e.g., Beck, Hawkins, & Silver, 1978; Bruffee, 1973; Elbow, 1973). One of the few research studies of the collaborative method was conducted by Clifford (1981). Clifford found that college students taught by a method including free writing and peer-group response wrote better essays than those students taught by a traditional method.

We know of no study of any method of teaching invention that does not claim success. But the many theoretical and pedagogical studies of invention appear to have had little impact on writing instruction in the schools. Applebee (1981) conducted a national study of 754 teachers and found that except for occasional brainstorming sessions by about 20% of responding teachers, invention skills are not formally taught. In observational studies Applebee has found that the average time teachers devoted to preparing their students for writing is just over three minutes. College writing instruction may place more emphasis on invention. In a national survey of 115 college writing teachers, Witte, Meyer, and Miller (1982) reported that 25.6% of the teachers listed teaching invention among the most successful aspects of their classes.

IMPLICATIONS FOR ASSESSMENT

Studies of planning at several age levels suggest that expert writers not only plan more extensively than inexperienced writers, but that they are also able to modify and elaborate their plans while they are writing. The protocols of children in the primary grades typically reflect only content (Burtis et al., in press). Even though children are clearly influenced by the rhetorical situation, this influence is apparently unconscious. Writers of about age 18 consciously plan, but they also have difficulty evaluating the rhetorical situation (Flower & Hayes, 1980a). Likewise, adult basic writers draw operative goals primarily from the writing assignment rather than from their representations of the rhetorical situation (Flower & Hayes, 1981c; Perl, 1978, 1979). Only expert writers seem to exhibit effective goal-directed planning that takes into account all of the major components of the rhetorical situation (Berkenkotter, 1981; Flower & Hayes, 1977, 1981c).

These findings have important implications for assessing writers' processes of composing. They suggest that researchers need to develop assessment instruments that will elicit information about the levels of consciousness writers employ during planning, and the time writers spend planning at various stages of their composing, about the rhetorical, linguistic, and aesthetic considerations that affect planning, and about the variety of strategies that writers employ in their planning.

The procedures used to date for describing composing have been the thinking-aloud procedure (e.g., Emig, 1971; Flower & Hayes, 1977, 1980a, 1980b, 1981b, 1981c; Perl, 1978, 1979; Pianko, 1977, 1979a) and the clinical interview (Bereiter & Scardamalia, 1983; Scardamalia & Bereiter, 1983b). Many researchers are enthusiastic about the potential of both procedures. For example, Scardamalia & Bereiter (1983a) find that young children like to discuss their strategies for reading in much the same way that psychologists discuss these strategies. A key issue is how well self-reports of process gathered under less rigorously controlled conditions might reveal changes in composing, an issue we return to in Chapters 6 and 10. Up to now, the techniques of content analysis developed for protocol research have not been considered for use in assessing writing skills. Part III of this book explores how research methods used for studying planning might be extended to writing assessment.

Chapter 3

Research on Producing Text

Of the three writing processes that have received most attention from researchers—planning, producing text, and revising—producing text is the most controversial and the least accessible. This difficulty is in one way paradoxical. Many people think of writing only as text production—the process of physically putting words on a page. In this view, production is a process distinct from planning, involving the transcription of ideas generated during planning. Some researchers, however, see a much more complex relationship between planning and production. In this view, planning and production cannot be so easily separated. Some researchers theorize that planning progresses from some abstract form through successive substantiations until words are formed on the page. Beaugrande and Dressler (1981) describe phases of text production such as planning, ideation, and parsing that do not run in a neat time sequence. They argue that these phases can interact simultaneously with dominance among the phases shifting rapidly. When inchoate ideas take form on the page, the writer must make certain decisions about the text that will follow or decide to perform local revisions. There is no point when production necessarily stops.

Producing text, in some quarters at least, is viewed as a process that is both extremely complex and very difficult to observe. In a review essay, MacNeilage and Ladefoged write that "very little is known about the production of language" (1978, p. 75). Further complicating efforts to study production are the many pragmatic factors (reviewed in Chapter 5) that make conversations "microcosms of the social order" (Butterworth, 1980, p. 2). Nevertheless, some solid work has been done that contrasts the nature of oral and written discourse production and investigates instruction in text-producing skills.

PSYCHOLINGUISTIC RESEARCH ON DISCOURSE PRODUCTION

Although there is a massive literature on comprehension, relatively few studies in psycholinguistics have addressed production. A few

43

lines of research in oral sentence production have developed, including work on lexical production (e.g., Garrett, 1975), syntax (e.g., Fay, 1981), semantics (e.g., Rosenberg, 1977), pauses (e.g., Goldman-Eisler, 1961), and speech errors (e.g., Fromkin, 1973). Most research follows a generative grammar model. Researchers theorize that people produce oral language in clause-like units (e.g., Fodor, Bever, & Garrett, 1974; Ford, 1982). The speaker monitors the meaning of the previous clause while producing subsequent clauses. The process of speech production, therefore, is dependent upon the limits of short-term memory. Daiute (1981) has found evidence from errors that suggests the same psychological model holds for writing. Errors in writing tend to occur after strong perceptual clauses, large numbers of words, and complex syntactic structures. Daiute suggests that in such complex sentences, writers lose the grammatical information necessary to complete the sentence before they finish.

A major criticism of American psycholinguistics is that its research program has been too much dominated by syntactic theory (e.g., Rommetveit, 1974). Even after psycholinguists rejected the direct application of Chomsky's theories (e.g., Bransford & Franks, 1971), researchers continued to analyze the psychological reality of linguistic units rather than to test theoretical models of production. Beaugrande (1982) criticizes psycholinguistic studies of production for looking at aspects of production in isolation. Beaugrande suggests that production processes may vary in different contexts and that different aspects of production may co-occur. Thus a major issue for current psycholinguistic research is whether the syntactic component of language production is autonomous. McDonald (1983) charges that

> modern theories of linguistic competence, though cast in a "generative" framework are not suited to the job of goal-directed generation because their formal structure does not permit them to address the central problem, i.e., *how specific utterances arise from specific communicative goals in a specific discourse context.* (emphasis in original, p. 209)

In contrast to the fragmented efforts to understand text production in American psycholinguistic research, a comprehensive theory of text production is one of the foundations of Soviet psycholinguistics. Work on text production in the Soviet Union follows from the theoretical framework set out by Vygotsky ([1934] 1962). This theory has motivated a great deal of neurolinguistic research, especially research in aphasia. Vygotsky's primary mechanism for explaining the development of speech is the notion of "inner speech."

Vygotsky conceives of thought as internal dialogues. These internal voices derive from voices the speaker has heard. Thus, for Vygotsky, there is no private language.

Since Vygotsky theorizes that speech is acquired through social interaction, his theory stresses functions and processes rather than linguistic structures. Vygotsky proposes that an utterance is formed in a series of stages, beginning with inner speech, then progressing to meanings of external words, and finally resulting in external words themselves. These notions have been modified in successive generations of Soviet research. Leont'ev (1977) describes general postulates for speech production. He delineates two sets of rules: a set of rules for representing the content in the predicative utterances of inner speech and a set of rules for translating inner speech into natural language. Inner speech is held to be greatly dependent on intent and the communicative situation. In this respect, Soviet theory has affinities to speech act theory (e.g., Austin, 1962; Searle, 1969). In fact, Leont'ev calls the focus of his research *speech activity* or *speech action* instead of psycholinguistics (Zebroski, 1981).

ORAL VERSUS WRITTEN DISCOURSE PRODUCTION

Much recent work examines differences between oral and written discourse. Two assumptions run through this literature: (a) that oral discourse is bound to the immediate context while written discourse is not (e.g., Olson, 1977; F. Smith, 1982), and (b) that cohesion in oral discourse is, in part, achieved through nonverbal means while cohesion in written discourse is achieved through explicit lexical and syntactic means (Chafe, 1982; Halliday & Hasan, 1976). Exceptions call both assumptions into question, with strategies of written texts occurring in oral discourse and conversational strategies occurring in written texts (Tannen, 1981, 1982a).

More important for the present discussion is that researchers have begun to study differences between oral and written discourse production. Nystrand (1982b, p. 6) points out that most accounts of discourse production, whether written or spoken, place production after the ideational fact. Production is often defined as the translation of ideas (usually in propositional form) into well formed sentences (Clark & Clark, 1977). Up to now most researchers have considered writing as if it were transcribed speech. Indeed, there are many aspects of oral and written discourse production that are similar. For example, the subprocesses of generating ideas, organizing, and goal setting discussed in Chapter 2 operate in both spoken and written language production. But there are also aspects of production in speech that differ from those in writing, aspects more profound than transcription formats and text types. As Nystrand notes, the standard psycholinguistic conception of language production as a transcription of ideas fails to recognize that the resources of language for discourse are not entirely subsidiary to thought but "actually shape the possibilities for and hence the conduct of discourse itself" (1982b, p. 7).

Nystrand (in preparation) elaborates this argument. Whereas transcription models handle certain discourse problems fairly well (e.g., narrative as characterized by some story grammars), relationships and differences between spoken and written language present more troublesome production issues. Spoken and written language cannot be differentiated at the level of plans, goals, and purposes, since, as language, they are equally purposeful. This is the chief reason that transcription models work as general models of discourse but provide only a rough account of production processes. An adequate account of the latter requires an alternative formulation of production—a model of discourse that adequately encompasses the species of discourse production (writing, speaking) as well as the genus (language) and can, for example, differentiate writing and speaking.

One way of studying differences between oral and written discourse production is to have people compose on the same subject in each medium. Scardamalia and Bereiter (discussed in Scardamalia, Bereiter, & Goelman, 1982) asked fourth- and sixth-grade children to produce texts in three ways: by writing, by dictation, and by "slow dictation"—dictation transcribed by the experimenter at the child's previously determined rate of writing. The medium had a great effect on the quantity of text produced. In normal dictation children produced texts 163% longer than in writing, and in slow dictation, texts 86% longer. Texts were also rated for overall quality, and the differences between media approached significance (p = .06). Texts produced by slow dictation were rated highest, followed by normal dictation and writing. Scardamalia and Bereiter concluded that freeing children from mechanical concerns improved writing quality but increasing the rate of production did not.

Scardamalia, Bereiter, and Goelman (1982) again tested the effects of medium, adding a further experimental intervention. When children were finished composing, they were asked to add more. The next two times the children stopped, they were again prompted to say or write more. As a result children produced much longer texts in every condition. The prompting led to texts twice as long in the writing and normal dictation conditions. Texts written or spoken before the three prompts were analyzed for quantity and quality. The results replicated the earlier Scardamalia and Bereiter experiment. For the extended compositions, however, the texts produced by writing were rated significantly higher (p = .016) than the dictated compositions. To probe the effect of prompting on ratings of quality, Scardamalia, Bereiter, and Goelman analyzed the children's texts for several features of content and structure. They found the added content for written texts to be more closely connected to the text produced initially than was the case for the dictated texts. They concluded that "signaling to produce more led children in writing to extend coherent strings whereas in the dictated compositions the initial coherent string was usually already ended" (1982, p. 200).

Scardamalia, Bereiter, and Goelman assume four postulates in their interpretation of these findings on the effects of medium:

1. that a written text is not a transcript of a text held in memory, but one possible realization of a more abstract set of plans;
2. that higher-level representations of text plans are not automatically stored but have to be constructed or reconstructed when needed;
3. that mental effort is required to shift from lower- to higher-level representations (e.g., to shift from debating about the spelling of a particular word back to the overall plan for a text segment);
4. and that mental representations vary a great deal according to the sophistication of writers, their familiarity with particular tasks, and their momentary needs.

Scardamalia, Bereiter, and Goelman theorize that since speech production is largely automatic, children engaging in normal dictation can remain at higher levels of representation and thereby produce much more relevant content. In slow dictation, the children are forced to wait and to engage in more reconstructions. In writing, children have the large additional burden of graphic representation. They are frequently forced to reconstruct the gist of their text, but apparently these successions of reconstructions better enable them to incorporate new information coherently into the fabric of the existing text.

INSTRUCTION IN PRODUCING TEXTS

The teaching of writing has long been associated with the teaching of skills such as forming letters on the page, placing them on the page neatly, and spelling and punctuating in accordance with conventions. Much has been written on the teaching of written conventions, such as spelling (Fergus, 1973; Frith, 1980), punctuation (Mills, 1974), and handwriting (Shaughnessy, 1977). Gould (1980) points out that such skills are not automatic for young children but require planning; therefore, for young learners, perhaps all aspects of producing texts are aspects of planning. With years of practice children form words on pages, make word and syntactic choices, spell, and punctuate with less and less conscious effort. Many plans for physically producing texts are gradually reduced to considerations such as "I don't have to write neatly since I'm going to type it after I finish." But researchers have repeatedly called attention to the fact that inexperienced adult writers frequently lack mastery over some production skills (Perl, 1979; Pianko 1979a, 1979b; Sawkins, 1971; Shaughnessy, 1977). They are unsure of spelling and punctuation, and they often struggle with word choice and syntactic form. Perl (1979) speculates that these preoccupations interrupt the flow of ideas, leading to the poorer quality of inexperienced writers' texts. Evidence for Perl's contention in children's writing, however, is inconclusive. Scardamalia (1981) claims that "recent evidence indicates that concerns with mechanics are not the major impediment to presentations of coherent ideas in discourse" (p. 100).

Studies of Error

Both first- and second-language writing research has long been concerned with the study of error. Error analysis, a procedure of analyzing written data to pinpoint students' writing difficulties, has a tradition reaching back to the early 1900s. From 1915 to 1933, error analysis was widely used in the United States in classes for students whose native language was English; in the mid-1960s, error analysis became common in language courses for non-native speakers. The general methodology of error analysis consists of the following six steps:

1. Student compositions are collected.
2. Errors are identified and labelled (e.g., "sentence fragment").
3. Errors are classified into types (e.g., "person and number agreement").
4. Relative frequencies for types of errors are determined.
5. Major areas of difficulties are identified.
6. These areas become the focus of instruction.

Soon after its reemergence as a tool for teaching second-language learners, several shortcomings of the method became apparent. First, simply determining what constitutes an "error" as opposed to a "mistake" caused by fatigue or carelessness is often a major problem. Second, categorizing errors is also frequently troublesome (Williams, 1981). Third, many so-called errors, such as "sentence fragments," occur frequently in published prose (Kline & Memering, 1977).

Hammarberg (1974), Bartholomae (1980), and others are critical of taking errors out of the contexts in which they occur. If, for example, students avoid some structure or mark of punctuation because they do not understand its use, error analysis cannot detect that difficulty. Only if the writer is willing to use a particular construction is error analysis able to detect the student's problem with it. The appearance of a type of error may in some cases be an indication that a student is trying something new (Kroll & Schafer, 1978). Maimon and Nodine (1978) find that error rates increase when students attempt to use unfamiliar syntactic structures in their compositions.

Syntactic Approaches to Writing Instruction

Another line of research influenced heavily by linguistics theorizes a close relationship between syntactic form and idea generation. One of the most influential theorists is Christensen (1967, 1968a). Christensen's interest in syntax began as a reaction to what he considered misguided advice about sentence structure in composition textbooks. Christensen (1968b) compared the syntax of major nonfiction writers and college students and found that the most important syntactic difference between the two groups of writers is the frequency and placement of nonrestrictive modifiers (cf. Faigley, 1979a; Wolk, 1970). Christensen developed a method of teaching writing that encourages students to use nonrestrictive modifiers (1968a; Christensen & Christensen, 1976), which was extended by others to larger units of discourse (D'Angelo, 1974; Grady, 1971; Karrfalt, 1968). He felt that practice using nonrestrictive modifiers could generate the supporting detail that is typically absent from student writing. Christensen's method has been criticized as applicable only for paraliterary discourse (e.g., Johnson, 1969; Tibbetts, 1970). But still uninvestigated directly is Christensen's most important claim: "solving the problem of *how to say* helps solve the problem of *what to say*" (1968a, p. vi).

Christensen called his method of teaching writing "generative rhetoric," although he did not make use of generative grammar theory. Other researchers were strongly influenced by Chomsky's (1957, 1965) work in transformational grammar. Hunt (1965) conducted a major study of written syntax of children and adults, charting what he called the development of "syntactic maturity." Subsequent studies using different methodologies supported the notion of syntactic maturity (Hunt, 1970; O'Donnell, Griffin, & Norris, 1967). Hunt (1977) later recognized that the use of nonrestrictive modifiers of the kind Christensen advocated greatly increases syntactic maturity as Hunt defined it. Hunt (1965) suggested that sentence-combining practice would enhance the syntactic maturity of developing writers. Mellon (1969) made the first pedagogical applications of Hunt's research in a year-long study of the effects of sentence-combining practice on the syntactic "fluency" of 247 seventh-grade students. (See Williams [1979] and Faigley [1980] for a discussion of the terms "maturity," "fluency," and "complexity" used in syntactic research.) Mellon observed far greater gains in 12 measures of syntactic fluency among students who were taught sentence combining than among students who were not taught the technique. Nevertheless, Mellon thought sentence combining to be an arhetorical activity, and he was concerned that sentence-combining practice not harm writing quality. O'Hare (1973) argued along the lines of Christensen that sentence-combining practice could positively affect writing quality. He reported significant gains in writing quality as well as gains in syntactic maturity among seventh-grade writers as a result of sentence-combining practice. Numerous sentence-combining studies at various grade levels (reviewed in Kerek, Daiker, & Morenberg, 1980) supported O'Hare's results with certain exceptions.

The Miami University study (Daiker, Kerek, & Morenberg, 1978; Kerek, Daiker, & Morenberg, 1979, 1980; Morenberg, Daiker, & Kerek, 1978) extended the potential of sentence combining to produce significant gains in syntactic maturity and overall writing quality to the college level. The Miami University investigators first assumed that the sentence combiners' gains in quality were related to the increases in Hunt's syntactic indices (Morenberg et al., 1978). Faigley (1979b, 1979c) examined syntactic indices as predictors of overall quality and found that Hunt's measures explained less than 3% of the raters' judgments of quality (see also Nold & Freedman, 1977; Witte & Faigley, 1983). W. Harris (1977) and Freedman (1979) conducted experiments to determine which internal factors in essays were significant influences upon raters. They rewrote essays to be strong or weak in content, organization, and sentence structure, and they found the influence of sentence structure considerably less important than the influences of content and organization upon raters' judgments of quality. When the Miami University investigators analyzed the relationship between syntactic maturity and quality in the data they collected, they too found the syntactic indices to be very poor predictors of overall quality (Kerek et al., 1980).

If syntactic differences have little influence upon judgments of writing quality, then how are gains in writing quality produced by syntactic approaches to college writing to be explained? Various explanations have been advanced, including the rhetorical assumptions introduced into sentence-combining pedagogy (Kerek et al., 1980; Kinneavy, 1979; Mellon, 1979). Other theories concern the composing process and are of most interest to the present review. Both Flower and Hayes (1980b) and Winterowd (1976) see the value of sentence combining in reducing the cognitive demands upon a writer. They propose that increasing students' ready store of sentence patterns improves the quality of their writing because students no longer have to spend as much planning effort on sentence-level considerations and can devote more mental capacity to "higher-level" planning concerns such as generating ideas, organizing, and goal setting.

Kerek (1981) extends the "cognitive load" hypothesis. He sees every writer operating within two kinds of constraints: developmental constraints—such as an 8-year-old's difficulty using left-branching structures—and rhetorical constraints—such as the demands of a particular situation. Kerek's distinction is similar to Flower's (1979) description of "writer-based" and "reader-based" prose. As children progress through the grades, developmental constraints govern less and less of their writing, and rhetorical constraints become more important. Moreover, Kerek's claim for the value of sentence combining goes beyond the reduction of cognitive demands. He theorizes that sentence-combining practice can "enlarge the students' syntactic repertoire and increase their capacity for syntactic processing, by maximizing their chunking ability and thus expanding the size of their mental 'armful'—the amount of information that they can pay attention to" (1981, pp. 105–106).

IMPLICATIONS FOR ASSESSMENT

The study of text production is met with numerous theoretical and methodological difficulties. Simple indices of error or syntax have proven to be of little value for understanding the production skills of adult writers. The major difficulty is the lack of a theory for discourse production. Psycholinguistics in the United States has thus far failed to offer a comprehensive theory of text production. Soviet psycholinguistic theory has been of value in understanding aphasia and other neurological aspects of production, but its current leader, Leont'ev (1977), admits that key aspects of the theory are not available for empirical investigation. Until better theoretical models of production emerge, assessment of text production skills in writing will remain on soft theoretical foundations.

Chapter 4

Research on Revision

According to Nold (1979), revising is "the retranscribing of text already produced after a portion of the already existing text is reviewed and found wanting" (p. 2). Revising involves both producing and planning, a fact that Emig (1971) among others acknowledges in her choice of the term "reformulation" rather than revision. The fact that revision can go on any time in the composing process, even before words are put on the page, is generally accepted. But those researching revision have, on the whole, dealt only with revisions of the written text. In spite of the difficulty of isolating revision for study, researchers have devoted a great deal of attention to this subprocess of composing.

Several researchers have stressed the role of "dissonance" in revision. R. Graves (1978) speaks of dissonance as the stimulation for correcting what is "wrong" in a text. He claims that when readers are dissatisfied with a flawed sentence, they "reconstruct, mentally, the existential situation," and then "recast the sentence, making its form reflect the situation" (p. 230). Other researchers consider dissonance as something much broader (Della-Piana, 1978; Flower & Hayes, 1981a; Perl, 1980; Sommers, 1978, 1980). In his examination of the revising of poetry, Della-Piana (1978) defines revision as "both the *discrimination* or sensing of something in a work that does not match what the poet intends or what the poem itself suggests and the *synthesis* that brings the writing closer to what is intended or suggests the way that this might be done" (p. 106). Sommers says that when the expert writers "recognize incongruities between intention and execution," the resulting dissonance "both provokes revision and promises, from itself, new meaning" (1980, p. 386). Perl (1980) describes dissonance as a "felt sense" that prompts the writer to move backward in the text.

This chapter reviews research that develops classifications for coding the kinds of revisions made by writers, studies of writers revising and the limitations of these studies, and research on the effects of instruction on revision.

SYSTEMS FOR CLASSIFYING REVISIONS

The effects of revision are tempting to examine because researchers can observe the record of revisions on the page. But as an object of study, revision has proven to be difficult and often frustrating to analyze. The seemingly clear surface record hides great underlying complexity. Nevertheless, researchers have tried to develop systems for classifying the types of changes writers make when they revise.

Literary scholars have long studied the manuscripts of literary works to discover what the writer actually wrote (often published versions are altered) and what can be inferred about the composition of the work. This interest has led to speculation about characteristic revision habits of various writers. But the scholarly controversies around some literary manuscripts imply that studies of literary revisions are labyrinthine undertakings. First, there is no way of knowing how many drafts were discarded during the writing of a work or even the sequence in which existing drafts were written. Beyond these questions a student of literary revision must develop some method for analyzing revisions. This task is also formidable. Often it is impossible to say with certainty whether a minor change in wording was performed to improve the rhythm of a particular sentence or to maintain some larger pattern in the text. One example of an attempt to classify literary revisions that illustrates these difficulties is Hildick (1965). Hildick developed a taxonomy with six kinds of revisions: (a) Tidying-up Changes ("correcting grammatical lapses," "refining puntuation," p. 13); (b) Roughening-up Changes ("loosening of a speech when it has been made too fluent for the character using it," p. 13); (c) Power Changes ("to achieve greater accuracy of expression . . . or greater force of argument," p. 14); (d) Structural Alterations (sweeping changes); (e) Ideologically Determined Changes (such as bowdlerizing); and (f) The Ragbag of Types (a miscellaneous category). These categories greatly overlap, a fact that Hildick admitted.

The problems are of only slightly less magnitude in studying revisions by children and most adult writers. For example, the National Assessment of Educational Progress (1977) classified the revisions of elementary and secondary students using categories such as "organizational," "stylistic," "continuational," and "holistic" changes. Like Hildick's categories, the NAEP classifications overlap and are impressionistic, and they too undercut conclusions based on the results of the study.

More rigourous efforts to develop reliable systems of classification are those of Sommers (1978, 1980), Bridwell (1980), and Faigley and

Witte (1981, 1984). Sommers classified changes by length and type of operation. For the latter she used the same categories—deletion, addition, substitution, and rearrangement—that Chomsky (1965) used to group syntactic transformations. Bridwell used the same scheme but added an additional length category for broad, text-motivated changes. Faigley and Witte classified changes according to their effect on the meaning of the text. They drew upon recent work in text structure (van Dijk, 1977, 1980) and inferencing (Crothers, 1979; Kintsch & van Dijk, 1978) in constructing a taxonomy of revisions. The main distinction in their taxonomy is between revisions that affect the meaning of a text and those that do not. They further subdivided meaning changes into revisions that affect the gist of a text and those more local in significance. They also characterized six types of revision operations: additions, deletions, substitutions, permutations, distributions, and consolidations.

STUDIES OF WRITERS REVISING

The Development of Revising

Children begin revising as soon as they begin writing. Calkins (1980), D. Graves (1975, 1979), J. Smith (1982), and Sowers (1979) observed that children in grades one through four were capable of revising and at times used sophisticated strategies. Graves has noted a developmental pattern of revising. When children begin to write words, their only revisions are adjustments in the form of letters. As they gain more proficiency in composing, their most common revisions are spelling changes, but sometimes very young children cross out words and substitute others. Later some young writers perform more advanced revisions such as rearranging sentences and paragraphs.

The development of revising abilities after the early grades through the end of high school is not well understood. The one major study of writers in these age groups was conducted by the National Assessment of Educational Progress (1977). The study included groups of 2,500 students at ages 9, 13, and 17. The 9- and 13-year-olds were first asked to write in pencil a science report about the moon and then asked to make any revisions in pen. The 17-year-olds followed the same procedure, except that their writing task was a note to a grocer about the sale of some rotten peaches to a child. Of the students writing the science report, the 13-year-olds revised more extensively, even though they were better prepared to write this report than the 9-year-olds. The 17-year-olds revised less than the 13-

year-olds. Nold (1981) attributed this result to the relatively easier writing task that the 17-year-olds were asked to do.

Many students leave high school with inadequate revising skills. Several researchers have asserted that high school and college writers in general do not know how to revise effectively. Crowley (1977) observed the composing processes of college freshmen for 3 years. She found that students wrote first drafts "straight through, sentence by sentence, in classic Sherman-through-Georgia fashion" (p. 167), and afterwards, their revisions were limited mainly to the correction of mechanical errors. Crowley reported that her students conceived of a second draft of a paper as "a neat recopying of the first" (p. 167). Bridwell (1980) also noted that many of the second drafts of 12th-grade students whose papers were rated low in overall quality were recopies of their preliminary drafts. Perl (1979), however, described a characteristic pattern of revision among unskilled college writers different from the one Crowley described. The students in Perl's study frequently interrupted the composing of the first draft to search for errors rather than writing their compositions straight through. This preoccupation with errors not only halted the development of lines of thought, but also led to changes that impaired the original text. Two other researchers (Bridwell, 1980; Mischel, 1974) reported cases of students rewriting papers from the beginning rather than revising the first draft. Bridwell surmised that such students either have too little interest in the topic or lack the requisite strategies to revise their essays.

Exactly what constitutes mature revision abilities remains uncertain. Two studies have suggested that expert writers are more inclined than nonexperts to make changes that affect the structure and content of a text. Sommers (1978) compared the revisions of 20 college freshmen and 20 experienced adult writers. The student writers typically viewed their first draft as conceptually finished, needing only mechanical corrections and lexical changes. Sommers called their strategies for revision a "thesaurus philosophy of writing" (1980, p. 387). Several other researchers have spoken of the predominance of mechanical and word-level revisions among inexperienced writers (e.g., Bridwell, 1980; Pianko, 1977, 1979a, 1979b; Perl, 1980; Stallard, 1974). The expert writers in Sommers' study tended to suppress concerns about mechanics and verbal precision until they had worked out the ideas of the text.

Sommers' conclusion that expert writers and inexperienced writers revise in different ways is supported to some extent by another study that describes through text analysis what Sommers learned through interviews. Faigley and Witte (1981) analyzed the effect on text structure of revisions of college freshmen, advanced college students, and expert adult writers. The advanced students turned out to be the most frequent revisers, making nonmeaning changes about twice as often as the expert adults and making about the same proportion of meaning changes. Revisions of the freshmen were predominantly nonmeaning changes. Faigley and Witte conducted a second study in which copies of the first drafts of three inexperienced writers were given to the expert adults with the request to revise the drafts as if they were their own texts. The experts exhibited considerable diversity in revising their own texts, but they revised the students' drafts in similar ways, condensing what the students had written and then elaborating to support the points that the students apparently wanted to make.

Beach (1976) also found evidence suggesting that experienced writers have different strategies for revision than inexperienced writers. Beach concluded that extensive revisers "conceived of revising as involving substantive changes in content and form" (1976, p. 164) while nonrevisers saw revising as making minor changes. Nonrevisers were "often unwilling to criticize themselves" and "rarely predicted changes for subsequent drafts" (1976, p. 164). Beach assumed that extensive revisers necessarily produce better quality papers, an assumption that has been rejected by several researchers including Beach himself in a later study. (For example, Bridwell [1980] discovered no correlation between the number of revisions and the quality of the final product in her study of high school seniors.)

A limitation of the Sommers, Faigley and Witte, Beach, and Flower and Hayes studies is that the experienced writers are either upper-division college students, journalists, fiction writers, or English teachers. Few studies have examined the revisions of other adult writers. Bazerman (in press) analyzed the historical context, notebooks, and preliminary draft leading to an article published in 1925 by the physicist, Arthur H. Compton. Compton reported in his article the results of several experiments conducted to answer challenges to an earlier experiment. Thus, the article had a clear rhetorical purpose—to convince remaining doubters of the validity of his earlier work. Bazerman found that Compton made his primary rhetorical decisions by designing the experiments to answer the objections of his critics. In the evolution of the article itself from notebooks to draft to published paper, Compton devoted most of his attention during revision to increasing the accuracy and detail and decreasing the personal claims of the written report. Bazerman concluded that once the experiments had run their course, Compton gained his rhetorical purpose by seeming to eschew rhetoric.

In a study of the composing processes of an engineer writing on the job, Selzer (1983) found that his one subject spent up to 80% of his time planning while writing documents other than routine correspondence. Revision took up less than 5% of total composing time and was limited to minor changes. Studies such as Bazerman's and Selzer's indicate that the call for more "naturalistic" research on composing should be heeded.

Effect of Medium on Revising

A few studies have examined the effect of medium on revising. Recent interest has focused on the use of computer text editors for composing (reviewed in Bridwell, Nancarrow, & Ross, 1984). Several researchers have argued that computer text editors are aids to revising because writers are freed from recopying (e.g., Bean, 1983; Daiute, 1983). For younger writers the time-consuming activity of recopying tends to discourage revising. The counterargument has been made by Gould (1980) in a study of the composing of business letters. Gould found that writers who used a text editor did indeed make more revisions, but these revisions often did not improve the final product. Gould speculated that the ease of revising on a computer at times encourages unnecessary revisions, diverting writers' attention from the more difficult activity of generating new text. Collier (1983) also observed that the use of a text editor by college students increased the number of revisions but did not enhance the quality of the final products. He found that students' efficiency and experimentation in revision did increase. Other studies that have explored the use of the computer as a guide for revising are discussed in the next section.

A few studies have considered differences between oral and written discourse production (e.g., Scardamalia, Bereiter, & Goelman, 1982; Gould, 1980). Revision is frequently not an issue in these studies, but perhaps it should be. Much written communication in business is now dictated, a technological change that discourages extensive revision. Writers who dictate to word-processing centers typically do not revise, or they make only small changes when they are given the transcribed version of their texts (Halpern & Liggett, 1984). Faigley and Miller (1982) interviewed a few writers on the job who are uncomfortable composing orally because they cannot easily revise or refer to previous text.

Textual Cues

Another line of research examines textual cues that prompt revision by asking subjects to revise test passages devised by researchers.

One approach used by makers of standardized tests is to require students to make interlinear revisions. For example, some versions of the English Composition Test contain 20-minute interlinear exercises for which students are asked to recognize errors in diction, verb tense, and style, cross out these errors, and insert corrections (Godshalk, Swineford, & Coffman, 1966). Another format for the same approach asks students to select among possible revisions (e.g., Matalene, 1982). A second approach is to ask students to revise a defective passage. This approach is widely used in second-language research with the goal of correlating performance on the instrument with overall writing proficiency (e.g., Arthur, 1980). Both approaches allow experimental control over numerous prompting factors, but critics raise the question of validity. Several studies have demonstrated that writers revise their own texts differently than they revise the texts of others (e.g., E. Bartlett, 1982; Faigley & Witte, 1981). Studies using "canned" passages, however, are at least of interest for what they tell us about how people revise the texts of others, an important concern for the study of collaborative writing.

Although a multitude of style manuals and composition handbooks offer advice on revising specific textual features (such as "Change passive sentences to the active voice"), few researchers have sought to identify what textual cues prompt revision. E. Bartlett (1982) presented a variety of textual problems to 250 children in grades four through seven to find out if certain problems are more difficult to detect in one's own writing than in the writing of others. In her experiments, children wrote a short text that they edited one week later. They were also asked to revise eight short texts devised by the researcher. Bartlett found that students detected both syntactic anomalies and referential ambiguities much more often in the texts of others. They rarely noted referential ambiguities in their own texts, probably because the references were clear to them.

Witte (1983) investigated how topical structure might influence revising decisions. Eighty students enrolled in college writing courses were given a short informative text that they were asked to revise so it would be easier to read and understand. Students' revisions were rated for overall quality, and the 20 texts with the lowest ratings and the 24 texts with the highest ratings were chosen for analysis. Several discourse variables identified by Daneš (1964) and adapted by Lautamatti (1978) were analyzed. Witte found that the high-rated revisions provided more elaboration for a limited number of subtopics from the original text and thus achieved better focus, while the low-rated revisions contained almost twice as many subtopics as the high-rated revisions. Witte speculated that students who received low scores failed to understand the focus or gist of the original text, accounting for the high number of subtopics and the arrangement of those subtopics.

Limitations of Observational Studies of Writers Revising

Applications of research on revision to writing instruction and writing assessment must be made cautiously. The corpus of research on revision contains three major limitations.

First, as noted earlier, few studies of revision consider persons other than student writers, academicians, and professional writers (especially noted literary figures). The complex uses of writing in technologically advanced countries, however, suggest that we need to now more about how these various functions of writing affect the ways people compose and revise.

Second, experimental studies of revision attempt to control for situational variables such as the motive for writing the text, familiarity with the medium and kind of writing task, the time allotted for drafting and revising, knowledge of the audience, and so on. In short, the writing situation in experimental studies is artificial. Observational studies of actual writing situations might produce different results from the same writers. A writer on the job, for instance, might rarely revise office memos but take an annual report through several drafts. In a revealing study, Berkenkotter obtained thinking-aloud protocols from Donald Murray during his normal writing routine (Berkenkotter & Murray, 1983). While he was being studied, Murray wrote three essays for which he spent only 3%, 3%, and 0% of total composing time revising. It is clear from this study that Murray's familiarity with article writing made extensive revising unnecessary. Just as an average writer can compose a routine business letter without revision, an experienced journalist such as Murray can draft an article without having to rework it.

The third limitation is related to the second. Some skilled writers compose successfully while making few changes in a text because they can retrieve or construct extensive plans. Gere (1982) studied a blind writer who is forced to write without revising, yet is an able and prolific writer. Murray has even changed his views on revising in light of his study with Berkenkotter. He now admits, "I suspect that when we begin to write in a new genre we have to do a great deal of revision, but that as we become familiar with a genre we can solve more writing problems in advance of a completed text. . . . Much of my revision is certainly a planning or prewriting activity" (Berkenkotter & Murray, pp. 170–171).

The three theoretical positions outlined in Chapter 1 point to these limitations. The literary view emphasizes the complexity and inaccessibility of the processes behind the behavior, the cognitive view reminds us of the procedural nature of some kinds of revision, and the social view exposes the artificiality of controlled studies of revision.

INSTRUCTION IN REVISION

Classroom studies of revision have the advantage of knowing the cause of revision. Students revise because teachers tell them to revise. The crucial question for these studies and for methods of teaching revision is "Why ask students to revise?" Researchers have attempted to answer this question in two ways. First, they have examined the general effect of revision on writing quality. Second, they have studied the interaction between writers and teachers and the use of procedural guides for revising.

Typical studies of the first kind are those by Buxton (1958) and Hansen (1978). Buxton devised an experiment with three groups of students. One group did no writing and served as a control group. Two treatment groups wrote an essay a week for 16 weeks. One of the treatment groups received extensive comments and revised their papers in class with teacher supervision. The other treatment group received minimal comments and did no revision. By the end of the term, both treatment groups wrote essays rated higher in quality than the control group, and the group that received detailed comments and revised wrote better than the group that did not.

Hansen reported very different results in a study which paired an experimental group that revised every paper and a control group that did not revise. Both groups improved in writing quality over one semester. Hansen concluded that what seemed to be the determining factor in the improvement in compositions of both groups was the extensive instruction in revising strategies that both groups received. One-fourth of class time was spent on this activity. She alleged that "if comprehension of revision techniques is achieved, the actual writing out of what has been comprehended may be irrelevant" (p. 960).

It is hard to draw general conclusions from these studies, however, because a number of important variables were left uncontrolled. Whether revising was or was not responsible for the effects cannot be determined. In addition, Fulkerson (1978) has questioned whether Hansen's judgments about students' revision skills from one piece of writing are valid.

Recent research has been directed toward more specific questions than whether students should or should not revise. In particular, researchers have examined the influences of teacher response and automatic response to students' writing and revising.

Teacher Response

Comments on student papers. Several empirical studies have examined the effect of teachers' comments on students' attitudes toward writing and the quality of their writing (reviewed in Ziv, 1981). Researchers have found that negative comments produce negative attitudes toward writing (e.g., Gee, 1972; Stevens, 1973; Taylor & Hoedt, 1966), but these researchers were not able to show that positive or negative comments influence the quality of student writing. Several studies have manipulated the types of comments that students receive, examining the effect on writing quality. For example, Bata (1972) tested for the effects of marginal, terminal, and mixed marginal and terminal comments on writing quality. No significant differences were observed for any of the conditions. In another approach, Arnold (1963) asked one group of 10th-grade students to revise using a teacher's comments while another group did not revise, but both groups wrote papers similar in quality after a year of instructional treatment. Beach (1979) similarly found little evidence that between draft teacher comments on high school students' essays produced differences in overall quality. A problem common to all of these studies is the narrow focus. Knoblauch and Brannon (1981) criticized such studies of teachers' comments for assuming that degrees of effectiveness could be distinguished "amidst such gross uncertainty about the value of *any* kind of commenting" (p. 2). They further charged that it is impossible to separate teachers' comments "from the whole environment of oral and written communication between teacher and student" (p. 2).

Teachers' comments have been blamed for students' failure to revise effectively. In a study of the functions of teachers' comments, Searle and Dillon (1980) found that the majority of comments were judgmental in nature, while practically none anticipated further revision. Sommers (1982) charged that many comments "take students' attention away from their own purposes in writing a particular text and focus that attention on the teacher's purpose in commenting" (p. 149). Criticism of teachers' comments denying students' intentions in writing is nothing new. In 1923, Leonard asked 181 high school teachers to "make whatever corrections and changes you would require a high school pupil to make" (p. 518) on a series of 50 sentences taken from literary essays. Leonard noted that "practically all the teachers fatigued themselves to a point close to insensibility by meticulous correction of a great number of idioms in sentences from DeQuincey, Lamb, Symonds, and authors of similar standing" (p. 518). In another experiment teachers "corrected" sets of high school themes. In describing the teachers' corrections, Leonard observed that "in many cases, they reveal awkward and even tactless minds which 'schoolmaster' and iron out what is pleasantly individual" (pp. 528–529).

One study examined the effects of teacher comments in relation to other aspects of instruction. Hillocks (1982b) conducted a complex experiment with three instructional treatments involving 278 seventh and eighth graders in 12 classes. The instructional period was 4 weeks, and all students wrote two pretest and two posttest essays. Students in half the classes were taught prewriting activities that included observing, listening, describing, and acting (see Hillocks, 1975); students in the other half received only the assignment. For the second treatment, students in half the classes revised all essays written between the pretests and posttests; the other students did not. Finally, half of the students received extensive comments on what they wrote; the other half did not. All instructional treatments achieved significant gains, but the gains for prewriting with revision, prewriting without revision, and assignment with revision groups were far greater than the assignment without revision group. Significant interactions occurred between instruction and revision and between instruction and comment. Hillocks' study has several implications for response and revision. First, it demonstrates that practice in revising can affect performance on subsequent new writing tasks. Second, it suggests that teacher comments can be effective if they are focused and are part of a broader instructional approach. Finally, Hillocks' study illustrates the necessity of studying isolated aspects of instruction, such as teacher comments, in the context of other factors.

Conferencing. Several researchers have found that teachers can lead young writers to revise extensively (e.g., Calkins, 1980; D. Graves, 1979). In a typical study, Kamler (1980) described the role of a primary teacher in influencing the revisions of a student who worked on a story about her cockatiel over a 3-week period. After writing the initial draft, the teacher first had the student read and discuss the story with a peer. Later, the student had two conferences about the paper with her teacher and, finally, met in a peer-group conference to discuss the paper. As a result of each conference, she made changes in her paper. Her composition evolved from a few unrelated, brief generalities about her bird to a much longer development of her topic including several accounts of the bird's activities. The student revised to add information, delete irrelevancies, clarify meaning, and supply transitions. Kamler claimed that what was most notable about the student's experience was not the product, but the "process that helped develop an inadequate beginning into a competent end" (p. 693). Several claims have also been made for the value of conferences in college-level writing courses (e.g., Arbur, 1977; Reigstad, 1980), but few researchers (e.g., Freedman, 1981) have actually studied what happens in conferences that are part of college writing courses.

Procedural Response

The introduction of computers as interactive tutors in elementary, secondary, and college classrooms has led to interest in automatic kinds of response to writing. Children in the early grades can learn to write on a computer quickly, and they are eager users when given the opportunity to communicate (Bradley, 1982). Some efforts are now being made to develop a comprehensive language-arts curriculum using computers (Rubin, 1982). Two kinds of computer response for revising are being tested. Students composing on the computer can call on "help" programs to aid them in revising. Second, students can call upon computer programs that analyze texts such as the Writer's Workbench (McDonald et al., 1982) to evaluate what they have written. They can then use this evaluation to help them revise.

Not all procedural response has to come from a computer. Scardamalia and Bereiter (1983b) employed another kind of procedural response in a study of what competencies children need to be able to revise. The subjects for the study were 90 children—30 each from grades 4, 6, and 8. While composing a paragraph on the topic, "Should children choose the subjects they study in school?" half of the students from each class were asked to stop after each sentence was written and perform three related tasks: (a) The students evaluated their sentences using eleven evaluation phrases supplied by the researcher, such as "People may not understand what I mean" or "This is good." (b) They then made a "tactical choice" of what to do with the sentence by using the six directives supplied by the researchers, e.g., "I'd better say more." (c) These students then either changed the sentence or generated the next one. Scardamalia and Bereiter called the process "Compare, Diagnose, and Operate," likening it to one of the operations that experienced writers generally perform when producing texts. These researchers found that students' evaluations of their papers agreed to a large extent with the assessments of an adult rater; however, students were generally unable to diagnose specific problems. Their difficulty with diagnosis seemed to be caused by their focusing on problems within individual sentences rather than considering the effect of particular sentences in the text as a whole. The C–D–O process is one of several intervention techniques or "facilitators" that Bereiter and Scardamalia have developed to reduce the demands of a writing task so that young writers can make better use of the knowledge and skills they have (see Bereiter & Scardamalia, 1982).

IMPLICATIONS FOR ASSESSMENT

Most observational and experimental studies of revision have been concerned with writers' behavior. These studies, however, give a conflicting record. For example, the kinds of revisions made by the engineer in Selzer's (1983) study are similar to the revisions of inexperienced college writers in Sommers' (1978) and Faigley and Witte's (1981) studies, and, indeed, to Murray's own habits of revision (Berkenkotter & Murray, 1983). Are we to conclude that these writers all revise in similar ways because the surface record is similar?

With more studies like Selzer's of professionals writing on the job, we might find that the most extensive revisers are persons newly hired. They would likely have the most difficulty with the written conventions of a particular workplace. As they internalize and become fluent in using these conventions, certain kinds of decisions should require less conscious attention, which is Murray's explanation of why he revises so little himself. As writers gain expertise in a particular kind of writing, they are better able to monitor a larger number of conventions and to make decisions before committing their ideas to the page.

Consequently, we should be as interested in the revisions writers do not make as in the ones they do. The focus of research on revision needs to move away from the record on the page toward the knowledge that writers have for evaluating and revising texts. Studies employing thinking-aloud protocols offer one approach to writers' knowledge. Other approaches are systematic interviews (Odell & Goswami, 1982) and carefully designed empirical studies. We need to know, for example, the importance of the ability to take an alternative point of view for effective revising. Kroll's research (1978), following the tradition of Piaget, suggests this ability develops relatively late. Other theorists, especially Ong (1975), maintain that the ability to take the reader's perspective is the result of a writer's extensive reading experiences. One recent experiment provided expert writers with verbal protocols of readers interpreting their texts (Swaney et al., 1981). Writers who were shown protocols made changes in response to misreadings, changes that improved ratings of comprehension. We need to know if younger writers are capable of using this kind of information to improve their texts. Clearly we need to know more about how knowledge of writing and strategies for composing develop before we can accurately assess writers' abilities to evaluate and revise their texts. It may be that the knowledge used for revising follows the acquisition of other kinds of knowledge.

Chapter 5

Research on
Writers' Knowledge

Up to now we have looked at studies that examine a variety of processes and subprocesses involved in composing. These processes often overlap and interact in complex ways. Although we have not tried to sort out the many sources of theoretical and methodological confusion in the studies we have described, it should be evident that terms such as "planning," "transcribing," and even "composing" often differ in meaning from researcher to researcher. These terms are often overlapping, and some researchers do not find it necessary to distinguish among them.

For example, Scardamalia, Bereiter, and Goelman (1982) offer a simple, but elegant, distinction for analyzing processes of composing. They group components concerned with "goals, plans, strategies, task-related knowledge and the like" under the heading of *metacomponents* (1982, p. 173). They call another set of components used to carry out the writer's decisions and plans *production factors*. Following this distinction, we can sort composing subprocesses for adult writers along these lines:

Production Factors	Metacomponents
psycho-motor activities	task-related knowledge
syntactic processes	subject-related knowledge
grapholect	audience-related knowledge
inferences	goal setting
short-term memory	organizing
etc.	etc.

From this brief list of metacomponents, we can see that knowledge of writing is of two kinds: knowledge of strategies for composing, which is often tacit knowledge; and knowledge about the subject matters, rhetorical goals, and organization of writing, which is sometimes declarative knowledge. Ryle (1949) described this distinction as the difference between knowing "how" and knowing "that." Polanyi (1958) makes a similar distinction that Reither (1981) and Britton (1982) have applied to composing and the teaching of writing. Recently, researchers in artificial intelligence have debated how to represent declarative and procedural knowledge, coming to the conclusion that they are not easily divisible (Winston, 1977). Understanding what a writer knows is essential to understanding why that writer does or does not make particular decisions and execute particular strategies during composing. In this chapter we highlight some of the issues in the vast literature on knowledge of language and the uses of language that are pertinent to the study of writing processes.

LANGUAGE SYSTEMS AND DISCOURSE

Knowledge of language systems and discourse is highly developed before children form their first letters on the page. Consequently, the nature and sequence of development of oral language strongly influences the development of writing abilities. We will briefly review some of the important work in language systems and discourse that has investigated these aspects of a writer's knowledge.

Language Systems

All healthy humans can talk; not all learn to read and write. Since Bloomfield's dictum that "Writing is not language" (1933, p. 21), the discipline of linguistics has focused on spoken, not written, language. A few contemporary linguists in both Europe (Stubbs, 1980; Vachek, 1973) and America (Read, 1981; Tannen [Ed.], 1982b) have finally broken the restriction on the study of written language just as earlier pioneers (e.g., Z. Harris, 1952) ventured beyond Bloomfield's restriction of linguistics to sentence level structures and below. Nevertheless, most linguists in America still observe the traditional boundaries of linguistics and generally ignore written language.

The traditional boundaries of linguistics do prove useful to the present discussion because they isolate those aspects of a writer's knowledge that all healthy children possess, whether literate or illiterate. These aspects include systems of phonology, lexical items, and syntax, which children acquire in developmental stages. Much is known about the sequence of development. In general, the rates of development vary greatly among the major components, with learners devoting more attention to phonology and vocabulary at earlier stages than to syntax. As learners become more proficient in using a particular system, that system becomes increasingly automatized, demanding less of the user's awareness (Shuy, 1981).

Writing instruction typically follows a pattern similar to oral language acquisition, where children first learn to make and recognize letters, then to write and recognize words, and finally to form sentences. But there are more differences than similarities between how children learn to talk and how they learn to write. Children learn to speak without instruction, but they must be taught to write. (However, writing can be learned outside of school settings, as Scribner and Cole [1981a] found true for the Vai.) Because children are taught to write after they learn how to speak, what they already know about language necessarily influences how they learn to write. Bissex and others (Gundlach, 1981; Read, 1980) point out that children in the first and second grades frequently invent spellings based on their knowledge of sound-letter correspondence. Bissex (1980) noted that her son Paul's first efforts at writing were not attempts to spell but to communicate (such as making a "welcome home" banner for mom). Before Paul entered the first grade, he wrote signs, lists, informative notes, labels, and captions, a story, a greeting card, a game, directions, and statements. The complexity of speech-writing relationships is also illustrated in written syntactic development. O'Donnell, Griffin, and Norris (1967) found that the written syntax of third graders was much simpler than their spoken syntax, but in the fifth and seventh grades, written syntax tended to be more complex. Loban (1976) reported similar findings in a study of language development from kindergarten through Grade 12, although he found that syntactic development in oral language is more regular than in written language.

The relationships between the development of oral and written language become more complex when students learn a written dialect that is different from their spoken dialect. Hirsch (1977) claims that all writers of English cope with this problem, but the problem is magnified for speakers whose spoken dialect differs markedly from the written dialect. Features of the spoken dialect appear inappropriately in writing. Whiteman (1981) calls this problem *dialect influence*. In a study of the written texts of lower-class black and white children, Whiteman found that certain kinds of errors, such as the omission of some inflectional suffixes, suggest both dialect influence and an overall pattern of writing development. Clearly, much remains to be learned about relationships between oral and written language development.

Discourse

Human ability to produce and understand language cannot be described solely in terms of traditional linguistic systems such as syntax and phonology. When we study how people use language to communicate, we study language as discourse. The following brief review of discourse research suggests that humans possess several kinds of complex knowledge about discourse, knowledge that is part of general language abilities. The point of our brief discussion is that writing is learned as part of a much broader spectrum of communicative abilities.

Discourse can be studied from several perspectives (see Dressler, 1978). First, discourse can be analyzed as a collection of formal systems. One frequently analyzed phenomenon is *cohesion*, which actually is a blanket term for several kinds of grammatical and semantic relationships. Beaugrande and Dressler (1981) distinguish between short-range and long-range cohesion. Short-range cohesion is maintained through grammatical dependencies and can be represented by grammatical (e.g., Beaugrande, 1980; Woods, 1970) or semantic networks (e.g., van Dijk, 1977; Frederiksen, 1977; Kintsch, 1974). Long-range cohesion is established primarily through various kinds of recurrence, especially the repetition of key words and concepts (Halliday & Hasan, 1976). Cohesion is also related to the distribution of "old" and "new" information in a text (Clark & Haviland, 1977; Daneš, 1970; Daneš, 1974; Palkova & Palek, 1978; Prince, 1981; Vachek, 1975). Old information is information the listener either knows or has been made aware of by previous mention in the text. Together, these relations not only provide the "glue" that holds sentences together, but also signal the discourse topic and mark other relationships.

Surface markers of cohesion are indications of a deeper *coherence*. Discourse is said to be coherent if it can be interpreted in a world that a listener knows or can imagine. If the interpretation of discourse were strictly a matter of logic, coherence would not be a difficult phenomenon to explain. But discourse often is not logical in structure, nor is it interpreted in ways comparable to formal logic. The concepts in discourse are often fuzzy and ill-defined, allowing many possibilities for interpretation. Furthermore, ways of establishing coherence differ from culture to culture (Chafe, 1980).

People derive meaning from writing by integrating concepts in the text with their knowledge of the world. Discourse typically is incomplete, and listeners rely upon their knowledge of the world and expectations about texts to make inferences (Clark, 1977; Crothers, 1978, 1979; Schank, 1975). In fact, explicit discourse is difficult to understand, not only because it is redundant, but also because listeners make unintended inferences (cf. Shuy & Larkin, 1978). Recent work in the field of artificial intelligence—the attempt to model human thought processes using computers—has demonstrated the extent to which listeners must contribute to the construction of meaning. Attempts to have computers tell stories, for example, illustrate that even simple folktales must be interpreted through subtle chains of reasoning (Black, Wilkes-Gibbs, & Gibbs, 1982).

Intentionality refers to the goal or motive underlying discourse. The study of intentions is often called *pragmatics* following Morris (1946). Children learn how to express intentions early in life (Bruner & Garton, 1978). Many recent studies have examined the relationship of communicative intentions to social structures (e.g., Halliday, 1978; Sinclair & Coulthard, 1975). The most extensive attempt to construct a theory of intentions in texts is speech-act theory (Austin, 1962; Bach & Harnish, 1979; Searle, 1969; Steinmann, 1982). Searle (1969) analyzes statements in four levels: as *utterance acts* possessing linguistic meaning (that is, texts that are grammatical), as *locutionary acts* possessing propositional content (that is, coherent texts), as *illocutionary acts* possessing intentions that the speaker wishes someone to recognize (such as requests), and as *perlocutionary acts* capable of bringing desired effects upon listeners (such as changing someone's beliefs). Speakers successfully communicate if listeners recognize their illocutionary intention, but speakers are successful as persuaders only if their listeners perform the speakers' perlocutionary intentions. In other words, the intent of a speaker's request may be clear, but the listener may not want to do what the speaker requests. Listeners rely upon shared assumptions when interpreting a speaker's intentions. Grice (1975) described four categories of mutual beliefs which he called the *cooperative principle.* They include *quantity* (Make your text no more or less informative than is required), *quality* (Say only what you believe to be true and have adequate evidence to support it), *relation* (Be relevant), and *manner* (Be brief and orderly; avoid obscurity and ambiguity).

Green (1982) claims that the ability to infer speakers' plans, goals, intentions, and purposes from their utterances and to plan and execute communication so that such inferences are most efficiently made is more important than knowledge of language itself. Green outlines four steps, which may occur unconsciously and simultaneously, for making any utterance. The communicator must select some constellation of aspects about the subject of the utterance, order this group of aspects, choose suitable expressions for them, and arrange the chosen expressions according to the rules of grammar and whatever principles of rhetoric are available and relevant. These four steps, she claims, are directed more by pragmatic knowledge of goals, plans, and intentions than by grammatical knowledge.

Thus, the ability to convey and recognize intentions is heavily dependent upon the mutual knowledge and beliefs of the speaker and listener. Listeners must be able to distinguish between literal and nonliteral usage and, at times, even interpret the motives of deliberately deceptive language.

WRITTEN TEXTS

Because writing abilities must be learned through instruction, the central question for those who teach writing is: "What knowledge must an effective speaker acquire to become an effective writer?" We maintain that knowledge of writing comprises much more than knowledge of the technology of writing. Effective writers must also know a great deal about the uses of writing in a particular discourse community, about potential readers in that community, and about specific subject matters.

Differences between Speech and Writing

The most obvious writing conventions are the visible aspects of written form such as graphemes (Vachek, 1973) and spelling (Frith, 1980). The technology of the alphabet is in itself a remarkable human achievement, which Havelock's studies of the development of the Greek alphabet (1963, 1976, 1981) have helped us to appreciate. But research on written texts and research on differences between speech and writing have demonstrated that conventions of writing extend far beyond the learning of orthography (reviewed in Akinnaso, 1982).

Several researchers have studied the lexical differences between spoken and written language. Drieman (1962) and Gibson, Gruner, Kibler, and Kelly (1966) each set up experiments in which university students, unaware that the purpose of the experiments was language analysis, spoke and wrote on the same topic. These researchers found written discourse to have more words, more polysyllabic words, and fewer personal words. Several other researchers have corroborated these findings. De Vito (1966, 1967), for example, found that written discourse is characterized by a greater number of abstract nouns. De Vito's findings may not be generalizable, however, because his subjects were university professors whose published academic papers were the data for the written text analysis. In another study of spoken and written vocabularies, Gruner, Kibler, and Gibson (1967) corroborated some of the earlier findings, specifically that written discourse contains fewer personal references. They found that writing is characterized by a more varied vocabulary, although they also found that the 25 most frequently used words in both oral and written discourse are similar (e.g., determiners, demonstratives, and pronouns). Akinnaso (1982) suggests that because words of Latin derivation are considered more formal, they occur more frequently in writing.

In addition to lexical differences, there are also several syntactic and semantic differences between written and spoken language. De Vito (1967), Goody (1980), O'Donnell (1974) and other researchers have found that the syntactic and semantic structures of written discourse are generally more elaborate, especially with respect to complex noun and verb structures. Research on style in written texts that focuses on features such as nonrestrictive modifiers and parallelism gives additional evidence for this claim (e.g., Christensen, 1967; Milic, 1965; Walker, 1970). Another syntactic feature that researchers have determined occurs more often in written texts is the subject–predicate construction. Spoken discourse, in contrast, relies more heavily on reference–proposition constructions. Ochs (1979a) attributes this difference to the degree to which the discourse is "planned": "In spontaneous communication, speakers . . . rely less heavily on syntax to articulate semantic relationships . . . Context is used to link referents (logical arguments) to their relevant predications" (p. 62). Other syntactic differences between spoken and written language noted by researchers are: (a) greater occurrence of passive verb constructions in written language, (b) greater occurrence of definite articles than demonstrative modifiers in written language, and (c) more frequent use of certain grammatical features such as attributive adjectives and participles in written language (O'Donnell, 1974; Ochs, 1979a).

Written texts are also said to differ from spoken discourse in logical organization. Olson (1977) claims that the presence of paragraphs, "topic sentences," and other organizational markers characterizes nonfiction written texts. Paragraph structure has been the subject of considerable research. In the mid-1960s three competing theories of paragraph structure were offered. Christensen (1965) advanced two possible relationships among sentences in a paragraph—coordinate and subordinate. Becker (1965) proposed a model of paragraph structure based on arrangements of semantic "slots"—

such as "topic–restriction–illustration" and "problem-solution." Rodgers (1966) offered a third view, arguing that paragraphs are orthographic conventions not controlled by rules governing their structure. Rodgers instead proposed a semantic unit centering on a single topic that may or may not constitute a paragraph. Each of the three theorists depended on the reader's ability to identify the discourse topic, and Christensen and Becker's theories included something like a topic sentence. But when Braddock (1974) surveyed a corpus of 25 essays from contemporary journals, he estimated that only 13% of contemporary nonfiction paragraphs begin with a topic sentence and only 3% end with one.

Other semantic aspects of written texts have been examined as well. Several schemes for describing the logical relationships between sentences have been offered (e.g., Larson, 1976; Pitkin, 1977a, 1977b; Winterowd, 1970). Approaches developed for the study of oral language have been applied to writing—approaches such as the analysis of lexical cohesion (e.g., Witte & Faigley, 1981), the analysis of "old" and "new" information (e.g., Dillon, 1981; Faigley & Witte, 1983; Vande Kopple, 1982), and the analysis of intentions (e.g., Larson, 1971). These studies emphasize the special characteristics of writing.

Another important difference between spoken and written language is genre. Kress (1982) observes that

> the child has to gain mastery over the forms and the possibilities of the different generic types, as part of the process of learning to write. The different genres each make their own demands in terms of their formal structures, their ordering of thematic material, their conception of knowledge. . . . The achievement of genre is a necessary and integral part of the achievement in writing; the two are inextricably interwoven. (p. 99)

Little work has considered these different demands, either from the standpoint of comprehension (e.g., Brewer, 1980; Meyer & Rice, 1982; Olson, Mack, & Duffy, 1981) or production (see "Organizing" in Chapter 2).

More recently, several researchers have argued that the structure of complicated texts can be signalled by the way information is displayed on the page (reviewed in Hartley, 1980). This line of research has drawn new attention to issues such as type font and size, page size, headings and subheadings, spacing, illustrations, tables, and other graphic materials. Even from this short review of the more obvious differences between speech and writing, we can begin to appreciate why writing is difficult to learn.

Cognitive Effects of Writing

A more global issue in speech-writing research centers on the cognitive consequences of being able to read and write. In his analysis of the intellectual life of ancient Greece, Havelock (1963, 1976) argues that the invention of the alphabet allowed the Greeks to externalize memory, thus freeing the mind for abstract thought. He claims that writing permitted thoughts to be compared and their structure analyzed. Goody (1968, 1977, 1980) takes a more extreme position, arguing that the development of writing led to the development of new cognitive structures. For example, Goody and Watt (1963) maintain that Aristotle's syllogistic reasoning was made possible by writing. Olson (1977, 1980) applies this view to contemporary education and social structures. He contends that oral language is fragmented and dependent on an immediate context. Written texts in contrast are said to be explicit because they cannot rely on paralinguistic cues and other contextual factors to make meaning. The demand for explicitness in written language created what Olson calls "objective knowledge." He sees people in literate cultures "as progressively more able to exist in a purely linguistically specified, hypothetical world" (p. 276).

Analysts of literacy who take the social view outlined in Chapter 1 discount both the cognitive "gulf" created by literacy and the notion that written texts are independent of context. Some of the strongest evidence against the cognitive argument has come from a study of the Vai in Liberia, a people who had developed literacy apart from schooling (Scribner & Cole, 1981a, 1981b). Scribner and Cole found that literacy produces some differences in certain contexts. Literates were more sensitive to the needs of their audiences and were able to contextualize information better than nonliterates. But in the important dimension of logical thinking, literates and illiterates did not differ in performance. Scribner and Cole observed that literacy did not create new cognitive abilities but tended to increase existing abilities. They argue that literacy should be understood as a set of skills similar to other skills such as those that enable one to play a musical instrument. They fault Olson for attempting to explain ontogenetic development on the basis of intellectual history and for attributing to literacy characteristics of thought that are associated with schooling. Olson's contention that in written language "all of the information relevant to the communication of intention must be present in the text" (p. 277) has also come under strong attack. Several theorists (e.g., Heath, 1980; Rader, 1982) argue that no discourse can be decontextualized, that every text is a negotiation of meaning between writer and reader. We will further discuss this notion in Chapter 6.

Beliefs and Attitudes about Writing

Writers not only acquire knowledge about writing, they also acquire beliefs and attitudes about writing that influence how they compose. Student writers often have misconceptions about composing, such as the belief that good writers produce finished texts in the first draft (Rose, 1980). Many people who believe that writing is difficult tend to avoid writing whenever possible. This anxiety toward writing has been described as *writing apprehension* (Daly & Miller, 1975). Highly apprehensive writers make academic choices and select careers perceived to require little writing (Daly & Shamo, 1976, 1978). Highly apprehensive writers also tend to score lower on standardized tests of writing related skills, and their written products are judged lower in quality for some types of writing (Faigley, Daly, & Witte, 1981).

In a modified case study of four writers assessed as high apprehensives and four writers assessed as low apprehensives, Selfe (1981) found that the high apprehensives had written less in college, disliked writing, procrastinated when forced to write, and feared having their writing evaluated by teachers. High writing apprehensives spent less time planning and revising than did the four low writing apprehensives. Studies of writing apprehension emphasize that what people believe to be true about their abilities as writers affects their performance.

FUNCTIONS OF WRITING

Writers have some motive for writing. Students write papers to fulfill assignments; people write letters to the editor to express anger; scientists write papers to inform other scientists of their work. We can examine functions of writing by focusing on the uses of writing in particular societies and by focusing on an individual writer's purposes for writing.

Social Uses of Writing

Purposes for writing shaped the development of writing systems. Recent scholarship has pushed back the history of writing systems some 5,000 years (Schmandt-Besserat, 1977). Schmandt-Besserat argues from archeological evidence that a precursor of writing developed about 8,500 B.C. in western Asia among farmers who devised an ingenious method of keeping track of their trading. They recorded livestock and other trade goods using a system of clay tokens. Much later (starting about 3,500 B.C.) these tokens began to take on new functions as trading became more extensive and covered broader distances. Tokens sealed in clay jars served the same function as a modern bill of lading. A jar accompanied a shipment and was broken at the time of delivery to insure that what was promised had actually been shipped. The problem with this system, however, was that the jars had to be broken to reveal their contents. The important step for the development of writing, according to Schmandt-Besserat, was when shippers began to use the tokens to imprint the outside of the jar, indicating what was inside. Eventually, the imprints replaced the function of the tokens, and clay tablets replaced clay jars. The critical link between these archaic recording systems and writing was the replacement of the three-dimensional token with the two-dimensional image.

The oldest surviving examples of actual writing date back 5,000 years to Mesopotamia. Again, these documents all have commercial purposes and deal with trading and accounts. Later, writing acquired additional functions. Oppheim (1977) notes that in ancient Mesopotamia and in other ancient civilizations of the Near East, writing was used for recording and communicating data, and for ceremonial purposes. The first function included recording for administrative purposes, codifying of laws, preserving sacred lore, and recording events. The second function included letters, edicts, and public announcements. The third function included inscriptions not intended to be read by ordinary citizens, such as inscriptions on amulets to ward off demons and sacred texts that were read by priests.

Writing took on new functions during the classical age in Greece. Writing extended beyond the subject matters of other ancient civilizations—commerce, government, and religion—to new areas such as literature, philosophy, history, and science. Much later, the uses of writing became considerably more diversified and extended to a much larger population as a result of printing (Eisenstein, 1979). We cannot pursue an extended discussion of these uses here. It seems clear, however, that commerical reasons for learning to read and write cannot explain the high rate of literacy that Western Europe and the American colonies had achieved by the middle of the 18th century. Scotland and Sweden—which were largely rural and unindustrialized—had among the highest rates of literacy in Europe, and by the end of the 18th century, a predominantly rural population in New England had almost universal male literacy (Lock-ridge, 1974). People learned to read and write because they understood literacy as a civic and religious responsibility.

By the end of the nineteenth century, however, the changing nature of the American economy and society brought changing attitudes toward writing (Heath, 1981). Writing skills became associated with "good character" and "good language." Ohmann (1976) associates these changing perceptions of writing with the rise of a managerial class during the second half of the nineteenth century:

> Writing took on new functions in nineteenth-century America. Complex industrial firms needed a corps of managers who could size up needs, organize material, marshal evidence, solve problems, make and communicate decisions. Government and other bureaucracies had a similar need for exposition and argument and allied skills. Writing was no longer mainly a private and public art, but a tool of production and management. (p. 93)

Ohmann sees the development and maintenance of composition courses as serving the needs of the industrial state.

The importance of writing as an on-the-job skill can explain perhaps better than any other single cause the proliferation of composition courses in American colleges and universities. In the years following World War II, demands for writing grew as bureaucracies grew in business and government. Writing skills were required of an expanding professional class (P. Anderson, 1980; Davis, 1977; Penrose, 1976; Rader & Wunsch, 1980; Stine & Skarzenski, 1979). Writing itself became a major economic product in the United States and other technologically advanced nations. The United States Bureau of Labor estimated that in 1930, 12.5 million workers were employed in the information sector of the American economy, 10.5 million in agriculture, 18 million in industry, and 10 million in services. In 1980, the Bureau of Labor estimated there were 45 million in the information sector, 2 million in agriculture, 21.5 million in industry, and 27.5 million in services (Bell, 1981, p. 522). As the United States moves toward a postindustrial economy, the functions of writing have become increasingly vital to national interests.

Uses of Writing for the Individual

Part of the process of learning to write is learning what functions writing serves. Specific functions for writing have been broadly classified in several different systems. Jakobson (1960), Kinneavy (1971), and Britton (1978; Britton et al., 1975) have advanced taxonomies of purposes for writing. Kinneavy's classification has as its theoretical basis the four components of the "communication triangle"—which, for written discourse, would include the writer, the reader, the subject, and the text itself. Each of these components, Kinneavy argues, must be present in order for communication to occur; and when a piece of discourse emphasizes one component more strongly than the others, different kinds of discourse result. Emphasis on the writer results in self-expressive discourse; emphasis on the reader results in persuasive discourse; emphasis on the subject results in informative discourse; and emphasis on the text results in literature.

The functions of writing for the individual writer can also be viewed in terms of *exigency*—what's at stake for the writer (Bitzer, 1968). For persons on the job, writing can be a way of accomplishing both short-range goals, such as asking a subordinate to do something, and a way of accomplishing long-range goals, such as enhancing one's reputation and advancing in a corporate hierarchy (Faigley & Miller, 1982). Historically, writing has served as a way of maintaining personal relationships among family and friends. Besides communicative and self-expressive uses, writing can be a way of discovering ideas. Writing allows us to reflect critically upon our ideas and recast them through successive drafts in a dialectical process.

The prompting impulse for a particular written text can be described as a *pragmatic goal*. Pragmatic goals, in turn, shape the operative goals that guide discourse production. Beaugrande (1980) provides an example of a pragmatic goal controlling several successive operative goals in his analysis of the discourse in Sidney Howard's *The Late Christopher Bean*. In this play a family during the depression learns that a destitute, fatally ill painter whom they sheltered has now become famous and that they might resume their former style of living if they could find and sell one of his paintings. The only canvas by the painter that remains in the house is a portrait owned by their maid. The family attempts one ruse after another to talk the maid into giving them the painting, each plan motivated by the same pragmatic goal. Pragmatic goals are not necessarily concealed; in fact, they are inferable in most discourse. The point we are making here is that pragmatic goals influence other decisions in planning, such as the choice of genre and medium.

Circumstances for Composing

Associated with knowledge of the functions of writing is knowledge of the circumstances for composing. Most studies of composing have dealt with school-sponsored writing where the circumstances for composing are controlled. For writing that is done outside of school, however, writers typically must manage these constraints as part of the writing task. One kind of constraint is the amount of time for writing. Researchers in composing have characterized production as ceasing when the writer is satisfied that the text adequately accomplishes the purpose for writing (Beaugrande & Dressler, 1981). Obviously, the decision to stop writing for experienced writers is influenced by how much time they have to write. Writers on the job frequently do not have time to revise (Faigley & Miller, 1982; Selzer, 1983). Time constraints also influence how a document is composed. Many executives are now required to dictate on the assumption that this method of composing saves time (Faigley & Miller, 1982; Gould, 1980).

Another rarely investigated factor is the nature of authorship. Faigley and Miller (1982) found that nearly 75% of the 200 college-trained writers they surveyed sometimes collaborate with at least one other person in composing. The nature of collaboration varies considerably. Sometimes several experts contribute a section to a report in their particular area of expertise, with the project leader integrating the sections into a coherent whole. In other cases, a superior edits the work of a subordinate. In still other cases, people work closely together through all phases of a writing project. Many companies and agencies have explicit review processes that a document must pass through. Documents produced by the government destined for the public often undergo lengthly review. This process has been the subject of recent research (Felker & Rose, 1981).

THE WRITER–READER RELATIONSHIP

When writers begin writing, they ideally know who will read their text and what relationship they hope to establish with those readers. In actual writing situations, questions concerning the relationship between the writer and potential readers are often complex and multifarious. During the writing of this book, for example, the authors frequently communicated while they were logged in to the same computer using a program that displayed what each person typed on everyone's screen. Rules of conversational turn-taking came into effect, and the resulting exchanges resembled transcribed telephone conversations. At the opposite extreme, writers of fiction cannot be sure of their readership because their work may continue to be read long after their lifetime. The inexplicitness of this kind of writer–reader relationship has forced some literary critics to argue for an "implied" reader (e.g., Iser, 1978).

Young writers often ignore all but immediate readers, taking the position that "if readers don't understand what I write, it's their problem." Effective written communication, however, always depends upon a reader's response to the text. Effective communicators, regardless of the medium, are sensitive to the knowledge and beliefs of the audience. For this reason, teachers and researchers who adhere to the cognitive or social views of composing described in Chapter 1 have examined how writers come to know and address specific audiences as they plan and generate written texts. Proponents of the literary view, on the other hand, often address questions of a writer's audience with the assumption that "the writer's audience is always a fiction" (Ong, 1975) and assume that a writer should be able to create an ideal audience in the same way that a writer can create an ideal persona.

Audience analysis was a foundation of classical rhetoric and has continued to occupy the attention of both theorists and researchers in rhetoric and cognitive psychology. But in spite of this concern, we still do not understand how successful orators or writers come to a sense of audience and use that awareness. Odell (1980) notes that very little research has addressed how knowledge of audience affects either written products or writing processes. And Park (1982) points out that the meanings of audience are unclear even to scholars who work with language and literature: the concept of audience may mean "actual people external to a text . . . whom the writer must accommodate," or it may suggest an audience implied by the text itself, "a set of suggested or evoked attitudes, interests, reactions, conditions of knowledge which may or may not fit with the qualities of actual readers or listeners" (p. 249). The notion of a "universal audience" advanced by Perelman (1969, 1982) does not go far toward answering the question of how a writer's sense of audience affects the text produced.

The Concept of Audience in Classical Rhetoric

Modern confusion about the meaning of audience results, at least in part, from the classical rhetoricians' treatments of the concept of audience strictly as a speaker-listener emotional relationship and from their failure to explain how a speaker can develop a sense of audience. Simply stated, the classical dictum was that a speaker should know his audience's character thoroughly and plan his rhetorical strategies according to that knowledge. Clearly, the ambiguity of this dictum has led to problems for later rhetoricians. Aristotle devotes 10 chapters of his *Rhetoric* (trans. 1954) to the emotions a speaker can arouse in an audience and spends 6 chapters on the types of social groups that audience members might fall into. However, as Ehninger (1968) has pointed out, Aristotle's *Rhetoric* is speaker- and subject-centered, treating the matter of audience naively. Since the *Rhetoric* deals only with the classes of listeners a Greek orator might encounter, Aristotle's theories cannot be understood to deal with all types of an audience's knowledge, reason, character, and emotion. The Roman rhetoricians expanded on Aristotle's work rather than altering it. Cicero, for example, introduces *De Oratore* (trans. 1959) with the claim that "all the mental emotions, with which nature has endowed the human race, are to be intimately understood, because it is in calming or kindling the feelings of the audience that the full power and science of oratory are brought into play" (I.v. 17).

The Development of Audience Awareness

The realization that no one, including classical rhetoricians, has addressed the problem of *how* a writer comes to know his audience has stimulated important work in cognitive-developmental psychology (discussed in Barritt & Kroll, 1978). In experiments on communication in children, Piaget ([1926] 1955) found that young children could rarely adapt a message to the needs of the listener. They seemed to assume "from the start that the [other] will grasp everything, will almost know beforehand all that should be known and will interpret every subtlety" (p. 115). Based on this finding and others, Piaget coined the term *egocentrism* to explain how young communicators could take only their own perspective and not recognize that of a listener. He explained further that, as children age and develop, they eventually learn how to *decenter*, to take another's perspective and adapt a message to it. In recent years, however, Piaget's sequence of cognitive development has been questioned by several studies which show that the stages of reasoning Piaget describes vary according to the content of specific tasks (reviewed in Shweder, 1982).

Flavell (1968) has described the development of role-taking abilities that lead to knowledge of audience as a five-step series: existence, need, prediction, maintenance, and application. The *existence* step involves knowing that there is such a thing as another's perspective and that the perceptions, thoughts, and feelings of another may not be the same as the writer's, a notion that corresponds to Piaget's notion of cognitive egocentrism (see Flavell, 1974). The *need* step represents the speaker's or writer's recognizing that the discourse situation calls for an analysis of another's perspective, and that such an analysis would enable the speaker or writer to achieve his or her desired goal(s). The *prediction* step involves knowing how to carry out this analysis, to discriminate with needed accuracy whatever the other's various attributes are. The *maintenance* step concerns knowing how to maintain this awareness, assuming that it competes with the speaker or writer's own point of view. Finally, the *application* step includes knowing how to apply knowledge of another's role to some end—for example, a written text.

Flavell suggests that these five steps constitute a cognitive-developmental pattern, yet he concedes that, especially in older children, a recognition that the message has not been successfully conveyed forces the speaker or writer to return to, and reassess, the need function.

The theories of early cognitive-developmentalists have partially answered the question of how communicators come to know their audience in a particular writing situation, yet some researchers have asserted that such concepts as egocentrism and role-taking appear too general to be of any great utility in understanding either the development of social perception or its relationship to communication. Delia and Clark (1977), for example, point out that a communicator's potential basis for knowing an audience rests not only on the differentiation of another's perspective or knowledge. They claim that a writer can form a notion of audience on the basis of *any* attribution of another's actions, roles, character, intentions, emotional state, or knowledge. They also argue that speakers and writers gain social understanding before they know how to use that understanding to control the content and structure of the texts they produce. A similar connection is made by Nystrand (1982b), who contends that the rhetorical study of audience—the investigation of how writers plan to achieve particular effects on readers—must be tied directly to the study of how potential readers affect writers and the texts they compose.

The Writer–Reader Relationship in a Written Text

While most theory and research on audience awareness has concentrated on the role of audience considerations in invention, a few researchers have emphasized the effects on text production. Nystrand (1982a) presents a taxonomy for analyzing errors on the basis of the writer-reader relationship. By cataloging the kinds of mismatches between "writers' words and readers' guesses" (p. 64), without attributing the cause of the mismatch to either the writer or reader, Nystrand concludes there are three kinds of distortions: (a) "simple misconstraint," which occurs as a result of the reader misinterpreting the text or the writer misleading the reader; (b) "impaction," which occurs when the text is overly dense for the reader; and (c) "rarefaction," which occurs when the reader needs additional information not provided in the text to understand it.

Other efforts to classify discourse according to the writer–reader relationship have examined individual text features. Linguists have examined the "I–you" relationship in texts, devising either discourse categories based on the "I–you" distinction (Longacre, 1976) or degrees of interactiveness with both "I" and "you" present in a text at one extreme and both absent at the other extreme (E. Smith, 1982; Tannen, 1982b). Smith concludes that texts are more or less interactive not by the raw number of "I's" and "you's" that a text contains, but by the relative prominence of references to the writer and reader in the overall text scheme.

Writers and Readers as Members of a Community

Finally, proponents of the social view of composing hold that since one's readers are frequently members of one's discourse community, many questions of how to conceptualize and address a specific audience are answered a priori by the contents and the conventions of the written text. Cicourel (1980) describes three models of social interaction which seem to characterize aspects of the social view of writer–reader relationships. First, a speech-act model of social interaction assumes that a reader who is a member of the writer's discourse community will be able to recognize the illocutionary intent of the writer's text. Second, the expansion model of social interaction suggests that writers and readers share a common knowledge base, an idea discussed in the following section; consequently, a writer may leave many details unsaid and still assume his reader will be able to understand the text. Third, the problem-solving model of social interaction incorporates notions from schema theory (Rumelhart, 1975), also discussed in the following section. The problem-solving model posits that members of the same discourse community have similar schemata for both the subject matters and the forms of written texts. As a result, writers can conceptualize and address readers based on their similar knowledge patterns.

SUBJECTS FOR WRITING

A writer's knowledge of subject matter exerts considerable influence over how he or she composes. For example, a writer uses different strategies for gathering content when writing about an unfamiliar subject than when writing on a familiar subject. Although considerations of subject-matter knowledge usually constitute a major portion of theories of rhetoric and composition, few researchers have considered subject matter other than in discussions of purpose. Only recently have questions emerged concerning how writers' knowledge of subject matter affects their composing processes and written products.

Treatment of Subject Matter in Rhetorical Theory

Subject matter was not so neglected in classical rhetoric. In the pre-Socratic period in classical Greece, there arose a set of stock arguments and examples that could be memorized and inserted *ex tempore* into an oration. These *topoi* served both as a guide for the speaker in filling out an argument and a guide for the listener in recognizing an argument. In early Greek rhetoric, the sophists gathered collections of *topoi* on various subjects pertaining to political, legal, and philosophical oratory. The *topoi* flourished in Roman rhetoric, where they were called *loci communes* or "commonplaces." In the later Middle Ages and in the Renaissance, commonplaces were collected in numerous manuals that were used to teach invention. During the 18th century, however, the commonplaces fell into disfavor. The rise of logic stemming from Descartes and Bacon led to increased emphasis upon direct observation. Major British rhetoricians of the 18th century—Smith, Campbell, Blair, and Witherspoon—were also logicians and followers of Locke. They either dismissed the commonplaces as incapable of accommodating originality or ignored them altogether (see Howell, 1971). By the 19th century, the commonplaces and treatment of specific subject matter had vanished from the curriculum.

In 20th-century theories of rhetoric and communication, ideas about the importance and effects of specific subject matter have appeared, but only conceptually; no theorist has defined operationally how specific subject matter knowledge helps shape composing. Jakobson's (1960) communication model suggests that a writer must know the context of communication, the content of a message, the means of making contact with a reader, and a code that will be acceptable. Similarly, Kinneavy's (1971) theory of discourse holds that "in informative and scientific discourse, the reality is represented" (p. 60). Moffett (1968) proposes four levels of "I–it" relationships that suggest levels of knowledge a writer must have about a subject; all four levels presuppose a writer has specific subject matter knowledge and can move from recording it to reporting it to generalizing about it to theorizing about it. Distinctive among modern rhetorical theorists' treatments of specific subject matters is the work of Perelman and Olbrechts-Tyteca ([1958] 1969). Perelman and Olbrechts-Tyteca maintain that all arguments, including empirical ones, begin with certain shared assumptions or agreements about the nature of the world. For example, geologists now assume that the Earth's crust consists of a series of moving plates, but in 1950 they would not have held this assumption. Perelman and Olbrechts-Tyteca claim that these assumptions are in themselves a kind of *topoi*.

Contemporary Views of Subject Matter

Even though composition research has largely neglected relationships between writing processes and subject matter knowledge, research in other fields has recently begun to influence ideas about composing. Several researchers have studied linguistic features characteristic of texts in specific subject areas. Prominent have been studies of the language of the professions (e.g., Alatis & Tucker, 1979; Di Pietro, 1982) and the language of public documents (Campbell & Holland, 1982; Redish, 1981). The goal of much of this research has been to make medical and legal language more accessible to lay audiences.

Schema theory. Other research has explored how knowledge of subject matter affects text comprehension and production. First, investigations of schema theory have demonstrated that writers' mental representations of knowledge in memory can affect the quality and quantity of their written products. Schema theory holds that writers bring different levels of knowledge to any writing task. The most general levels—schemata—represent the writers' general world view based on previous personal experience. Schemata, moreover, are organized into subschemata that are arranged hierarchically and represent more specific levels of knowledge (R. Anderson, 1978; Rumelhart & Ortony, 1977). Schema theory draws heavily on the memory research of F. Bartlett (1932) and the theory of frames proposed by Minsky (1975). According to Minsky, a frame represents a network of features in one's memory that is activated when one needs to understand a situation. The highest level of this network includes obligatory variables, inherent features of the situation. The second level contains optional features that are assigned importance if the situation demands it. Finally, the third level includes deviant features that prompt a person to activate new schemata in order to understand a situation.

An example might serve to demonstrate how this highly abstract theory applies to investigations of writers' knowledge of a specific subject matter. Suppose students living in New York City were asked to write an essay on urban public transportation. The schemata they might activate to accomplish this task would include several layers of subschemata, comprising knowledge of the several kinds of public transportation, typical routes and capacities for each kind, and personal experiences of using urban public transportation. Students who live in rural areas would likely have some general knowledge of public transportation, but they might not know, for instance, that subways often emerge from underground when they leave downtown areas.

Most applications of schema theory have investigated the relationship between knowledge of a subject and comprehension (see the discussion of coherence above). Few studies, however, have investigated the relationship between knowledge of a particular subject and generating a text about that subject. In one such study, Voss, Vesonder, and Spilich (1980) tested 20 subjects to determine their level of knowledge about baseball. Half were designated as high knowledge (HK), the other half as low knowledge (LK). All subjects were asked to write a narrative about a half-inning of a fictitious baseball game. Basing their analyses on the subjects' abilities to fill "slots" in a problem-solving model, the investigators found that HK subjects produced significantly more specific propositions about causal "auxiliary actions" in the game itself while LK subjects produced significantly more propositions about nongame-relevant activities, such as crowd size and fan reaction. Voss, Vesonder, and Spilich attributed these differences to the HK subjects' larger "problem space"—in other words, their knowledge of possible settings and actions in a baseball game—and to their greater ability to monitor their selected paths through the problem-solving model—in other words, their greater knowledge of possible alternatives in a game.

Sociology of knowledge and field theory. A second area of investigation that has begun to raise questions about relationships between writers' knowledge of subject matter and their composing has been opened by sociologists of knowledge and by studies of "field theory" in speech communication. Generally, explanations of the sociology of knowledge and field theory embrace what we have called the social view of composing, a view which holds that since writers are members of particular discourse communities, much of their work is guided by the assumptions shared by the members of these communities. In particular, studies of the sociology of knowledge and field theory stress that since discourse communities usually form within specific disciplines, professions, or schools of thought, members of the communities must know not only a considerable body of propositional knowledge that is common within the community, but also specific procedures for discovering and verifying that knowledge.

Most studies of the sociology of knowledge have centered on the sociology of science (reviewed in Bazerman, 1983). In general, these studies emphasize that all scientific observations are theory-laden; consequently, all published reports of scientific investigations derive from the shared knowledge of the scientific community to which the reports are directed (cf. Hanson, 1958). A frequently cited theorist who describes this idea is Thomas Kuhn. Kuhn (1977) uses the term *disciplinary matrix* to describe the complex of knowledge and thinking patterns that a discipline shares. Bazerman (1983) explains how the concept of a disciplinary matrix affects writers:

> Because the shared features of a disciplinary matrix often lie below conscious articulation, writing within each discipline can only be fully understood by those who share the matrix. Communication between participants in separate disciplinary matrices is rife with misunderstanding and unresolvable conflict—unresolvable because there is no neutral terminology that will allow for determination of mutually acceptable criteria of adjudication. (p. 161)

Kuhn's disciplinary matrix accurately describes the operations of one kind of scientific discourse community.

Field theory resembles the sociology of knowledge in its claim that particular discourse communities have distinctive patterns of knowledge that members must know; field theory, however, takes the argument one step farther by contending that discourse communities are actually created by their members' communication patterns. In one recent explanation of field theory, Willard (1982) claims that speakers' or writers' membership in an "argument community" affects their perspectives on subject matters they must treat in discourse. He understands fields as "real sociological entities" in which members are unified by "common beliefs, standards, rhetorical appeals, relationships, and political aims" (p. 28). Fields supply ways of interpreting reality. They represent schools of thought rather than individual disciplines. Willard claims that "a psychologist who is a constructivist has more in common with constructivists in other disciplines than with another psychologist who is a behaviorist" (p. 39). Fields also sanction certain knowledge as provisionally true, and since writers are usually read by members of the same field, fields are rhetorical in their operation. Willard writes that "a claim's authority inheres in the fact that it is believed; belief is legitimized by its conventional fit into a field's standards" (p. 40).

Both sociology of knowledge and field theory could provide the intellectual framework for establishing writing-across-the-curriculum programs in secondary and higher education. In their present form, many writing-across-the-curriculum programs operate from the general assumption that "writing is good for you" rather than basing instruction on any specific disciplinary theory of writing.

IMPLICATIONS FOR ASSESSMENT

In this chapter we have broadly considered the different kinds of knowledge writers use in producing texts. We examined the complex relationships between writing skills and general language abilities. We also explored how writers understand writing as a social act. We argued that successful writers must be aware of the functions of writing in a particular discourse community; they must know what written texts are typically expected to accomplish by the persons who create and exchange them. Accordingly, writers must attempt to adjust their written texts to the needs and expectations of particular readers. Finally, to the extent that the discourse community is defined by a body of shared subject matter, writers must be aware of and control the ways in which this shared body of knowledge necessarily influences the form and substance of the texts they produce.

The broad kinds of knowledge outlined in this chapter suggest some of the difficulties that evaluators of writing skills face. One implication for writing assessment is that notions of writing "competence" must be advanced in terms of the skills required to function in particular discourse communities. The knowledge required to use writing in professional and private life varies in subtle ways from community to community. For this reason we believe that evaluators of writing must turn to descriptive assessments of mature writing skills. In the next chapter, we examine methodologies that might be employed toward this end.

Chapter 6

Methodologies for Assessing Knowledge and Processes of Composing

We pointed out in the last chapter that a writer's knowledge extends beyond familiarity with a grapholect and strategies for producing text. A writer must know how writing is used in a discourse community, what functions it can fulfill, and how to create meaning for specific readers on specific subject matters. Since any effort to assess writing skills necessarily makes certain assumptions about a writer's discourse community, the ultimate context for assessment must be the writer's discourse community and the communities in which that writer wishes to participate. In this chapter we examine the immediate context for assessing student writing skills—the context of the classroom. Within that context, we discuss three methodologies for assessing writers' knowledge and processes of composing—observational studies in the ethnographic tradition, congnitive and metacognitive assessment using writers' verbal reports, and rhetorical text analysis. We argue that these methodologies could be used profitably in the assessment of writing abilities.

THE CLASSROOM AS A DISCOURSE COMMUNITY

A one-dimensional model of the classroom as a dispensary of knowledge is inadequate for understanding how classrooms influence writing abilities. Classrooms are processes—dynamic entities that affect and are affected by such surrounding contexts as the curriculum for their content area, the programs and curricula of the rest of the school, college, or university, and the society at large (Witte & Faigley, 1983). More important, classrooms are discourse communities and extensions of discourse communities. In classrooms students learn how to read and write and how to talk about reading and writing. They learn to use codes that are intelligible for discourse communities beyond the classroom. They learn to produce messages with definite forms that move through accepted channels and that say something about something.

The relationship between the discourse community of the classroom and a larger community is evident in most college courses that have a writing component beyond the use of essay examinations for testing. One mission of freshman writing courses is to convey certain conventions and uses of writing in the larger college discourse community. The heavy emphasis on the expository essay in freshman writing courses is often justified by the argument that students will need to know how to write expository prose in future college classes. Upper-division courses in students' major disciplines that contain writing components typically introduce students to conventions, uses, and ways of thinking in writing that are characteristic of that discipline. For example, upper-division engineering courses may require technical reports similar to those actually prepared by engineers in the discipline. Advanced social work classes frequently require students to write grant proposals like those that practicing social workers write to procure funding. Upper-division students in experimental psychology usually report their research in formats similar to those found in professional journals in the field.

Learning to write in the classroom involves interactions among teachers and writers, among textbooks and writers, among writers and writers, among writers and their own and others' texts, and among writers and texts and the culture at large. Different writing courses and programs frequently emphasize one or more of these interactive systems as most important. Mosenthal's (1983) model of classroom writing competence provides one available representation of the several contexts that interact in a writing classroom. Mosenthal's model, which he calls the Context Pyramid, includes five major components:

1. The writers themselves, including such factors as age, sex, background knowledge, IQ, reading ability, scholastic ability, grade level, and processes that writers use to produce texts.
2. The writing materials, including the remembered or produced picture, incident, idea, or text the writers are writing about, and the writers' text output.
3. The writing task, including the instructions and specifications for following the instructions.
4. The situation organizer (that is, the teacher).
5. The setting, including where the writers write and where the teacher prompts and evaluates the writing.

In Mosenthal's model, the teacher exerts significant control over materials, tasks, and settings. But Mosenthal's model does not suggest that the writing classroom as a discourse community operates soley by the students' following the teacher as giver of knowledge. Students acquire knowledge from several different sources. Mosenthal delineates four of them: the students' prior knowledge (we would assume knowledge of both the subject matter of the composition and of the procedures for creating such a text), the external stimulus of the writing task, the written text itself, and the social situation. Mosenthal includes "interactions among situation organizer, the setting, and the writer" (p. 33) in this fourth meaning source. We would add that he should also include interactions among writers themselves.

Considering the writing classroom as a discourse community allows one to see the deficiencies of much past writing research. Mosenthal asserts that too often writing researchers have tried to assess writing courses and programs by adopting a policy of "partial specification" (p. 35), selecting one context (such as the teacher) as the cause of writing competence, and one context (such as the students' written text) as the "effect" of writing instruction, then considering only the interactions between the two contexts. Mosenthal argues instead that researchers need to posit "a descriptive and operational definition of writing and classroom writing competence that considers all the meaning sources and the writing processes" (p. 51). In other words, he contends that writing research needs to investigate interactions among all components of the classroom discourse community.

In the sections that follow, we offer three methodologies that could be employed to investigate such phenomena.

METHODS

Observation and Microethnography

Understanding the classroom as a discourse community requires methods of research that reach beyond the individual student to the contexts for composing. To meet this need, some researchers have turned to the long tradition of ethnographic investigation in anthropology, sociology, and linguistics.

Since many researchers in education now claim to take an ethnographic approach and yet operate in very different manners, we will qualify what we mean by ethnography. To an anthropologist, according to Conklin (1968), ethnography involves the attempt to "record and describe the culturally significant behaviors of a particular society" (p. 172). Conklin continues:

> Ideally, this description, an ethnography, requires a long period of intimate study and residence in a small, well-defined community, knowledge of the spoken language, and the employment of a wide range of observational techniques including prolonged face-to-face contacts with members of the local group, direct participation in some of that group's activities, and a greater emphasis on intensive work with informants than on the use of documentary or survey data. (p. 172)

The key to successful ethnography, then, is participant observation of a culture and its phenomena.

An investigation such as Conklin describes would produce what linguistic anthropologist Hymes (1980) calls a "comprehensive" ethnography, a careful and "thick" description (Geertz, 1973) of all aspects of the specific culture. Hymes contends that the distinguishing characteristic of an ethnographic investigation is that it is open-ended: "initial questions may change during inquiry" (p. 92). According to Hymes, the validity of an ethnographic description depends on an "accurate knowledge of the meanings and behaviors of those who participate in them" (p. 93). The reliability of an ethnography—the degree to which other researchers similarly describe the same culture—depends on how accurately the original ethnographer articulates his or her method, (Kantor, Kirby, & Goetz, 1981).

Drawing on anthropology, researchers of language and education have adopted ethnographic methods in a variety of investigations. For example, Heath (1980, 1982) studied the meanings of school and community literacy in a long-term study of reading and writing in the Piedmont region of the Carolinas. Hymes and others (1981) investigated school discourse and patterns of acquisition of reading and writing skills in the Philadelphia schools. Florio and Clark (1982) studied the functions of writing in an elementary classroom.

Ethnographies of school writing proceed with an awareness that writing courses have goals that determine the curriculum or content of the course. These goals consist of the explicit goals of a writing program (e.g., those stated in a program description) as well as the goals, either explicit or implicit, of the instructor. All goals must necessarily be influenced by the society and the supporting institution. We suggested in Chapter 1 that teachers or researchers might be able to articulate the explicit goals of a writing class according to the view of composing that the course maintains. These possible views include the literary view, which suggests that instruction should emphasize the personal growth of the writer; the cognitive view, which holds that writers should be led to increased knowledge of their capabilities for communicating with the world; and the social view, which suggests that writers should be taught how to become successful members of particular discourse communities.

In a study of writing instruction that takes the ethnographic perspective, there are a number of issues related to the stated goals of a writing course on which researchers can focus attention. For example, they could investigate how the various writing contexts described above (e.g., writing tasks) affect students' perceptions of the importance of these goals. They could study how the instruction either directly or indirectly led to the accomplishment of these goals. They could also investigate in what ways the explicit goals are and are not operating in the classroom.

What types of data might a researcher collect in such studies? Florio and Clark (1982) collected five kinds:

1. Ethnographic field notes resulting from extensive participant observation in each classroom.
2. Selected videotapes of everyday life in the classroom.
3. Weekly journals kept by the focal teacher describing instruction in general and the teaching of writing in particular.
4. Interviews with teachers about the content of journals and videotapes.
5. Collections of students' written work and discussion with students about their work. (p. 118)

To these data sources, we could add the following: regular journals kept by students describing their writing instruction, products, and processes; interviews with students about their perceptions of good written products and good writing practices; and responses of students to various instruments that ask them to discuss and evaluate their writing.

How might a researcher analyze these data? Hymes (1980) argues that typology is central to any analysis of ethnographic data. Basso (1974) calls for a study of "acts of writing, or writing events . . . which are recognized as distinct by members of the society under study" (p. 428). In short, the researcher would need to classify findings in response to the question, "What counts as X?" For example, Florio and Clark were interested in discovering the functions of writing in an elementary classroom; consequently, they classified the writing they observed into "writing to participate in a community, writing to know oneself and others, writing to occupy free time, and writing to demonstrate academic competence" (p. 115).

Verbal Reports in Cognitive Research

While ethnographers make generous use of informants to learn more about a culture, cognitive psychologists also use verbal reports in studying cognitive operations. We regard the collection and analysis of verbal reports as a useful method for discovering information about both cognitive and metacognitive aspects of writers' knowledge and writing processes.

The use of verbal reports has a long history in the study of creative processes such as writing. Nearly a half century ago, Patrick (1937) asked poets and artists to provide verbal reports while they were working. Patrick analyzed these reports for evidence of the stages of creative thought that had been proposed by Wallas (1926). A decade later, de Groot (1965) began collecting verbal reports from expert chess players as they planned their moves. Then, in the 1950s, Newell and Simon began collecting verbal reports of people playing chess and solving arithmetic and logic problems. Newell and Simon's investigations culminated in their seminal text, *Human Problem Solving* (1972).

The most extensive use of subjects' verbal reports in composing research, of course, has come in the form of the "thinking-aloud protocol." We have discussed several studies using this research tool in Chapters 2, 3, and 4, and we return to a discussion of the methodology in Chapter 10. Swarts, Flower, and Hayes (1984) contend that the major benefit of the thinking-aloud protocol is that "it allows the writing researcher to observe not only cognitive processes and their organization in the act of composing, but [also] the development of the writer's ideas" (p. 54). Swarts, Flower, and Hayes suggest that thinking-aloud protocols can be used in exploratory studies of composing, in studies that produce a taxonomy of writing behaviors and strategies, in studies that test a hypothesis about composing processes, in studies that compare expert writers with novice writers, and in studies that aim to produce a model of the composing process.

Other types of verbal reports, however, can also be effective tools for assessing writers' knowledge and composing processes. Ericsson and Simon (1980) propose three methods of eliciting verbal reports in addition to the thinking-aloud protocol. Since the aim of the thinking-aloud protocol is to ask subjects to describe their activities, not to analyze them, Ericsson and Simon explain that researchers can probe subjects directly while they are performing the task under investigation. This concurrent probing seeks specific information from the subjects, presumably information representing the knowledge they would need to continue performing the task. Second, Ericsson and Simon propose that researchers can engage in retrospective probing, asking the subject for information immediately after completing the task. Finally, Ericsson and Simon explain that research using verbal reports as data can employ interpretive probing, a type of retrospective probing that asks subjects to analyze different approaches they may have taken while performing the task.

Ericsson and Simon openly acknowledge that the reliability and validity of verbal reports have been challenged for more than half a century. However, they conclude that when verbal reports are carefully elicited and interpreted in the contexts in which they were obtained, they can provide valid and reliable data about cognitive processes. Perkins (1981) comes to a similar conclusion:

> Asking people to think aloud or report their thoughts immediately after episodes of invention does not substantially disrupt the activity or yield substantially distorted results. (p. 32)

Text Analysis

The recent shift in emphasis to cognitive processes in composing and social contexts for writing has come in large part at the expense of text analysis. Text analysis fell into disfavor for two reasons. It can offer only indirect evidence about processes of composing, and often that evidence is unreliable. More important, most analyses of student texts have applied formal systems borrowed from structural or transformational linguistics. Becker's (1965) scheme for describing paragraph structure and Hunt's (1965) T-unit analysis are but two examples. We noted in Chapter 3 that these applications are plagued with methodological difficulties and tell us little about differences among types of texts or among adult writers. At first, these problems seemed resolvable with formal analyses that extend beyond the sentence level. Halliday and Hasan's (1976) method for analyzing cohesion is one such system. But when cohesion analysis was used to answer questions concerning actual texts, it too proved to be shot through with conceptual difficulties (Morgan & Sellner, 1980; Witte & Faigley, 1981).

Formal linguistic systems fail to uncover essential differences among texts because most are not designed to take into account the functions and contexts of language use. They can tell us little about why a particular written text might be effective or ineffective in a given situation. Much of the meaning in a text comes from the recognition of its context and from connections to the reader's previous knowledge. Many of the relationships within a text are inferred, not overtly signalled. Examples are easy to think of. Let's take a very simple text—a stop sign. The meaning of "STOP" painted on a red octagonal sign placed at an intersection is a set of procedures that might be listed as follows:

1. Put on your brakes so that your vehicle comes to a complete stop.
2. Look for vehicles that are approaching in either direction.
3. Proceed through the intersection if no vehicles are approaching.

In addition we have a great deal of other knowledge about stop signs. For instance, people know they must come to a complete stop if a policeman is present or else risk getting a traffic ticket.

Now imagine another situation—an organized march against nuclear weapons in the downtown area of a major city in the United States. One of the demonstrators is carrying a stop sign. In this case, most observers understand the sign to mean "stop building nuclear weapons" or "stop war." People would obtain either of these meanings from the immediate context and perhaps from their memory of "stop war" signs as protests against the Vietnam War. But if the stop sign is carried by a person at the front of the march wearing the appropriate clothing or badges of an official, and if that person turned to those behind him at an intersection, they might interpret that act as a signal to stop walking. A stop sign could mean stop doing almost anything, an ambiguity that is on occasion exploited by cartoonists. But in everyday experience, stop signs are unambiguous. They are transparent examples of the fact that meaning cannot be separated from context and use.

Difficulties in most formal systems for analyzing text arise from the assumption that texts are conduits of meaning (Reddy, 1979). Texts are thought to be like aqueducts. The writer pours in meaning and the reader extracts it. If the aqueduct is damaged, the reader will lose some of the meaning. Likewise, if the meaning has to travel great distances across time and cultures, some of the meaning will likely evaporate.

But the aqueduct analogy is inappropriate for the experience of reading. In Chapter 5 we reviewed research demonstrating that inferences derivable from a text are essential in constructing meaning. Schank and Abelson (1977) have shown that many inferences are necessary to interpret ordinary discourse. From a pair of sentences like "John and Mary went out for Beef Wellington on their twenty-fifth anniversary. Afterwards, they went dancing," we make a great many inferences: they were celebrating being married 25 years; they went to a fancy restaurant; the restaurant had waiters; they ordered from a menu; the waiters brought them their food; and so on. Another way the aqueduct metaphor fails is that texts sometimes carry *more* meaning than the writer intended. Unconscious humor is one such instance. For example, a college student wrote "men and women could not have intimate relationships if it weren't for communication, the end product of good writing skills." (We will not speculate on the possible effectiveness of such incentives in the teaching of writing.)

Consequently, to accomplish the purposes they intend, writers must guide readers' expectations in texts. Nystrand (in preparation) argues that writers negotiate key text points with readers by either *elaborating* or *segmenting*. When writers elaborate, they provide contexts for new information they present. When writers segment (by using headings, paragraphing, and other graphic aids), they divide the text into manageable units for the reader. One key text point is always at the beginning. The writer must establish some common ground with the reader, which may be as simple as signaling a genre (e.g., "Once upon a time"). But often establishing common ground is a much more complex process. For example, a college student whose father was an attorney began an essay about an unpopular case his father had taken on:

> I was on the road, going home to celebrate something important when I heard on the radio that a fisherman in Seadrift had been shot and killed by a Vietnamese crabber. I remember that I was infuriated. Those little bastards, I thought, we pluck them out of the ocean and what do they do? Start shooting Americans.

The student found out when he arrived at home that his father was going to defend the Vietnamese crabber. The remainder of the essay described how the student's perceptions of the case and the people involved changed during the course of the trial.

The complex nature of texts has caused many researchers to turn away from formal analytical systems to alternative methods of analysis. For example, Hymes (1974) employs the rhetorical theory of Burke. More recently, Agar and Hobbs (1982) have adapted concepts from artificial intelligence research and literary criticism for use in text analysis.

IMPLICATIONS FOR ASSESSMENT

Since writing is a learned set of skills, not an innate ability, comprehensive assessment of writing skills must be understood in terms of the educational goals of a society and the chief expression of those goals—the schools. To study the relationship of writers to their society and how writers learn to use writing, ethnographic methods can be employed fruitfully. Because writing is closely related to natural language abilities, it is useful to study writing from the cognitive perspective using methodologies developed to answer questions from that perspective. Finally, the product of writing is a text. The success or failure of the writer's purpose usually depends on the text, and it is important to understand how texts fulfill purposes.

Thus we see all three methodologies as valuable in assessing writers' knowledge and processes of composing. Ethnographic research methodologies have already been adapted for use in classroom settings. A collection of essays edited by Spindler (1982) outlines both theories and methodologies of educational ethnography. In Parts II and III, we adapt verbal reports and text analysis for classroom use. Part II presents an application of text analysis to student texts written for specific situations and readers. Part III employs verbal reports to assess the conscious knowledge that writers use in text production. Our efforts are exploratory, but we do hope to show the potential of these approaches.

Part II
Assessing Changes
in Writers' Knowledge

Up to now, we have deliberately taken a broad perspective in an attempt to outline the complexities of composing processes and writers' knowledge. Part of our motive was to suggest that any assessment of writing must acknowledge these complexities. In Part II, we narrow our focus to provide a concrete example of a methodology that might be used to assess writers' skills in producing texts. The following chapters describe an approach to assessing writing skills that is based on analysis of discourse features. Because we measure skills demonstrated in performance, we call the approach "Performative Assessment." Our efforts represent a first step toward what we hope will be a practical approach to writing evaluation. We set out the justification for Performative Assessment, present examples that demonstrate the approach, and offer some preliminary evidence that our measures can be scored reliably. It is important to keep in mind that since the instruments we present were developed to assess the writing skills emphasized in regular freshman composition courses at the University of Texas, this investigation is exploratory and limited in scope. We do believe, however, that with further testing the approach to assessment we propose here can lead to more accurate and informative assessments of specific text production skills for different kinds of writing.

In Chapter 7, we review existing procedures for evaluating written products, and we outline the development of Performative Assessment as an alternative to existing methods of assessing writing performance. Chapter 8 introduces the Performative Assessment writing tasks and scoring rubrics. Finally, Chapter 9 discusses how Performative Assessment can be used in evaluating and teaching writing.

The Development of
Performative Assessment

In this chapter we review issues in the direct and indirect assessment of writing skills, and we discuss in detail methodological issues that affect any assessment of writing performance. We outline the steps in the development of Performative Assessment writing tasks and scoring rubrics.

THE NEED FOR DESCRIPTIVE WRITING ASSESSMENT

A consequence of the renewed emphasis on writing has been a revival of interest in testing. Several recent articles on testing examine the issues surrounding direct versus indirect assessment. The debate over using writing samples versus objective tests to measure writing ability is an old one, and most of the recent work has reiterated issues discussed in the past. The arguments pro and con have become familiar to us (e.g., Breland & Gaynor, 1979; Stiggins, 1982). Defenders of indirect assessment point to its greater reliability and its success in predicting future grades. Furthermore, indirect assessments in the form of standardized tests are much cheaper to administer and score. But many English teachers have remained skeptical of indirect assessments. Their main complaint has been that indirect assessments are not valid; they cannot accept a test of writing that requires students to generate no text of their own.

Obscured in this debate are the reasons for evaluating student writing in the first place. Most work has assumed that the purpose of assessment is to test *general proficiency* in writing, either at the time students enter college or at the time they exit certain courses. But another major reason to assess writing is to *describe* students' skills in specific areas. Such descriptions may range from a teacher's informal assessment at the beginning of a writing course to the nationwide assessment of the strengths and weaknesses in the writing of young Americans. Descriptive assessments seek to determine the areas in which a student's writing needs to improve rather than to determine which student writers are competent or incompetent.

The strengths of various methods of testing have been discussed primarily in terms of assessing general proficiency. But if these methods of evaluation are used for descriptive assessments, their weaknesses are evident. Standardized tests may produce results that are said to correlate highly with direct assessments of writing, but their ability to produce descriptive information is restricted primarily to low-level writing skills. In spite of some efforts to extend the scope of standardized tests of writing (e.g., Matalene, 1982), they remain useful primarily for measuring a student's ability to recognize standard punctuation and usage. For this reason, standardized tests have also been attacked as culturally and socially biased.

Even though methods of direct assessment have been looked upon with more favor, they also have serious limitations when used for descriptive assessment. The most widely used method of direct assessment is holistic scoring, the impressionistic rating of essays for overall quality (Cooper, 1977; Godshalk, Swineford, & Coffman, 1966). In its most common form, two readers rate each essay on a 1–4 or 1–6 point scale, with the essay going to a third reader if the raters differ by more than a point. The essays are rated relative to each other; in other words, a "4" or "6" paper is good in relation to the other papers in the set being evaluated, and a "1" is poor. Raters usually are trained in an initial session in which they are presented essays representing the range of quality in the essays they will assess. The training can produce a substantially high agreement among raters, especially if raters in long sessions are periodically retrained, ratings are monitored to insure consistent standards, and wide disagreements are adjudicated by an additional rating. Although such norm-referenced holistic evaluations of general proficiency may be suitable for some evaluation purposes, they are of little value in descriptive assessment because they furnish no information about *why* a paper is assigned a particular score.

A second method of direct assessment—analytic scoring—attempts to overcome the descriptive limitations of holistic scoring by isolating and assessing particular qualities of written texts. The best known analytic scale was developed on the basis of research by Diederich, French, and Carlton (1961). Diederich et al. had 53 readers from six different fields rate 300 college-level essays on a 1–9 scale. Factor analysis was used to sort the readers into groups on the basis of their tendency to agree with one another. Readers' written comments were then analyzed to determine what accounted for the ratings of quality. Five factors emerged and were given the following labels—Ideas, Form, Flavor, Mechanics, and Wording. A rating instrument consisting of these five categories was then devised and tested for a year in three high schools (Diederich, 1964). On the basis of a factor analysis of teachers' ratings, the five-factor scale was collapsed into a two-factor scale consisting of one factor for "General Merit" and one for "Mechanics." The components of the General Merit factor, however, consisted of four of the original factors—Ideas, Organization (Form), Flavor, and Wording. The final version of the scale (Diederich, 1966) was as follows:

	Low		Middle		High
Ideas	2	4	6	8	10
Organization	2	4	6	8	10
Wording	1	2	3	4	5
Flavor	1	2	3	4	5
Usage	1	2	3	4	5
Punctuation	1	2	3	4	5
Spelling	1	2	3	4	5
Handwriting	1	2	3	4	5

On the insistence of the teachers, "Ideas" and "Organization" received double weight on the scale, and a category for "Handwriting" was added. (Handwriting did not figure in the original scale since the essays on which it was based were typed prior to rating.)

Although analytic scoring schemes provide more descriptive information than holistic evaluations, they too have been criticized. Analytic categories such as "flavor" are difficult to set apart from categories such as "wording." Another serious objection is that criteria for assessing writing quality may vary across different types of writing or even across different writing tasks of the same general type. For instance, organization might have more relative importance in some kinds of texts than in others. Thus Diederich's assumption that an analytic scale generated for one writing task can be applied to other writing tasks has been questioned (Odell & Cooper, 1980).

A third method of direct assessment, in turn, attempts to overcome some of the limitations of holistic and analytic scoring. Primary-Trait Scoring, developed by Lloyd-Jones (1977) and others (Klaus et al., 1979; Mullis, 1980), was used in the second and third rounds of the National Assessment of Educational Progress. Unlike analytic scoring, Primary Trait Scoring does not assume that different writing tasks should be rated according to similar criteria. Separate Primary-Trait Scoring criteria must be developed for each writing task. As originally conceived, Primary-Trait Scoring is designed to assess a writer's ability to produce written texts for particular audiences and purposes. The Primary-Trait scoring system is based on characteristics in students' written responses to specific tasks. In this respect, Primary-Trait Scoring is different from holistic and analytic scoring in that it is a *criterion-referenced* rather than a *norm-referenced* measure. Although this distinction is implicit in the literature on Primary-Trait Scoring, it is not explained in detail. Nonetheless, the shift to a criterion-referenced scoring system marks a major change in the measurement of writing abilities.

Both holistic and analytic scoring systems place student essays on a continuum of relative quality, but neither describes student performance in terms of specific text features. In contrast, Primary-Trait Scoring specifies particular characteristics in student writing. For example, on one writing task scored by the Primary-Trait system, a paper rated "2" on a 4 point scale "takes a position and gives one unelaborated reason" (Lloyd-Jones, 1977, p. 61). Primary-Trait Scoring guides, once developed, can be applied to a single student essay without reference to other student essays. Holistic scoring, on the other hand, always requires that a single paper be measured in reference to other papers.

Holistic scoring, analytic scoring, and Primary-Trait scoring each address an important aspect of the large complex of skills known as "writing ability." Holistic scoring produces a measure of overall proficiency relative to other papers judged in a given rating session. Analytic scoring yields more information regarding particular features of papers that are being scored. Finally, Primary-Trait Scoring assesses a writer's ability to manage the constraints imposed by particular rhetorical situations. The development of these systems of scoring written products represents a progression toward increasingly informative measures of writing abilities and toward measures that are more sensitive to the complex relationships between the writer's knowledge and intentions and the reader's expectations.

Our purpose in this section is to introduce a method of evaluating writing that extends this line of theory and research in writing assessment. "Performative Assessment" writing tasks require students to employ specific text-production skills in response to carefully controlled rhetorical situations. "Performative Assessment" scoring rubrics allow raters to assess these skills by identifying text features that characterize different levels of performance.

Like Primary-Trait Scoring, Performative Assessment instruments are criterion-referenced. The development of criterion-referenced testing was closely associated with the movement to identify learning outcomes in terms of behavioral objectives that followed the publication of Bloom's *Taxonomy of Educational Objectives* (B. Bloom, 1956). Whereas norm-referenced testing involves rank-ordering individuals in relation to others who take the same test, criterion-referenced testing involves judgments of individual performance that are not related to the performance of others. The main assumption behind criterion-referenced testing is that teachers and evaluators are able to describe expected instructional outcomes in precise terms. Criterion-referenced testing theory holds that students can be adequately evaluated only in terms of established descriptions of what they can and cannot *do*.

Although both Primary-Trait Scoring and Performative Assessment are criterion-referenced, there are important differences between our approach and Primary-Trait Scoring. First, we proceed from different assumptions about what we want to measure. Since Primary-Trait Scoring attempts to "evaluate the capacity to write for precisely defined purposes" (Mullis, 1980, p. 9), the skills needed to complete a typical Primary-Trait Scoring task are conflated with the purpose and audience named in the task. Primary-Trait Scoring guides are designed to assess "how well [students] fulfilled the purpose of a particular task" (Mullis, 1980, p. 8). Performative Assessment scoring rubrics do not ask raters to make global judgments about how well writers meet specific purposes. Instead, Performative Assessment attempts to define and measure certain text-production skills involved in fulfilling particular discourse purposes.

Second, Primary-Trait Scoring tasks used by the NAEP have not always carefully controlled for discourse audiences and purposes. For example, here is a task used during the second round of the NAEP (Klaus et al., 1979):

> Sometimes people write just for the fun of it. This is a chance for you to have some fun writing.
>
> Pretend that you are a pair of tennis shoes. You've done all kinds of things with your owner in all kinds of weather. Now you are being picked up again by your owner. Tell what you, as the tennis shoes, think about what's going to happen to you. Tell how you feel about your owner. (p. 14)

The authors later called this task one of their most successful (Klaus et al., 1979). Although this task makes an explicit call for expressive writing, it does not specify an audience. The audience conceivably could be the owner, the writer him/herself, or some third party. In addition, it is not altogether clear whether the task measures writing abilities or personality development since responses to the task were "scored in terms of criteria appropriate to role playing in writing" (NAEP, 1976, p. 17). In a supplementary analysis, the NAEP further classified responses by personality types "in order to characterize the inventiveness that went into the role playing" (p. 19). These types ranged from "battered, abused" to "athletic, competitive." These supplementary analyses—presumably intended to give more information about role elaboration—suggest instead that other factors were conflated with students' abilities to write for an expressive purpose.

Third, Primary-Trait Scoring assumes that a single "primary" dimension can be identified along which papers differ (Humes, 1980). Performative Assessment is based on the assumption that there are multiple dimensions that make up such a "Primary Trait." Isolating and measuring these component subskills in terms of the features that characterize student texts is the chief goal of Performative Assessment.

AIMS OF PERFORMATIVE ASSESSMENT

We tried to develop a methodology for differentiating and assessing the skills that are lumped together in Primary-Trait Scoring. The instruments presented in the next chapter were designed to assess general writing skills taught in the beginning freshman English course at the University of Texas. These skills are of two kinds. First the program focuses on certain basic thinking processes reflected in organizational patterns in writing (see Hillocks, 1982). These processes include classifying, reasoning deductively, reasoning inductively, and constructing hypotheses. Although we assume that college students can write texts that incorporate these processes, we see our efforts as directed not toward measuring cognitive processes themselves but toward measuring the *skills* required to effect these processes in extended written texts. It is in this sense that we use the term "skills." We did not assume that students who fail to produce texts of a certain quality are deficient in those kinds of reasoning. What we attempt to measure are the skills needed to incorporate such reasoning processes in extended written texts, not the reasoning processes themselves.

Second, the beginning composition course at Texas focuses on writers' skills in meeting the needs and expectations of particular readers. Primary-Trait Scoring was in part designed to measure these skills through global judgments about a writers' success in achieving a particular purpose. Again, we have tried to isolate more narrowly defined skills in our Addressing-a-Specific-Audience instruments. We have applied work in text analysis that investigates how a writer prescribes a context for potential readers and guides the expectations of the reader.

To the extent that other writing courses proceed from the same assumptions as the beginning freshman English courses at Texas, the instruments that we constructed may be valid for measuring the skills taught in those courses. Many freshman English courses, however, are based on different assumptions, especially those based on the literary view of composing described in Chapter 1. Nevertheless, our aim was to develop an assessment *procedure* that could be used in a wide variety of writing courses, not to develop instruments that define writing abilities as the presence or absence of one set of skills. We see our research-based approach to assessment as more important than the instruments we produced. In Chapter 9 we discuss how Performative Assessment can be used to evaluate writing in specific subject domains.

ISSUES OF RELIABILITY AND VALIDITY

Performative Assessment grows out of three years of testing various approaches to evaluating specific text-production skills. A detailed account of the procedures we use to create and test the Performative Assessment instruments is in order because our methodology is what enables us to make certain claims about the reliability and validity of the instruments. In the procedures we followed to develop the Performative Assessment instruments and our account of these procedures, as well as in our reports of certain statistical tests in the next chapter, we have observed as carefully as possible the guidelines set forth in the American Psychological Association's *Standards for Educational and Psychological Tests* (1974).

Reliability

Most discussions of the reliability of essay tests, especially debates concerning direct versus indirect assessment, have to do with only one aspect of test reliability—scoring reliability. Although there is always the chance of some degree of scoring error associated with objective tests, an even greater degree of scoring error attends the rating of essay tests. Methods of counteracting sources of error in essay scoring typically include careful selection and training of raters, and in some cases, scoring guides designed to move raters toward greater consistency and agreement in their judgments of written texts. We have used all three methods, and the scoring reliabilities for individual Performative Assessment instruments are reported in the next chapter.

Scoring reliability is an important facet of test reliability—especially for essay tests of writing skills. Another important aspect of test reliability, however, and one that is typically overlooked in discussions of essay tests, has to do with consistency over time. Does the instrument yield the same results across successive administrations? Although there are several methods of demonstrating this aspect of reliability for objective tests, procedures for determining the reliability of essay tests have not been firmly established.

We attempted to gauge the reliability of the Performative Assessment instruments by developing matched pairs of writing tasks to measure a single writing skill and its component subskills. For example, we developed two Classification tasks with the intention that the two forms would be equivalent. We did the same for the Induction, Deduction, Constructing-a-Hypothesis, and Addressing-a-Specific-Audience instruments as well. Students in freshman English classes at the University of Texas wrote in response to one of the two tasks. Statistical analyses were then conducted to determine whether the two forms of each task yielded equivalent results. Admittedly, our assumption of the comparability of the Freshman English classes used to test the instruments constitutes something of a leap of faith. We do know, however, that all students in these regular Freshman English classes had scores under 550 on the English Composition Test and that all classes used the same syllabus. The principal motivation behind our sampling techniques was to make the best use of what was available to us in a "natural" setting.

Our assumption was that if there were no significant differences in scores on the parallel forms, then the writing tasks could be assumed to be reliable across successive administrations. This procedure represents a compromise between the well-known split-halves method of demonstrating test reliability and the equivalent forms method of determining internal consistency (Popham, 1981). We split instruments designed to assess a particular writing skill into two equivalent "halves," or two separate writing tasks, and then tested the two forms for equivalence. This method was necessary in part because a test–retest method (wherein subjects would have written on the *same* form of the writing task after a short interval) would have been unduly influenced by a practice effect. Although it would have been desirable to have administered each of the two different forms to several freshman writing classes, we had neither the time nor the resources to do so. Given these limitations, we consider the tests of equivalent forms of each instrument to be at least some indication of its reliability. The results of these tests of equivalence are reported after the discussion of each instrument in the next chapter.

Validity

As with questions of reliability, issues surrounding the validity of essay tests of writing skills are usually raised in the context of debates on direct versus indirect measures. Those who hold that objective tests are invalid usually consider essay tests to be valid by definition. Proponents of essay tests argue that if an instrument requires students to produce a written text, then the instrument can be considered a valid test of writing ability.

This assumption, however, obscures the fact that there are several different types of validity that should be considered in the validation of testing instruments. The APA *Standards* emphasizes three: criterion-related validity, content validity, and construct validity. Criterion-related validity has to do with the extent to which scores on a particular test can predict performance on other current or future tests. (Hence criterion-related validity is further broken down into concurrent and predictive validity). Criterion-related validity is not an issue with regard to the Performative Assessment instruments since we were not interested in relationships between these instruments and tests of other skills. Both construct and content validity, however, are important concerns in relation to the Performative Assessment instruments because of our claim to have isolated and tested certain skills and subskills from the larger domain of "writing abilities." Once again, our methods of developing and testing the instruments play a key role in determining their validity.

According to the APA standards,

> Evidence of content validity is required when the test user wishes to estimate how an individual performs in the universe of situations the test is intended to represent. Content validity is most commonly evaluated for tests of skill or knowledge. . . . To demonstrate the content validity of a set of test scores, one must show that the behaviors demonstrated in testing constitute a representative sample of behaviors to be exhibited in a desired performance domain. . . . An investigation of content validity requires that the test developer or test user specify his objectives and carefully define the performance domain in light of those objectives. (p. 28)

A more straightforward question of the content validity of a test might be: Does the test measure knowledge or skills that subjects might reasonably be expected to possess and demonstrate? In other words, is the test appropriate for those who will be asked to take it? Our efforts to insure the content validity of the Performative Assessment instruments were aimed in two directions: first, we sought to devise instruments that would measure skills college freshmen could be expected to have; second, we developed instruments to assess skills that would be influenced by the instruction students would receive in their Freshman English courses at the University of Texas.

Evidence that the Performative Assessment instruments measure skills that college freshmen could reasonably be expected to have comes mainly from the expert judgments of those who have served as consultants at several different stages of our research or who read and responded to earlier versions of this section. Each of the consultants who reviewed the instruments found them to be suitable for college freshmen.

In addition to the judgment of experts regarding our instruments—which alone might be held to constitute merely the type of "face" validity eschewed by the APA *Standards*—there is evidence that the Performative Assessment instruments measure skills that are the target of instruction in the Freshman English courses for which they were developed. The syllabus written for the course (Kinneavy, 1982) contains units that emphasize the types of thinking and writing skills tested by each of our instruments.

Unit IV of the syllabus, for example, covers "Classifying and Defining." One of the objectives of the unit reads as follows: "In classifying, the student should be able to use the 'principle of division,' avoid overlapping classes, and use classifications that are relevant to the purpose of the theme." This objective parallels very closely the skills measured by our Classification instrument. Unit VII covers "The Inductive Theme." One objective of the unit is that "the student should be able to use the traditional inductive organizational structure: introduction, thesis, definition of terms, procedures for gathering data, presentation of data, analysis of data, conclusion." With the exception of the concern with "procedures for gathering data" (all data are provided in the Performative Assessment instruments), this objective parallels the skills addressed by our Induction instrument. Other units in the syllabus include "Deduction," "Persuasion," and "Exploring a Topic," which are paralleled respectively by our Deduction, Audience, and Constructing-a-Hypothesis tasks. Because the Performative Assessment instruments are designed to test skills that college freshmen could be expected to possess by the end of a typical college writing class, and because they so closely parallel the instructional objectives of the particular Freshman English course for which they were designed, we conclude the instruments are content valid.

The definition of construct validity provided by the APA *Standards* runs as follows:

> A psychological construct is an idea developed or "constructed" as a work of informed, scientific imagination; that is, it is a theoretical idea developed to explain and to organize some aspects of existing knowledge. Terms such as "anxiety," "clerical aptitude," or "reading readiness" refer to such constructs . . . (p. 29)

For the Performative Assessment instruments, questions of construct validity have to do with whether the instruments in fact test the skills (constructs) and component subskills they were designed to test. Does the Classification instrument, for example, test students' ability to furnish categories for a supplied list of items, classify individual items appropriately, and produce an extended text that informs a reader of these operations?

Our efforts to insure the construct validity of the Performative Assessment instruments have taken several forms. First, we tried at all phases of the development of the Performative Assessment instruments to have our work reviewed by other researchers who were familiar with problems in writing assessment. In addition to having our work reviewed by on-site consultants or readers, we attempted to incorporate certain features into the instruments themselves that would help to insure their construct validity. In the writing tasks for each instrument, we tried to control for the amount of outside knowledge students would need to respond to the task successfully. By providing all or nearly all the factual information needed to write on the task, we were able to focus the instrument on the specific skills we wanted to test. Eliminating a confound between the skills we sought to measure and students' general knowledge lends support to our claim to have isolated and measured those skills.

Perhaps our most important argument for the construct validity of the Performative Assessment instruments rests on the scoring rubrics for each instrument. These rubrics enable trained raters to judge different levels of performance on the writing tasks. Each scoring rubric identifies four or five subskills that are components of the more general skill, or construct, engaged by the writing tasks. For each of the subskills on the rubrics, four levels of proficiency are described in terms of text features exhibited in student responses to the writing tasks. When raters score student essays using the rubrics, they essentially try to match the features of individual papers with the prototypical descriptions provided in the rubric. Although agreement among raters is of course not perfect, we are satisfied that the scoring rubrics include the key subskills called forth by the writing tasks. The fact that we have been able to identify and describe a set of dimensions for each instrument along which performance levels clearly vary gives evidence for the construct validity of the instruments.

Finally, there is some empirical evidence to substantiate claims of construct validity for some of the Performative Assessment instruments. Following the APA *Standards*, Popham suggests that:

> More often than not, construct validation studies are of the following sorts:
> 1. *Intervention Studies*: Attempts to demonstrate that examinees respond differently to the measure after receiving some sort of treatment.
> 2. *Differential-Population Studies*: Efforts to show that individuals representing distinct populations score differently on the measure.
> 3. *Related-Measures Studies*: Correlations, positive or negative depending on the measures, between examinees' scores on the test and their scores on other measures. (p. 114)

As mentioned earlier, we have done no "related measures studies." We do have some evidence, however, that the skills measured by the Performative Assessment instruments are sensitive to instructional intervention, and that students at different levels of ability score differently on the instruments we have been able to test in this manner. Scores on the second of each of the pairs of writing tasks administered at the end of a term, for example, are higher than scores on the first task at the beginning of the term. (In somes cases, these differences are statistically significant.) In addition, students representing three different ability levels (basic writers, regular Freshman English students, and Advanced Composition students) score differently on our Audience tasks.

STEPS IN DEVELOPING PERFORMATIVE ASSESSMENT INSTRUMENTS

We now turn to the procedures we followed to develop the Performative Assessment instruments. Each instrument evolved through the series of steps described below.

The first step in developing the Performative Assessment instruments was to identify a text-production skill that we wanted to measure. Once we had identified a particular skill, the second step was to devise a pair of writing tasks that we believed would elicit this skill. As mentioned earlier, we tried to create tasks that would not require writers to have specialized knowledge or interests by supplying most of the information that writers would need to complete the task.

When we agreed that the writing tasks called upon students to exercise the skill that we wanted to test, we made trial runs. We gathered numerous samples (usually over 100) in an attempt to represent the various levels of performance of lower-division college students. We read the responses and made further adjustments to the tasks. When we were satisfied that the tasks required students to use the skill we wanted to measure, we collected more writing samples, from which we tried to identify the component subskills that were necessary to complete the task and which could differentiate responses to the task.

The third major step was to develop scoring rubrics for each pair of tasks based on these subskills. On the basis of a careful reading of student essays, we distinguished four levels of proficiency that would describe the range of responses for each subskill. We chose to distinguish four levels of performance as a minimum number to insure adequate variance for our statistical analyses. We identified specific features of student essays that were typical of these levels of performance.

A example might clarify what we mean by identifying levels of performance on the basis of text features. In one of our initial efforts we devised a scoring rubric for a conventional description task that asked students to describe a place others would find interesting. (We did not test this rubric.) After reading a number of student essays on this topic, we concluded that one of the important subskills in successfully completing the task is the ability to orient the reader and move through the description in a systematic way. Below are descriptions of the features that characterize four levels of performance on this particular subskill.

Orienting the Reader and Moving Through the Description
(1 = low; 4 = high).

1. The writer does not establish an initial point of reference and seems to move randomly through a description of various aspects of the thing or scene.
2. The writer shows some awareness that providing a point of reference for subsequent descriptions is necessary but soon

abandons efforts to orient the reader and resorts to seemingly random movement through the description.

3. The writer identifies a particular feature and uses it as an initial point of reference. In moving through the description, however, the writer occasionally fails to reorient the reader when introducing a new aspect of the object or scene.

4. The writer identifies a particular feature and uses it as an initial point of reference. The writer then moves smoothly through the description by carefully reorienting the reader with each new aspect of the object or scene that is introduced.

Each scoring rubric describes levels of performance for three or four such text-production subskills.

The fourth step in developing Performative Assessment instruments was to use the rubrics to score student essays. We all scored a sampling of responses for each task and then compared our results. When we disagreed, we tried to identify what caused the disagreement. In many cases, these discussions led to changes in the rubrics.

The fifth step was to conduct a rating session in which raters who were unfamiliar with our instruments and procedures were trained to score writing samples using our rubrics. After they had scored sets of papers from each task, we gathered comments from raters on our tasks and rubrics, and we analyzed their ratings for interrater reliability.

The sixth step was to revise our tasks and rubrics in light of these analyses. In our initial set of Deduction tasks, for example, one task proved to be much more difficult for students to write than the other. We had to replace the very difficult task with one that was more comparable to the easier task. (Such a problem still exists for our "Constructing-a-Hypothesis" tasks.) In other cases we had to revise our rubric categories and refine our descriptions of levels of performance.

The seventh and final step was to collect additional writing samples and have them rated in a session with raters who once again did not know about the development of the instruments. From these sessions we computed scoring reliabilities for each rubric and tested the pairs of writing tasks to determine whether they were equivalent. Interrater reliability statistics and the results of tests for equivalence are reported after discussions of particular instruments in the next chapter. Descriptive statistics for all instruments are reported in Appendix A.

Chapter 8

The Performative
Assessment Instruments

Each of the Performative Assessment instruments presented in this chapter consists of two parts: (a) a pair of writing tasks and (b) scoring rubrics for each task. The scoring rubrics describe prototypical levels on a continuum of performance (for a discussion of scoring "prototypes," see Myers, 1983). Although the rubric descriptions of prototypical levels of performance were derived from analyses of student texts, they do not necessarily include all features that characterize particular levels of performance. Our intention was not to provide an exhaustive list of types of responses to the writing tasks, since such an effort would certainly have been futile. Instead, our goal was to provide "benchmarks" that would enable raters to identify and assess skills in terms of text features.

On the Performative Assessment instruments that assess writers' abilities to effect certain thinking processes in written texts, the first category in each of the scoring rubrics concerns the extent to which students respond effectively to the rhetorical situation described in the writing task. This category assesses an aspect of writing performance that would figure importantly in nearly any writing task, something very similar to what Primary-Trait scoring attempts to measure. Subsequent categories assess particular skills required in producing an effective response to the writing task. In addition, we designed writing tasks and rubrics that probe what it means to address an audience effectively. We found that responding to a rhetorical situation requires multiple skills, some of which we tried to define in our Addressing-a-Specific-Audience instruments.

CLASSIFICATION

Classifying is one of the fundamental processes of thinking. When children first learn language, they learn to classify. Two-year-olds, for example, may call all liquids "juice." Later, they may distinguish two categories of liquids, which they might call "juice" and "milk." By the time they enter school, they will have labels for nearly all the liquids they drink and many other liquids as well.

Classifying as a way of organizing a piece of discourse, however, requires skills beyond those of distinguishing likenesses and differences. Writers must create groups that are recognizable to potential readers. These groups must follow from some implicit or explicit principle of categorization, and writers must signal relationships among the groups. Finally, the categories are expected to serve some purpose. For example, a physician classifies pneumonias as viral, bacterial, or chemical in order to treat them appropriately.

Our Classification tasks focus on students' skills in forming and distinguishing groups for an informative purpose. The first of the Classification tasks requires students to classify 12 dangers inherent in running. To minimize the problem of varying levels of subject-matter knowledge (in this case, knowledge of jogging), we provided the content necessary to complete the task. The principal requirement of the task, then, is to identify appropriate categories and then classify each of the 12 dangers accordingly.

The second Classification task is identical to the first in form and purpose, but differs in content. For this task students are required to classify not dangers but benefits of running. The two Classification tasks appear below.

Classification Task 1

You work for your college newspaper. Your assignment is to use the notes below to write a short article that classifies the major dangers of running. Your article will appear in a special supplement on sports activities. Determine the categories you need and include each of the ideas listed below under one of the categories.

- Older runners often run too far too fast and risk heart attacks.
- Because tired runners often do not look when they cross streets, they are sometimes hit by cars.
- Some people find runners to be snobbish toward nonrunners.
- Women running alone have been prime victims of rapists.
- Regular running can strain joints, which can become a serious problem in later life.
- It has been suggested that runners have higher divorce rates than nonrunners.

- Running for some people becomes an end in itself, leading them to neglect their jobs and other responsibilities.
- Runners often suffer heat exhaustion and heat stroke in hot weather.
- Runners are often bitten by dogs.
- Runners suffer from blisters, heel spurs, and shin splints.
- Running after eating a meal can cause indigestion.
- Running has become so commercialized that many of the "extras" are now unaffordable.

Classification Task 2

You work for your college newspaper. Your assignment is to use the notes below to write a short article that classifies the major benefits of running. Your article will appear in a special supplement on sports activities. Determine the categories you need and include each of the ideas listed below under one of the categories.

- Many people run to relieve tension.
- Regular running reduces blood pressure.
- Running is a relatively inexpensive hobby.
- Regular running can reduce cholesterol and triglyceride (fat) levels.
- Some businessmen find that they become more productive on the job when they run regularly.
- Many people find it easier to quit smoking when they run regularly.
- Some people run regularly in groups, combining exercise with conversation.
- Some runners enjoy "runner's high," a feeling of exhilaration that comes with running.
- Running uses calories at a high rate.
- Couples who run together find that they can talk without being interrupted.
- Active runners have greater stamina.
- Running long distances gives people confidence to attempt other difficult goals.

Scoring Rubric for Classification Tasks

The Classification tasks described above are so closely parallel that a single scoring rubric will accommodate both tasks.

Category "A" on the scoring rubric below evaluates how effectively students meet the demands of the rhetorical situation. Each of the four values on the 1–4 scoring range is described in terms of the features that typically characterize each type of response.

Category "B" addresses how well students establish categories necessary for classifying the items presented in the task. Responses to the requirement of the establishing categories range from establishing no categories at all to establishing an adequate number of *conceptually distinct* categories.

Category "C" concerns the extent to which students successfully place individual items into appropriate categories. To some extent, of course, category "C" depends upon category "B." Yet category "C" is necessary because there are numerous cases in which students establish categories but then fail to include particular items in the categories they have established.

Classification Scoring Rubric

Rate individual papers on each of the variables described below.
(1 = least effective; 4 = most effective)

A. Meeting the Demands of the Rhetorical Situation

1. The writer provides no introduction.
2. The writer provides an introduction, but it suggests that he/she knows *neither* the collegiate audience nor the circumstances (i.e., writing an article for a sports supplement) of the writing task.
3. The writer provides an introduction which shows that he/she recognizes *either* the collegiate audience or the circumstances of the writing task.
4. The writer provides an introduction which shows that he/she recognizes *both* the collegiate audience and the circumstances of the writing task.

B. Establishing Categories

1. The writer establishes no categories, but instead simply lists benefits or dangers in no discernible groups.
2. The writer groups items but does not name categories. Or, the writer establishes some categories, but not enough to accommodate all items. Or, the writer names all categories, but all the categories are not conceptually distinct.

3. The writer groups items into conceptually distinct categories and names some, but not all, of the categories.
4. The writer groups all items into conceptually distinct categories and names all the categories.

C. Classifying Individual Items

1. The writer is unable to classify items because categories have not been established.
2. The writer classifies some items appropriately into categories that have been established, but fails to include 3 or more items in his/her paper.
3. The writer classifies most items appropriately into categories that have been established.
4. The writer classifies all items appropriately into categories that have been established.

Preliminary testing of the Classification tasks and scoring rubric indicates that the rubric enables trained raters to score papers reliably. Two raters unfamiliar with our project scored the writing samples using the rubric. Interrater reliability was computed to be .82 for category "A," .79 for category "B," and .77 for category "C."[1] Interrater reliability for the task as a whole (i.e. with scores for all categories summed for individual raters) is .83. (Descriptive statistics for all the Performative Assessment instruments can be found in Appendix A.)

We also tested the two forms of the Classification task for equivalence by asking students from two different Freshman English sections to complete either Task 1 or Task 2. Scores assigned by the raters for rubric categories "B" and "C" were summed to yield a total score on the Classification task ranging from 4 to 16. (Category "A" was eliminated from this analysis since we were interested primarily in the specific classification skills assessed by the instrument.) A t-test of the total scores of students who completed Task 1 (n = 10) and students who completed Task 2 (n = 21) showed no differences between the two groups: $t(29) = 1.61$, $p < .118$.

In addition to the t-test of mean differences, we also conducted

---

[1]The reliability figures reported throughout this chapter are Pearson correlation coefficients, which represent the reliability of a single rating. The Pearson correlations could be "stepped-up" using the Spearman-Brown formula, but we elected to report the more conservative estimates of reliability. Disagreements of more than one point were adjudicated with a third rating. This was necessary for less than 10% of all pairs of judgments.

a multivariate analysis of variance using the summed scores of the two raters on rubric categories "B" and "C" as dependent variables. The multivariate test showed no significant differences between the two groups: $F(3,28) = 1.51$, $p < .238$. Neither of the univariate tests showed significant differences at or beyond the .05 level.

Since our judgment about whether the two Classification tasks are equivalent rests on our finding no statistically significant differences between the two groups who wrote on the task, it is important to make sure that our findings genuinely result from the nature of the tasks and not from the size of our sample. In other words, to avoid a Type II statistical error, we need to be certain that we did not fail to uncover differences merely because our sample size was inadequate. Cohen (1977) discusses procedures for statistical power analysis that are appropriate in cases such as this. He suggests that statistical power is a function of several variables: (a) the significance criterion chosen by the investigator (in our case, .05); (b) sample size; and (c) the magnitude of the observed effect. For the Classification tasks, the effect size is moderate (.57 on a 0–1 scale). The statistical power of our *t*-test of mean differences, given our sample size and the effect size, is .33. This means that we had a 33% chance of finding statistically significant differences. Given Cohen's suggestion that an adequate power coefficient should be .80 or above we cannot conclude that the two forms of the Categorizing task are equivalent. Further studies employing a larger sample—at least 40 students per group—will be necessary to answer the question decisively.

WRITING AN INDUCTIVE ARGUMENT

Our Induction tasks require students to assess an array of data and come to a generalization. We debated for a long time whether to use the labels "inductive" and "deductive." Several philosophers (e.g., Popper, 1963; Toulmin, 1958) have dismissed the inductive versus deductive distinction because inductive reasoning requires prior beliefs just as does deductive reasoning. Other efforts aimed at formulating a unified theory of human reasoning, however, have kept the inductive versus deductive distinction as fundamental (e.g., Sternberg, 1977). Because the beginning composition course at Texas distinguishes induction and deduction, we maintained these labels for our tasks, even though we tend to see our Induction, Deduction, and Constructing-a-Hypothesis tasks as closely related.

The distinction between our Induction and Deduction tasks might be clarified by applying Toulmin's (1958) model of argument. Toulmin's model assumes that all arguments consist of *claims, grounds,* and *warrants.* Claims are assertions put forth for public acceptance. Grounds are the facts or data for supporting an argument. Both the Induction and Deduction tasks call for students to make claims on the basis of grounds provided in the tasks. Warrants are the means for arguing from grounds to a claim. Warrants may be explicit (such as laws) or they may be implicit (such as the common sense paths of reasoning that allow us to draw inferences). Our Deduction tasks differ from our Induction tasks primarily in that certain warrants are made explicit in the Deduction tasks.

In the first Induction task, data are provided for four black-and-white television sets. Students must evaluate the data on four different characteristics of the sets and determine which set is the best buy. For the second task, students are asked to evaluate four different instructors. This second task is similar to the first inasmuch as there are four items to be evaluated and four categories for which data are provided. In addition to arriving inductively at a generalization by using the data provided, students must frame the presentation of the data for each task in such a way that it meets the constraints of the audience and purpose as outlined in the assignment. The two Induction tasks appear below.

Induction Task 1

You work for an organization that rates consumer products and publishes a monthly magazine. You have been asked to write an article for the magazine that makes a recommendation on which 19-inch, black-and-white television set to buy. Assume the table below will be included in the article. Your job is to discuss and interpret the test data and prices in order to make your recommendation. You must rank the televisions in 1,2,3,4 order, and you are expected to explain your choices. Be explicit in your reasoning so the reader knows how you made your decisions.

Brand Name	Picture Quality	Cabinet	Frequency of Repairs	Price
Astrovision	A	C	D	$210
Diamond	C	A	B	$180
Star	C	D	B	$100
Cosmoscreen	B	B	C	$285

Performance of black-and-white television sets. Key: A = Best; B = Better than Average; C = Average; D = Below Average; E = Worst.

Induction Task 2

You work for a student organization that is ranking faculty members for your school's annual teaching award. Your job is to use the data from student evaluations given below to make a recommendation on which instructor should receive this year's award. You must rank the instructors in 1,2,3,4 order, and you are expected to explain your choices. Be explicit in your reasoning so the reader knows how you made your choices.

Name	The instructor expected a reasonable amount of work and clearly explained the grading policy.	The instructor was enthusiastic about the subject.	The instructor explained the course material clearly.	The instructor showed genuine interest in students and was available outside of class.
Fred Jackson	B	E	A	B
Karen Thomas	A	D	B	C
James Radney	B	A	B	E
Jane Benson	D	C	C	A

Student evaluations of faculty. Key: A = Best; B = Better than Average; C = Average; D = Below Average; E = Worst.

Scoring Rubrics for Induction Tasks

The scoring rubrics for the two Induction tasks differ only in content. The variables about which raters must make decisions are identical in both rubrics; the only differences are that the first rubric deals with black and white televisions and the second deals with instructors.

The first category in the rubrics (Category "A") once again deals with students' skill in handling the demands of audience and purpose set forth in the writing task.

Category "B" is perhaps the most important one in the rubric. We found that one of the features that most clearly distinguishes responses to the writing tasks is how well students are able to establish priorities among the categories for which data are provided. In terms of the written responses, this was largely a matter of rendering explicit the criteria that were used in arriving at judgments regarding the television sets or the teachers. In order to evaluate the data that were provided in the writing tasks and arrive at a final recommendation, students had to determine the relative importance of each of the variables. As the rubric suggests, some students were unable to establish any priorities among the variables, while others were able to construct elaborate weighting systems and to make explicit how such criteria figured in their final determinations.

The third category in the rubrics deals with how well students relate their evaluations of particular variables to particular television sets or teachers. Not only is it necessary to establish priorities among the variables, but it is also necessary for students to make clear how these priorities affect the evaluation of *each* of the television sets and teachers.

The final category links the larger rhetorical concerns with the inductive evaluation process. In order to respond successfully to the task, students must make a final recommendation on which television set to by or which instructor should receive the teaching award. In addition, the strongest responses to the task allude to the discussion that has preceded the final recommendation. Effective recommendations, then, simultaneously achieve the purpose of the writing assignment and signal the conclusion of the discourse by way of summarizing.

Induction Scoring Rubrics

Task 1: Black-and-White Televisions

Rate individual papers on each of the variables described below.
(1 = least effective; 4 = most effective)

A. Meeting the Demands of the Rhetorical Situation

1. The writer does not provide an introduction that describes the task-at-hand, i.e., the rating of black & white television sets for prospective buyers.
2. The writer provides a brief, inadequate introductory sentence or two. The introduction might contain some vague generalizations about watching television.
3. The writer provides an introduction but fails to describe the task-at-hand in detail and/or fails to suggest that the essay is written for a particular audience.
4. The writer provides an introduction that describes the task-at-hand. It is clear from the introduction that the audience is assumed to be a magazine reader potentially interested in buying a black & white television.

B. Establishing Priorities Among Features

1. The writer establishes no priorities among features.
2. The writer suggests that *one* particular feature was an important factor in determining how a particular television set was ranked, but does not apply this evaluation to all sets in any systematic fashion.
3. The writer suggests that two or three of the features were important factors in determining how the televisions were ranked, but still neglects one or two features in his or her evaluations.
4. The writer clearly establishes a priority system for weighting the various features for which ratings are given (e.g., price is more important than repair record).

C. Rating Individual Television Sets

1. The writer discusses the features of the televisions, but in no apparent order of importance. Individual features are occasionally neglected, and no clear 1–2–3–4 ranking is demonstrated.
2. The writer mentions all of the rating categories in the discussion of particular televsion sets, but merely repeats from the task itself how each set rated in each category. A 1–2–3–4 ranking is established, but the reasons for the ranking are not clear.
3. The writer discusses all four categories for which ratings are given but occasinally leaves gaps in his or her explanation of their relative importance with regard to each of the television sets. Some reasons for the 1–2–3–4 ranking may not be evident.
4. The writer discusses the four features for which ratings are given and their *relative* importance with regard to each of the television sets. The television sets are rank-ordered, and the reasons for the 1-2-3-4 ranking are explicit.

D. Making a Recommendation on Which Television Set to Buy

1. The writer does *not* make a clear recommendation on which television set the reader should buy.
2. The writer makes a recommendation, but it is not supported by a discussion of the data.
3. The writer makes a recommendation, but there is no *explicit*

indication that the recommendation derives from the discussion of the data.

4. The writer makes a clear recommendation on which black & white television set to buy. The recommendation is patterned inductively, i.e., "Given these data, the best set to buy is . . ." Moreover, the recommendation serves as a conclusion to both the inductive evaluation and the paper as a whole.

Task 2: Faculty Teaching Awards

Rate individual papers on each of the variables described below.
(1 = least effective; 4 = most effective)

A. Meeting the Demands of the Rhetorical Situation

1. The writer does not provide an introduction that describes the task-at-hand, i.e. the rating of faculty members to determine which instructor should receive the teaching award.
2. The writer provides a brief, inadequate introductory sentence or two.
3. The writer provides an introduction but fails to describe the task-at-hand in detail and/or fails to suggest that the essay is written for a particular audience.
4. The writer provides an introduction that fully describes the task-at-hand. It is clear from the introduction that the audience is assumed to be other members of the committee charged with recommending a recipient of the teaching award.

B. Establishing Priorities Among Rating Categories

1. The writer establishes no priorities among rating categories.
2. The writer suggests that *one* particular rating category was an important factor in determining how a particular teacher was ranked, but does not apply this evaluation to all of the teachers in any systematic fashion.
3. The writer suggests that two or three of the features were important factors in determining how the teachers were ranked, but still neglects one or two features in his or her evaluations.
4. The writer clearly establishes a priority system for weighting the various categories for which ratings are given (e.g., clarity and effectiveness of presentation are more important than enthusiasm).

C. Rating Individual Teachers

1. The writer mentions the rating categories in the discussion of particular teachers, but in no apparent order of importance. Individual categories are occasionally neglected, and no clear 1–2–3–4 ranking is demonstrated.
2. The writer mentions all of the rating categories in the discussion of particular teachers, but merely repeats from the task itself how each teacher rated in each category. A 1–2–3–4 ranking is established, but the reasons for the ranking are not clear.
3. The writer discusses all four features for which ratings are given but occasionally leaves gaps in his or her explanation of their relative importance with regard to each of the teachers. Some reasons for the 1–2–3–4 ranking may not be evident.
4. The writer discusses each teacher in terms of the categories for which ratings are given, stressing the *relative* importance of each of the categories. The teachers are rank-ordered, and the reasons for the 1–2–3–4 ranking are explicit.

D. Making a Recommendation for the Award

1. The writer does *not* make a clear recommendation on which teacher should receive the award. Often the writer "cops out," using such statements as "after all, it's the reader's decision."
2. The writer makes a recommendation, but it is not supported by a discussion of the data.
3. The writer makes a recommendation, but there is no *explicit* indication that the recommendation derives from the discussion of the data.
4. The writer makes a clear recommendation on which instructor should receive the teaching award. The recommendation is patterned inductively, i.e., "Given these data, the teacher who should receive the award is . . . " Moreover, the recommendation serves as a conclusion to both the inductive evaluation and the paper as a whole.

Preliminary testing of the Induction tasks and scoring rubrics indicates that both tasks can be scored reliably. A summary table of interrater reliability figures for individual categories and whole instruments appears in Table 8.1.

Table 8.1. Induction Instrument Scoring Reliabilities

Rubric Categories	Task 1 (TVs)	Task 2 (Tchrs)
Category "A"	.87	.70
Category "B"	.74	.90
Category "C"	.57	.65
Category "D"	.69	.47
Total	.84	.88

Tests for the equivalence of the two Induction instruments suggest that the two tasks are not significantly different. Two comparable groups wrote in response to one of the two forms under pre-test conditions (Task 1, $n = 22$; Task 2, $n = 9$). Scores assigned by two independent raters on rubric categories "B," "C," and "D" were summed to yield a total score on the Induction task ranging from 6 to 24. A t-test of total mean scores of the two groups revealed no significant differences: $t(29) = -.58$, $p < .565$.

In addition, a multivariate analysis of variance using total scores on individual categories as dependent variables showed no significant differences between groups: $F(4, 26) = .97$, $p < .438$. None of the univariate tests on individual categories was significant at or beyond the .05 level.

Once again we conducted tests of statistical power to make certain we would not commit a Type II error if we concluded on the basis of our t-test that the two forms of the Induction task are not significantly different. Both our effect size (.22) and statistical power (.08) are quite low. In this case, however, it is important to examine the effect size more closely. Daly and Hexamer (1983) suggest that an important consideration is whether a certain effect size is conceptually meaningful. They argue that "it is very possible, with large power, to obtain highly significant effects in terms of statistical criteria but for that effect to be relatively meaningless—meaningless in the sense that it accounts for so little of the variability or is of so low a magnitude as to add virtually nothing to our knowledge" (p. 163). The mean difference between the two groups taking the two forms of the Induction task as a pre-test was only .7, a difference we judge to be quite insubstantial on the 6–24 scale. A sample size of over 350 per group would be required to reach statistical significance with this effect size, but statistical significance given the magnitude of the effect would be superfluous. We therefore conclude that since the mean differences between the two different forms of the Induction task are so small, the two forms are comparable with regard to their call for students to assess an array of data and present judgments based on those data to a reader. The fact that the two Induction writing tasks are equivalent means the two forms could be used for pre/post testing. The equivalence of the two forms also provides some evidence of test–retest reliability (see Chapter 7). Samples of scored Induction essays appear in Appendix B.

WRITING A DEDUCTIVE ARGUMENT

The Performative Assessment instruments below are designed to elicit writing that is patterned deductively. Students are given regulations that define certain types of behavior, along with a narrative describing a series of events. The requirement of the task is to determine whether the behaviors described in the narrative fit the definitions described in the regulations and to reach a final conclusion based on this "fit."

Students must organize their findings in a text that is suitable to be read before a committee charged with making a determination on an individual's guilt or innocence according to the regulations.

Deduction Task 1

Assume the following regulations regarding academic cheating apply to the situation below.

Cheating on a test includes:

1. The use during a test of materials not authorized by the person giving the test.
2. The possession during a test of materials not authorized by the person giving the test.
3. Copying from another student's paper.
4. Collaborating with or seeking aid from another student during a test without authorization.

Students guilty of cheating automatically fail the course and are subject to more severe penalties.

Charlie Roberts had had trouble with Zoology all semester, and now that the final was approaching, he began to get desperate. One day he approached his friend Jack Cline and suggested the two attempt to exchange answers during the test.

Not wanting to offend Charlie, Jack never explicitly refused to cooperate with Charlie in the scheme. He was decidedly uneasy about it, however, and attempted to compromise by offering Charlie his class notes to use in preparing for the test.

During the test, Charlie was caught using a set of class notes and automatically failed both the test and the course.

When the professor examined the notes Charlie had used during the test, he discovered they belonged to Jack. As a result of the discovery, the professor also failed Jack, claiming that he too had cheated on the test.

Jack felt he was innocent and followed the university's procedures for appeal to the Faculty Disciplinary Committee, which is responsible for making a decision in cases involving academic cheating. You are the student member of that committee.

The chair has asked you to prepare a written statement on whether Jack is innocent or guilty that will be presented before the Committee. Defend your opinion on the basis of the university's regulations on cheating.

Deduction Task 2

Under certain circumstances, public school teachers are allowed to deduct educational costs on their income tax returns. You are the citizen member of an Internal Revenue Service board of examiners, and you must rule on the following controversial case.

Assume these regulations regarding income tax deductions apply to the case described below:

A citizen may deduct the expenses of taking college classes if he or she is taking the coursework in order to:

1. Maintain or improve skills required in his or her present employment; OR
2. Keep his or her current employment status or salary; OR
3. Meet the requirements of his or her current employer.

However, the expenses may *not* be deducted if:

A. The courses are required in order to meet the minimum educational requirements of the person's employment; OR
B. The education would qualify the person for a new trade or business. A change of duties is not considered to be a new

trade or business if the new duties involve the same general work as the person did previously.

Mr. Barker is a 7th grade teacher at an elementary school that has grades kindergarten through 8. The county school administration he works for has decided to reorganize so that all of its elementary schools have only grades kindergarten through 6; consequently, Mr. Barker will be moved to a new school and will become a junior high school teacher. To continue teaching 7th graders under this new system, Mr. Barker must get a secondary school teaching certificate, and, in order to get this certificate, he must take a college course entitled "Methods and Materials for Teaching Junior High School Students."

On his income tax return, Mr. Barker deducted his tuition and book expenses. The Internal Revenue Service decided to investigate Mr. Barker. The IRS claimed that the course he took qualified him for a new trade or business; consequently, he was not permitted to deduct the expenses. Mr. Barker disagreed with this ruling and appealed his case to the board of examiners on which you are the citizens' representative.

Your job is to write a statement to be presented before the board of examiners that gives your opinion on whether Mr. Barker was in violation of federal tax laws or whether he was within his rights in deducting the college expenses. Defend your opinion on the basis of the guidelines presented above.

Scoring Rubrics for Deduction Tasks

The Deduction scoring rubrics begin with a consideration of how well students accommodate the rhetorical situation to which they are asked to respond (Category A). The most successful essays make it clear (either implicitly or explicitly) that the writer is addressing a committee charged with hearing the case described in the narrative. Furthermore, there is a clear description of the specific problem the committee is considering and a recognition throughout the essay that the committee is responsible for making a final determination of innocence or guilt.

Category B on the scoring rubrics is concerned with the writer's discussion of the regulations presented in the writing task. The most successful writers are aware of the need to make the regulations a part of their own text by summarizing the regulations for the audience and by demonstrating their understanding of them.

Category C involves the application of the regulations to particular behaviors. Here, the successful writers are explicit in describing the closeness of the "fit" between the regulations and the behaviors described in the narrative.

Finally, Category D assesses the extent to which the writer is explicit about having made a final determination regarding guilt or innocence. The most successful writers not only make a final judgment but clearly relate that judgment to the foregoing discussion of particular behaviors and the regulations outlined in the writing task.

Deduction Scoring Rubrics

Task 1: Academic Cheating

Rate individual papers on each of the variables described below.
(1 = Least effective; 4 = most effective)

A. Meeting the Demands of the Rhetorical Situation

1. The writer does not identify him/herself as a member of the university disciplinary council *and* does not identify the task-at-hand.
2. The writer does not identify him/herself as a member of the university disciplinary council *or* does not fully describe the task-at-hand.
3. The writer identifies him/herself as a member of the university disciplinary council and provides an introductory statement that describes the task-at-hand.
4. The writer identifies him/herself as a member of the university disciplinary council and provides an introductory statement that describes the task-at-hand. In addition, throughout the paper, the writer makes occasional reference to the audience, acknowledging that he/she is leading them through an argument and that the council as a whole is responsible for making a determination on Jack's guilt or innocence.

B. Discussing the Regulations Regarding Academic Cheating

1. The writer neglects to discuss some of the regulations as outlined in the writing task.
2. The writer mentions the regulations, but merely reiterates them verbatim from the writing task.

3. The writer discusses all of the regulations regarding academic cheating, but does not demonstrate his/her understanding of them.
4. The writer discusses all of the regulations regarding academic cheating as outlined in the writing task in such a way as to demonstrate his/her understanding of them. It is also clear from this discussion of the regulations that the writer is summarizing the regulations for the audience.

C. Relating the Regulations to Jack's Behavior

1. The writer ignores the regulations themselves and merely retells the story of Jack and Charlie.
2. The writer alludes to the regulations, but does not relate any particular regulations to Jack's behavior.
3. The writer relates one or two regulations to Jack's behavior.
4. The writer relates all the regulations to Jack's behavior, stating the particular sections that apply.

D. Drawing Conclusions from the Regulations as Applied to Jack's Behavior

1. The writer draws no explicit conclusions regarding Jack's behavior.
2. The writer expresses a personal opinion that Jack is innocent or guilty, but does not state that the disciplinary council must make a final recommendation regarding Jack's case.
3. The writer concludes that, overall, Jack is innocent (or guilty) of the charges brought against him and states that the disciplinary council must make a final recommendation, i.e., that Jack should be exonerated or disciplined.
4. The writer draws explicit conclusions from the discussion of the regulations regarding academic cheating as applied to Jack's behavior and clearly states that the disciplinary council must make a final recommendation. These conclusions result from syllogistic reasoning, e.g.: Cheating consists of 'X'; Jack did (or did not) do 'X'; therefore, Jack did (or did not) cheat.

Task 2: Income Tax

Rate individual papers on each of the variables described below. (1 = least effective; 4 = most effective)

A. Meeting the Demands of the Rhetorical Situation

1. The writer does not identify him/herself as a member of the board of examiners *and* does not identify the task-at-hand.
2. The writer does not identify him/herself as a member of the board of examiners *or* does not fully describe the task-at-hand.
3. The writer identifies him/herself as a member of the board of examiners and provides an introductory statement that describes the task-at-hand.
4. The writer identifies him/herself as a member of the board of examiners and provides an introductory statement that describes the task-at-hand. In addition, throughout the paper, the writer makes occasional reference to the audience, acknowledging that he/she is leading them through an argument, and that the board as a whole is responsible for making a determination on Mr. Barker's guilt or innocence.

B. Discussing the Regulations Regarding Income Tax Deductions

1. The writer neglects to discuss some of the regulations as outlined in the writing task.
2. The writer mentions the regulations, but merely reiterates them verbatim from the writing task.
3. The writer discusses all of the regulations regarding income tax deductions, but does not demonstrate his/her understanding of them.
4. The writer discusses all of the regulations regarding income tax deductions as outlined in the writing task in such a way as to demonstrate his/her understanding of them. It is also clear from this discussion of the regulations that the writer is summarizing them for the audience.

C. Relating the Regulations to Mr. Barker's Behavior

1. The writer ignores the regulations themselves and merely retells the story of Mr. Barker's job change.
2. The writer alludes to the regulations, but does not relate any particular regulations to Mr. Barker's behavior.
3. The writer relates one or two regulations to Mr. Barker's behavior.
4. The writer relates all the regulations to Mr. Barker's behavior, stating the particular sections that apply.

D. Drawing Conclusions from the Regulations as Applied to Mr. Barker's Behavior

1. The writer draws no explicit conclusions regarding Mr. Barker's behavior.
2. The writer expresses a personal opinion that Mr. Barker is innocent or guilty, but does not state that the board of examiners must make a final recommendation regarding Jack's case.
3. The writer concludes that, overall, Mr. Barker is innocent (or guilty) of the charges brought against him and states that the board of examiners must make a final recommendation, i.e., that Mr. Barker should be exonerated or disciplined.
4. The writer draws explicit conclusions from the discussion of the regulations regarding income tax deductions as applied to Mr. Barker's behavior and clearly states that the disciplinary council must make a final recommendation. These conclusions result from syllogistic reasoning, e.g.:
   Permissible deductions consist of 'X'; Mr. Barker did (did not) make deductions in accordance with these guidelines; therefore, Mr. Barker did (did not) cheat on his income tax.

Preliminary testing suggests that the two Deduction tasks can be scored reliably. A table showing interrater reliability figures for individual rubric categories and total instruments appears in Table 8.2.

We lacked appropriate data to test the two Deduction tasks for equivalence (see Appendix A).

CONSTRUCTING A HYPOTHESIS

The tasks requiring students to construct a hypothesis are related to the Induction and Deduction tasks but are different in focus and method. Like the Induction and Deduction tasks, the Constructing-a-Hypothesis tasks require students to create evaluation arguments. Like the Induction tasks, they ask students to make an evaluative generalization based on specific data. Like the Deduction tasks, they ask students to use general principles—in these cases, principles of simple economic supply and demand and public opinion—to judge a specific situation.

We believe, however, that the tasks for constructing a hypothesis differ from the other reasoning tasks in that the former require writers to construct and evaluate hypotheses that can explain causation.

Table 8.2. Deduction Instrument Scoring Reliabilities

Rubric Categories	Task 1 (Cheating)	Task 2 (Income Tax)
Category "A"	.65	.75
Category "B"	.81	.94
Category "C"	.86	.74
Cateogry "D"	.68	.73
Total	.85	.94

In both of the tasks that follow, students are given charts containing numerical data and are asked to construct a hypothesis that might account for the data.

Constructing-a-Hypothesis Task 1

You are working on a special issue of a magazine that will examine major economic trends that occurred from 1971–1980. You have found out that in 1971, 1.6 trillion kilowatt-hours of electricity were produced; in 1976, 2.0 trillion kilowatt-hours; and in 1981, 2.3 trillion kilowatt hours. You are now looking at the sources of energy used for the production of electricity. The table below gives the percentage of electricity produced according to the power source.

Year	Coal	Gas and Oil	Nuclear	Hydro
1971	44%	38%	2%	16%
1976	46%	28%	12%	14%
1981	56%	24%	8%	12%

Your job is to explain why most electricity in the United States was produced using coal by the end of the 1980. Give the cause or causes for this increased use of coal to make electricity. Be explicit so that the reader can follow the steps in your reasoning.

Constructing-a-Hypothesis Task 2

You are a writer for a magazine that publishes news and feature stories about product marketing practices, and you are working on a special issue of the magazine entitled "Success Stories in Marketing." You have done some research and have found the following two tables. Your job is to explain in your article how the Japanese captured most of the American market for motorcycles. Give the cause or causes for the increasing sales of Japanese cycles. Be explicit so that the reader can follow the steps in your reasoning.

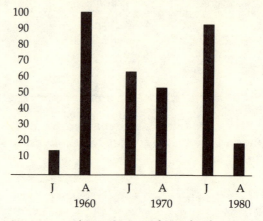

Percentage of American-Market Sales for Japanese (J) and American (A) Motorcycles (1960–1980)

Size	1960	1965	1970	1975	1980
Large Bikes	A=$1200 No J Model	A=$1275 No J Model	A=$1350 J=$1250	A=$1500 J=$1325	A=$1750 J=$1600
Mid-Range	A=$600 No J Model	A=$650 J=$525	A=$750 J=$600	A=$825 J=$710	A=$1150 J=$1075
Mini-Bikes	No A Model J=$200	No A Model J=$225	A=$400 J=$300	A=$500 J=$425	A=$575 J=$525

Average Prices of Motorcycles According to Size (J = Japanese; A = American)

Scoring Rubrics for Constructing-a-Hypothesis Tasks

Since the tasks requiring students to construct a hypothesis are essentially argumentative writing tasks, we have adapted Toulmin's (1958) model of argument as a basis for three of the four categories on the scoring rubrics. The rubrics for the two tasks are conceptually identical; the only differences between them result from necessary references to the specific tasks.

Category A, as in all the Performative Assessment rubrics, deals with how well students respond to the rhetorical situation they are confronted with. In these tasks the most successful writers demonstrate that they are writing for a specialized magazine in order to hypothesize a specific cause for the situation described in the task.

Category B assesses the hypothesis the writer claims will explain the data. The most successful writers present a hypothesis that includes elements of the specific grounds in support of the hypothesis. In other words, the successful writers' general claims hint at the specific supporting detail that will follow.

Category C investigates the extent to which the writer provides specific grounds to support the claim that has been made. While reading sample papers, we noticed that many students fail to provide these specific grounds, even though their generalized claim suggested that they were going to.

Category D assesses whether the student has provided a sufficient link between the specific grounds and the general claim. Again, we found that many students fail to establish these logical connections and consequently create an incomplete argument. The scoring rubrics for the Hypothesis tasks appear below.

Constructing-A-Hypothesis Scoring Rubrics

Task 1: Coal Use in Producing Electricity

Rate individual papers on each of the variables described below.
(1 = least effective; 4 = most effective)

A. Meeting the Demands of the Rhetorical Situation

1. The writer does not provide an introduction that describes the task-at-hand, i.e., hypothesizing why the use of coal has increased.
2. The writer provides a brief, inadequate introductory sentence or two. The introduction may contain some generalizations about energy consumption and efficiency, but the generalizations are vague.
3. The writer provides an introduction but fails to describe the task-at-hand in detail and/or fails to suggest that the essay is written for a particular audience.
4. The writer provides an introduction that fully describes the task-at-hand. It is clear from the introduction that the audience is assumed to be readers of an economic journal interested in issues of energy production and consumption and environmental concerns.

B. Hypothesizing a Cause for the Increased Use of Coal

1. The writer hypothesizes no cause for an increased use of coal.
2. The writer hypothesizes a cause for the increased use of coal, but the hypothesis is constructed only on the intrinsic qualities of coal use and does not mention qualities of any of the other power sources.
3. The writer hypothesizes a cause for the increased use of coal; the hypothesis mentions intrinsic qualities of coal use *and* qualities of *one* of the other power sources.
4. The writer hypothesizes a cause for the increased use of coal; the hypothesis mentions intrinsic qualities of coal use and qualities of *all three* other power sources.

C. Providing Specific Grounds for the Hypothesis

1. The writer provides no specific details to support the hypothesis.
2. The writer attempts to provide specific details to support the hypothesis, but he or she supplies only the percentages given in the chart. In effect the reasoning is circular: coal use increased because its percentage of use increased.
3. The writer provides at least *one* specific assertion about coal use (e.g., it is cheaper, easily accessible, easily transportable, in abundant supply) plus at least *one* specific assertion about *one* of the other power sources: gas and oil (e.g., decreasing supply, Arab embargo, nationalist attitude against import dependency, higher prices), nuclear (e.g., great expense, possibility of danger, Three Mile Island incident, opposition from activist groups), or hydro (e.g., geographic constraints, dwindling supply of sufficient water, low efficiency, higher expense).
4. The writer provides at least *one* specific assertion about coal use and least *one* specific assertion about *each* of the other three power sources. See #3 above for typical examples of specific assertions.

D. Providing General Warrants to Justify the Grounds

1. The writer provides no general explanation of the grounds.
2. The writer merely repeats facts from the given data in a narrative form, without trying to provide a general explanation.
3. The writer provides the general reasoning to justify the grounds; however, the reasoning considers only questions of the expense and economics of electricity production.

4. The writer provides general reasoning to justify the grounds, explaining general principles of economics *as well as* principles of sensitivity to public opinion about the safety of the environment *or* about opposition to import dependency.

Task 2: *Japanese Domination of the Motorcycle Market*

Rate individual papers on each of the variables described below.
(1 = least effective; 4 = most effective)

A. Meeting the Demands of the Rhetorical Situation

1. The writer does not provides an introduction that describes the task-at-hand, i.e., hypothesizing why the Japanese motorcycle companies have dominated the market.
2. The writer provides a brief, inadequate introductory sentence or two. The introduction may contain some generalizations about purchasing and riding motorcycles, but the generalizations are vague.
3. The writer provides an introduction but fails to describe the task-at-hand in detail and/or fails to suggest that the essay is written for a particular audience.
4. The writer provides an introduction that fully describes the task-at-hand. It is clear from the introduction that the audience is assumed to be readers of an economic journal interested in marketing practices of major corporations.

B. Hypothesizing a Cause for the Japanese Domination

1. The writer hypothesizes no cause for the Japanese companies' domination of the market.
2. The writer hypothesizes a cause for the Japanese companies' domination of the market, but the cause is clearly extrinsic to the given data.
3. The writer hypothesizes a cause for the Japanese companies' domination of the market, but the hypothesis mentions only the consistently lower prices of the Japanese products.
4. The writer hypothesizes a cause for the Japanese companies' domination of the market; the hypothesis mentions both the lower prices and the Japanese' successful marketing strategy.

C. Providing Specific Grounds for the Hypothesis

1. The writer provides no specific details to support the hypothesis.
2. The writer attempts to provide specific details to support the

hypothesis, but he or she supplies only the figures from the *upper* chart in the task. In effect the reasoning is circular: the Japanese gained domination because their market shares increased.

3. The writer provides specific details to support the hypothesis, supplying examples both from the figures in the upper chart and the consistently lower prices in the lower chart.
4. The writer provides specific details to support the hypothesis, supplying examples from the figures in the upper chart, the consistently lower prices in the lower chart, *and* a specific explanation of the marketing strategy of capturing the bottom end of the motorcycle market before moving into production of more expensive motorcycles.

D. Providing General Warrants to Justify the Grounds

1. The writer provides no general explanation of the grounds.
2. The writer merely repeats facts from the given data in a narrative form, without trying to provide a general explanation.
3. The writer provides general reasoning to justify the grounds; however, the reasoning is based only on the assumption that consumers want a lower-priced, good quality product.
4. The writer provides general reasoning to justify the grounds, explaining that consumers want a lower-priced, good quality product *and* that consumers grew up with Japanese motorcycles, buying first their smaller models and then moving up to larger models.

Scoring reliabilities for the Constructing-a-Hypothesis instruments appear in Table 8.3.

We also ran tests to determine whether the two Hypothesis tasks are equivalent. Two comparable groups of freshman composition students were given one of the two tasks (Task 1, $n = 16$; Task 2, $n = 16$). The scores of two raters on rubric categories "B," "C," and "D" were summed to yield a total score on the Hypothesis task ranging from 6 to 24. A t-test of scores from these two groups showed the groups to differ significantly: $t(30) = 3.05$, $p < .005$.

A multivariate analysis of variance using summed scores on rubric categories "B," "C," and "D" as dependent variables also showed significant differences between the two groups: $F(3, 28) = 12.16$, $p < .001$. Univariate analyses of individual category scores revealed that categories "C" and "D" contributed most to these differences—category "C": $F(1,30) = 4.69$, $p < .038$; category "D": $F(1,30) = 19.02$, $p < .001$.

Since the mean difference between the two groups (3.13) is con-

Table 8.3.   Constructing-a-Hypothesis Instrument Scoring Reliabilities

Rubric Categories	Task 1 (Coal)	Task 2 (Cycles)
Category "A"	.65	.81
Category "B"	.70	.33
Category "C"	.87	.81
Category "D"	.64	.57
Total	.82	.71

ceptually meaningful and the effect size is high (.81), we conclude from these tests that the two Constructing-a-Hypothesis tasks are not equivalent and therefore stand in need of further testing and refinement.

The Constructing-a-Hypothesis tasks demand more extensive use of general knowledge than is required by the other Performative Assessment tasks. This demand may explain why the two Constructing-a-Hypothesis tasks are not equivalent. We suspect that the students are more likely to be familiar with the energy issues referred to in Task 1 than they are with the economic and marketing principles underlying Task 2. Another explanation may be that Task 2 simply requires students to process more information than Task 1.

At any rate, the Constructing-a-Hypothesis tasks do demonstrate the importance of the procedures for task and rubric development described in Chapter 7. The Hypothesis tasks were judged to be equivalent by us and by others we consulted, but the detailed analyses we performed reveal that they are not. We left these tasks "unfinished" to show the developmental process that we followed for our other tasks. Our next step for these instruments would be to revise the tasks and begin another round of collecting responses.

ADDRESSING A SPECIFIC AUDIENCE

The Performative Assessment instruments for addressing a specific audience differ from the other instruments both in the kind of skills that they measure and in the nature of the tasks themselves. We tried several approaches to assessing writers' skills in addressing specific audiences. The approach we found to work best requires students to write for two different audiences on the same subject. We tried asking students to write to audiences with different levels of knowledge about a particular subject (such as children and adults), but these tasks proved to be difficult both to write and to score. We opted instead for tasks that require students to write to audiences with approximately the same level of knowledge but with different views on a particular subject. These tasks were far more successful.

Specifically, we asked students to assume the role of a civil servant who must answer letters from two individuals who are displeased with a decision made by the public agency where the writer works. The tasks put the writer in a situation where he or she must answer people with different views. The point of this exercise is not to force the writer to take a "chameleon's" stance on the particular issue. We do not ask students to do what Plato accused the Sophists of advocating—to placate audiences with rhetorical artifice. Rather, we take the position of Aristotle that rhetoric is a means of understanding and addressing the argument of the other. Each Audience task contains two letters. In each letter are three arguments that the writer must acknowledge and address.

Audience Task 1

During the past 10 years, a dispute has been raging in western Washington between two groups of outdoors enthusiasts—the hikers and the bikers. The controversy concerns whether the motorcyclists should be allowed to ride their dirt bikes on the several hiking trails leading into the Cascade Crest area in the Snoqualmie National Forest. Previously, the National Forest Service officials had banned the bikers from all 52 of the trails. Recently, however, the Forest Service modified its position and decided to open 25 of the trails to cyclists.

You are the district ranger from the Snoqualmie National Forest, and you have recently received the two letters that follow. Your job is to reply to the letters. You must write one to the hikers and one to the bikers. Your job is to convince them that the decision to open the trails is a good decision.

Letter 1
District Ranger, Snoqualmie National Forest
U.S. Forest Service
905 Second Avenue
Seattle, Washington 98104

Dear Sir:

Speaking for all the members of my organization, I cannot believe that the National Forest Service gave in to the pressure of various motorcycle organizations and opened the 25 trails in the Cascade Crest area to motorized use.

Over the years, the amount of hikable trail mileage near Cascade Crest has been severely reduced by logging roads. Now your action threatens to reduce the amount even further by turning available hiking trails into miniature dirt-bike racing tracks.

The members of my organization have always gone to the wildlands at least partly to escape from machines and all they symbolize. Now there will be no place where people can get away from machines.

Until recently, our organization had planned on holding a national convention of hikers next year in the Cascade Crest area. Such a convention would have brought great prestige to your forest and great profits to the merchants of the small towns surrounding the forest, towns which are already suffering from a depression in the lumbering industry. Your decision to open the trails has put this convention in grave jeopardy, and consequently, we may have to find another site for our meeting.

I urge you strongly to rescind your decision and once again ban the bikers from the trails. I look forward to hearing from you at your earliest convenience.

Sincerely,
Dennis Abercrombie, President
Western Washington Hiking Association

Letter 2
District Ranger, Snoqualmie National Forest
U.S. Forest Service
905 Second Avenue
Seattle, Washington 98104

Sir:

Your decision to open only 25 trails in the Cascade Crest area is horrible. Although such a limited access to the trails is better than no access at all, you are still discrimating against us bikers by keeping 27 of the best trails closed to us.

I'm afraid, my friend, that you have some pretty fouled-up ideas about dirt biking. We cause no more noise pollution than your backpackers do when they bring all those blaring radios and crying children with them.

If you would only open up all your trails to us bikers, I'm sure you could attract cyclists from all over the country to your forest. But with less than half the trails open, it's hardly worth the effort to come out there. If you want to cater to real outdoors people, open all the trails.

I hope you realize, sir, that if you deny us bikers access to all the trails, you are letting only one kind of people enjoy the wilderness— the hikers. Why should casual strollers with 60-pound packs on their backs be the only ones to enjoy the forest? Let everyone use all of it!

Yours for biking,
A.K. Rutherford
President of Seattle Dirt Bikers

Audience Task 2

During the past 10 years, the federally-funded Great Plains Water Project has been under construction in North Dakota. The project was originally intended to irrigate 1,300 farms by means of a 60-mile main canal and a network of feeder ditches. In addition, the project would have created four new man-made lakes in the region. Originally scheduled to cost $145 million, the total cost of the project has grown to $500 million. Consequently, the directors of the project have decided not to finish the entire project. Instead, they have decided to finish only the 60-mile main canal, at a cost of $106 million, to provide irrigation to 120 farms bordering on the canal. No new lakes will be constructed and no feeder ditches will lead to outlying farms.

You are the district officer for the Great Plains Water Project, and you have recently receved the two letters that follow. Your job is to reply to the letters. You must write one to the farmer and one to the Audubon Society. Your job is to convince them that the decision to complete only part of the project was a good decision.

Letter 1
District Officer, Great Plains Water Project
1000 Spruce St.
Fargo, N. D. 58201

Dear Sir:

The members of my organization and I are greatly distressed by the Bureau of Reclamation's decision to complete a substantial part of the Great Plains Water Project. You recall, of course, from our earlier correspondence that the National Audubon Society has favored terminating the entire project.

We contend that there are several reasons why your bureau should abandon your plans completely. Our foremost concern is that the 60-mile canal will destroy valuable wildlife habitats. Studies over several years have demonstrated that the central North Dakota farmlands are major stopping points in the northbound migration flights of both sandhill cranes and the nearly-extinct whooping cranes. The canal seriously threatens to upset the ecological balance of the Great Plains.

We also hold that, in these days when the federal government is trying to reduce its expenditures, the Great Plains Water Project does not make financial sense. Since the completion that you propose will benefit only 120 farms, the project as you envision it will eventually demand almost one million dollars per farm. In addition, much electricity will be required to pump the water from the Missouri River to the farms along the canal. Furthermore, maintenance of the canal will be expensive since the banks are already slipping into the water.

The partial completion that you propose will be counterproductive for farming as a whole in the Great Plains. Although your plans would provide irrigation for 120 farms, the completion of the main canal would result in a net reduction of 8,148 acres of cropland and 34,172 acres of grassland in North Dakota. In other words, the farmlands of the Great Plains are already productive—why destroy what is already good?

We believe that these reasons are cause enough to abandon all plans to complete even a portion of the Great Plains Water Project. Our organization intends to continue lobbying in Congress for this goal. We urge you, as director of the Bureau of Reclamation, to consider our reasons and act wisely for the sake of a sound environment and a sound economy.

Sincerely,
Mary Williamson, President
National Audubon Society

Letter 2
District Officer, Great Plains Water Project
1000 Spruce St.
Fargo, N. D. 58201

Dear Mr. District Officer:

My name is Olaf Petersen, and I am one of the farmers in Tyler County, North Dakota who would have received irrigation from the Great Plains Water Project if you had decided to finish the whole thing. I don't mind telling you that I am awful mad that you decided not to.

I have been a good U.S. taxpayer for more than 40 years, and I hate to see my good tax dollars going to waste. I read in the paper last week where the Government has already spent 100 million dollars to complete part of the project. Why can't we spend some more and finish it so that more of us farmers can benefit? As it is now, it seems that my tax dollars are paying for water for someone else.

You people in Washington talk all the time about how the U.S. should take up its burden and help to relieve the world hunger problem. Well, if we had this water from the Great Plains Water Project up in the central part of North Dakota, we could increase production on our farms enough to yield bumper crops every year. We could then have enough food to feed hungry Americans and send food to hungry people abroad.

By not finishing the project, not only do you take water from farming away from us—you also take away water for recreation. I read where your original plan was to create four big lakes while you were building the ditches and pipelines. These lakes would have been wonderful—they could have been stocked with fish and used for boating. I guess that fun has no place in the federal budget!

As I said before, I am a good U.S. taxpayer who only wants to farm his land and enjoy his outdoor life. If you would complete the entire Great Plains Water Project, I could do both. I ask you sincerely to reconsider your plans and go ahead with the whole thing.

Yours truly,
Olaf Petersen
R.D. #4, Tyler County
Tyler City, North Dakota 58905

Scoring Rubrics for Audience Tasks

In constructing the scoring rubrics for these tasks, we have operated on the assumption that the ability to address a specific audience can best be assessed when a student is required to address separate audiences whose concerns and arguments are very different. Consequently, we direct our raters to consider the two letters as a single piece of discourse and rate them as if they are one.

Category A assesses how well writers represent the rhetorical situation in which they have been placed. Successful writers convey a message that could be paraphrased as follows: "You wrote to me, so I am writing back to you. We are at odds over this issue, but perhaps I can clarify the position of the agency I represent."

Category B both quantifies how many of the audiences' propositions—a total of six for the two letters—the student addresses effectively and assesses how well the writer demonstrates an understanding of the propositions.

Category C investigates the extent to which the writer is able to express and reasonably support why the contested action was taken. In reading sample papers, we found that some students fabricated information not contained in the task in order to avoid addressing the audiences' statements or to appease the audiences. We did not deem this an acceptable strategy for explaining why the protested action was taken.

Category D finds its basis in Hairston's (1978) treatment of Rogerian argument. The category assesses the extent to which writers can address the conflict between themselves and the audiences and the extent to which they attempt to secure the good will of the audiences. In some papers, we discovered that writers lectured and berated the audiences, a strategy we believe detracts from a writer's ability to mediate two conflicting positions.

Addressing Specific Audiences Scoring Rubrics

Task 1: Hikers and Bikers

Rate papers on each of the variables described below. Consider the two letters as one extended piece of discourse.
(1 = least effective; 4 = most effective)

A. Defining the Issue and the Rhetorical Situation

1. The writer provides no statements summarizing the situational context of the letters—i.e., that the writer is responding to the audiences' previous letters—and fails to define the issue under consideration.
2. The writer provides only a sketchy suggestion of the situational context and/or fails to define the issue under consideration.
3. The writer summarizes the situational context of the letters effectively and defines the issue under consideration.
4. The writer summarizes the situational context of the letters effectively. In addition, the writer not only defines the issue under consideration, but also demonstrates a willingness to provide a full account of why the protested action was taken.

B. Addressing the Audiences' Positions

Following are the propositions in each letter that should be addressed.

Letter One
a. The action of the Snoqualmie National Forest threatens to reduce the amount of available mileage open for hiking.

b. The members of the hiking association will not be able to escape from "machines and all they symbolize."

c. The convention which the hikers were planning to hold has now been put in jeopardy.

Letter Two

a. The bikers claim they cause no more noise pollution than some campers do.

b. The bikers won't find it worth their effort to come to the forest if only half the trails are open to them.

c. The forest service's decision discriminates against the bikers by allowing only the hikers to enjoy the forest.

1. The writer mentions none of the audiences' points and makes no attempt to demonstrate an understanding of the audiences' positions.

2. The writer mentions one, two, or three of the audiences' points.

3. The writer mentions four, five, or six of the audiences' points.

4. The writer verbally acknowledges all six of the audiences' points and demonstrates an understanding of these beliefs.

C. Stating the Writer's Position

1. The writer offers neither reasons nor support for why the protested action was taken. In addition, the writer sometimes fabricates information in order to avoid the issue at hand.

2. The writer offers very general reasons for why the protested action was taken, but does not elaborate on these reasons with supporting detail. In addition, the writer sometimes fabricates information in order to avoid the issue at hand.

3. The writer offers specific reasons but not support for why the protested action was taken. He or she doesn't fabricate to avoid the issue.

4. The writer offers specific reasons and support for why the protested action was taken. He or she doesn't fabricate to avoid the issue.

D. Addressing the Conflict Between the Writer's Position and the Audiences' Positions

1. The writer makes no attempt to show that the positions have common goals or values (e.g., preserving the beauty and recreational potential of the forest). In addition, the writer sometimes lectures or chastises the audiences.

2. The writer attempts to show that the positions have some common goals and values. In addition, however, the writer sometimes lectures or chastises the audiences.
3. The writer attempts to show that the positions have some common goals and values. The writer does not lecture or chastise.
4. The writer attempts to show that the two positions have some common goals and values. The writer does not lecture or chastise and includes in the letters some discourse designed to secure the good will of the audiences.

Task 2: Water Project

Rate papers on each of the variables described below. Consider the two letters as one extended piece of discourse.
(1 = least effective; 4 = most effective).

A. Defining the Issue and the Rhetorical Situation

1. The writer provides no statements summarizing the situational context of the letters—i.e., that the writer is responding to the audiences' previous letters—and fails to define the issue under consideration.
2. The writer provides only a sketchy suggestion of the situational context and/or fails to define the issue under consideration.
3. The writer summarizes the situational context of the letters effectively and defines the issue under consideration.
4. The writer summarizes the situational context of the letters effectively. In addition, the writer not only defines the issue under consideration, but also demonstrates a willingness to provide an account of why the protested action was taken.

B. Addressing the Audiences' Positions

Following are the propositions in each letter that should be addressed.

Letter One
a. Even partial completion of the canal threatens to upset ecological balance and destroy migratory stopping places for cranes.
b. The decision to complete part of the canal doesn't make financial sense.

c. The decision to complete part of the canal would be counterproductive to farming in the region.

Letter Two
a. The farmer's tax dollars seem to be paying for water for someone else.
b. Full completion of the project would help alleviate world hunger; partial completion won't help that much.
c. Failure to complete the full project will take away possibilities for recreation for the farmer.

1. The writer mentions none of the audiences' points and makes no attempt to demonstrate an understanding of the audiences' positions.
2. The writer mentions one, two, or three of the audiences' points.
3. The writer mentions four, five, or six of the audiences' points.
4. The writer verbally acknowledges all six of the audiences' points and demonstrates an understanding of these beliefs.

C. Stating the Writer's Position

1. The writer offers neither reasons nor support for why the protested action was taken. In addition, the writer sometimes fabricates information in order to avoid the issue at hand.
2. The writer offers general reasons for why the protested action was taken, but does not elaborate on these reasons with supporting detail. In addition, the writer sometimes fabricates information in order to avoid the issue at hand.
3. The writer offers specific reasons but not support for why the protested action was taken. He or she doesn't fabricate.
4. The writer offers specific reasons and support for why the protested action was taken. He or she doesn't fabricate.

D. Addressing the Conflict Between the Writer's Position and the Audiences' Positions.

1. The writer makes no attempt to show that the positions have common goals or values (e.g., using tax dollars for the common good). In addition, the writer sometimes lectures or chastises the audiences.
2. The writer attempts to show that the positions have some common goals and values. In addititon, however, the writer sometimes lectures or chastises the audiences.

3. The writer attempts to show that the positions have some common goals and values. The writer does not lecture or chastise.
4. The writer attempts to show that the positions have some common goals and values. The writer does not lecture or chastise and includes in the letters some discourse designed to secure the good will of the audiences.

Interrater reliabilities for the two Audience tasks suggest that the rubrics enable raters to score papers reliably. Scoring reliabilities for the Audience tasks are presented in Table 8.4.

Table 8.4   Audience Instrument Scoring Reliabilities

Rubric Categories	Task 1 (Hikers & Bikers)	Task 2 (Water Project)
Category "A"	.73	.66
Category "B"	.77	.81
Category "C"	.78	.75
Category "D"	.77	.54
Total	.85	.80

The Audience tasks were also tested for equivalence. Two comparable groups of students wrote in response to one of the two Audience tasks (Task 1, $n = 16$; Task 2, $n = 16$). Two raters' scores on all four rubric categories were summed to yield a total score on the Audience task ranging from 8 to 32. A t-test computed with the total scores from the two groups showed no significant differences: $t(30) = .77$, $p < .446$. A multivariate analysis of variance using summed scores on the four rubric categories as dependent measures also showed no significant differences: $F(4,27) = 2.50$, $p < .066$. In addition, none of the univariate tests on individual rubric categories was significant at or beyond the .05 level.

Our statistical power analysis for the Audience tasks, however, leads us to qualify the results of the t-test. The effect size of the mean differences between the two tasks (1.94) is moderately high (.42 on the 0–1 index). Given our sample size (16 per group) our statistical power is only .19, which prevents our concluding that the two forms of the Audience task are equivalent. Further testing with a larger sample size (approximately 88 per group) will be needed to determine the issue finally. Samples of rated Audience tasks appear in Appendix C.

Chapter 9

Using Performative Assessment for Teaching and Evaluating Writing

At the beginning of Part II, we named two primary reasons for evaluating writing. First, we observed that most formal assessments of writing abilities are concerned with some measure of overall proficiency. Such assessments are commonly used for assigning students to particular courses or for certifying students' progress. Second, we noted that writing assessments are also used for describing students' individual strengths and weaknesses in written composition. We also observed that current widely used methods for evaluating student writing have serious shortcomings in assessing text-production skills.

In this chapter, we describe how Performative Assessment can be used to assess text-production skills for several evaluation purposes, including diagnostic, formative (in-progress), and summative (final) evaluations. We also discuss how Performative Assessment can clarify some of the goals of writing instruction and how it can be used as an instructional tool. Finally, we will look at aspects of Performative Assessment that need further development and note some potential areas for research.

USES IN ASSESSMENT

Diagnostic and formative evaluations. We explained in Chapter 7 that criterion-referenced scoring can provide more information about a writing sample than other kinds of assessment. Such information may not be necessary for all evaluation purposes (e.g., advanced placement), but it is often desirable for those who are responsible for teaching and designing writing courses. Teachers who are familiar with the needs of individual students can better teach those students. Likewise, those who design writing programs have a great advantage if they know what skills students are likely to possess.

One of the goals of Performative Assessment is to provide such information.

Scores on one or more of the Performative Assessment instruments might be tabulated to give a profile of individual students and groups of students. Charts might be devised to show which students achieve certain levels of performance on particular instruments. The following chart gives an example of how scores of individual students on separate rubric categories might be recorded.

Similar analyses might be carried out during the course of instruction to provide formative evaluations of students' progress.

Summative evaluations. In addition to its uses in diagnostic and formative evaluations, Performative Assessment has potential for use in summative evaluations of students' writing abilities. At the conclusion of a unit or course, tables such as the one presented above could be used to show the number and percentage of students who have reached certain levels of performance. Evaluators who use Performative Assessment in summative evaluations can describe changes in students' writing in specific terms.

Another advantage of Performative Assessment is that scores on the various rubric categories for a particular instrument constitute a logically defined multivariate data set that provides considerably more information than a single holistic score. As a result, multivariate analysis of variance procedures can be used to conduct more powerful statistical tests of group and pre/post differences than can be conducted with only a single dependent measure. At the same time, univariate tests on individual rubric categories can identify particular skills in which students have (or have not) made improvement.

Repeated measures analysis-of-variance techniques might be employed, for example, to assess student growth across time. Pilot testing has yielded preliminary evidence that Performative Assessment instruments are suitable for measuring changes in students' composing skills in this manner. Although our pilot testing was not conducted under rigourous experimental conditions (i.e., we did not have experimental and control groups), the Performative Assessment instruments appear to be sensitive to changes in writers' knowledge that occur as a result of instruction. For example, students who wrote in response to the Induction and Classification tasks at the beginning and at the end of a college semester in a split-halves design made statistically significant pre/post gains. (We lacked appropriate data to test for pre/post differences with the Deduction and Constructing-a-Hypothesis tasks). Because we did not test the instruments under strict experimental conditions, we cannot attribute pre/post differences solely to instruction in the skills that are measured by particular instruments. Our results do indicate, however, that Performative Assessment can be a valuable tool for evaluating some aspects of writing abilities.

Administering the writing tasks. To use Performative Assessment instruments for purposes of evaluation, several procedures should be followed. Students should write in controlled conditions. Although they might be told beforehand that they will write the following day, students should not be given the writing task itself until they are seated for the writing session. At least 40 minutes should be allowed for the Classification, Induction, Deduction, and Construction-a-Hypothesis tasks. At least 60 minutes should be allowed for the Audience tasks since the writer must produce two separate texts. In some cases, more time may be preferred; in our view, it would be reasonable to allow up to 90 minutes for any of the Performative Assessment writing tasks.

Scoring writing samples. Procedures for scoring Performative Assessment writing samples are similar to those that have been developed for other types of scoring. Raters should be trained using sample texts that will not be included in the actual rating session. Texts chosen for training should represent the entire range of written responses so that raters receive as much practice as possible in making judgments regarding individual rubric categories. After a few sample texts are scored independently, a trainer should lead raters in a group discussion of their decisions in order to move raters toward consensus. Raters should be encouraged to talk in some detail about any difficulties they may have had in reaching decisions on particular papers. In addition, raters should be urged to make annotations on the scoring rubrics that will enable them to recall the gist of these training discussions. At this time as well, any necessary adjustments can be made in the scoring rubrics. After this initial discussion, a new set of training papers should be scored, followed by another round of discussion of individual raters' scores. Ample time should be allowed for training—at least one hour in most cases. If the rating session will last more than several hours, raters should periodically recalibrate themselves by scoring and discussing a few training papers. One problem that can arise in any descriptive assessment is the possible discrepancy between the presence and absence of a particular text feature and perceptions of overall quality. In most cases, however, descriptive judgments are in accord with impressions of overall quality.

It may be desirable in some cases to adjust the scoring rubrics to reflect the emphasis given certain skills in particular instructional sequences or courses. For example, to assess a course in which considerable attention is given to logical patterns of organization, it may be appropriate to give more weight to the Induction and Deduction rubric categories that assess these skills most directly. Similarly, for a course that emphasizes rhetorical propriety, it may be suitable to give more weight to the Audience rubric categories that assess tone and the writer/reader relationship.

USES IN TEACHING WRITING

Because Performative Assessment scoring rubrics specify characteristics in student texts that signal different levels of performance, they identify what students need to accomplish in a given writing task. Such criteria are not stated abstractly (in terms such as "Be clear" or "Use effective transitions") but in concrete terms that suggest to students precisely what a given writing situation demands. The value of criterion-referenced scoring guides in writing instruction has been pointed out by Johannessen, Kahn, and Walter (1982) and the developers of Primary-Trait scoring (Klaus et al., 1979).

Johannessen et al. describe an approach to developing instructional materials that is similar to the development of our scoring rubrics. First, they design a writing assignment that elicits a specific type of "composing skill." Then they have students write on that assignment and sort the papers into four or five levels or performance. Within these levels they identify specific "thinking strategies" required of that level of performance. For example, they find that the highest level of performance on an extended definition task requires "formulating criteria, generating examples that illustrate the criteria, inventing contrasting examples, and relating all the points through clear reasoning" (p. 10). Johannessen et al. recommend that after teachers identify the requisite thinking strategies for a particular writing task, they design activities to give students practice in those strategies (cf. Hillocks, 1975, 1979).

We took a somewhat different approach to instruction. We asked students to examine actual writing samples and to generate scoring rubrics based on their sense of which texts were most effective. We used the following procedure. During the first class meeting after students had written in response to a Performative Assessment task, the instructor brought to class at least two sample essays, representing a successful and an unsuccessful response, duplicated for distribution to the students. (These samples were not taken from the class itself, but from a collection of previous sample papers.) The instructor asked the students to read the samples and describe their general impressions of how the papers differed. The instructor then moved to more specific questions that focused on particular skills called for in the task.

For example, if the class was investigating essays from a classification task, the instructor asked which paper did a better job at establishing categories. When students responded that one paper did this better, the instructor asked the students to point out specific text features in the better essay. The instructor then asked students to describe how the poorer paper could be revised to improve its deficiencies. Next, the instructor asked which paper did the better job of classifying individual items. Again, when students praised one paper, the instructor questioned them about the paper's observable text features and asked them to recommend revisions on the poorer paper. The instructor concluded the discussion of the writing samples by focusing on Category A of the rubric, the one that asesses how well a writer has established the rhetorical context in a given essay. The instructor reminded students during this discussion that establishing the rhetorical context is important in almost every piece of writing and was not limited to this one task.

For the class session following this discussion of the sample texts, the instructor came to class with copies of the scoring rubric. Two options were then open to the instructor: students could score their own or each others's essays using the scoring rubric, or they could revise their essays using the scoring rubric as a guide.

We also found that the procedures for developing Performative Assessment scoring rubrics can be used to uncover the qualities of effective responses to other writing assignments. In Chapter 7, for example, we alluded to a rubric for a conventional description task that we had developed. We have found this procedure to work well with a variety of writing tasks.

THE POTENTIAL FOR PERFORMATIVE ASSESSMENT

We have tried in Part II to set out a direction for writing assessment that extends the progression from holistic scoring to analytic scoring to Primary-Trait Scoring. We suggested that criterion-referenced scoring holds great promise both for providing more information about student writing to teachers and evaluators and for clarifying the goals of writing instruction. But we also argued that the potential for criterion-referenced scoring could not be realized until teachers and evaluators have a better understanding of what they seek to teach and measure. The idea of Performative Asssssment has been not to invent an entirely new way of assessing writing but to define more precisely the skills measured in previous approaches to writing assessment.

Again, we stress that the shape of the instruments and rubrics presented in Chapter 8 was determined by the curriculum of a particular course. We do not see Performative Assessment as measuring any kind of abstract cognitive development such as the sequence theorized by Piaget. The skills we sought to measure are the global ones taught in typical college freshman courses. In order for Performative Assessment to become a practical and generally useful approach to teaching and evaluating writing, we need to know more about the range of global writing skills and the relationships among those skills.

We also see Performative Assessment as a valuable tool for assessing writing in specific subject domains. One assumption of writing-across-the-curriculum is that requisite writing skills differ among disciplines. As an example we will use the conventions for reporting experimental research in psychology. The first chapter of the *Publication Manual of the American Psychological Association* (1974) describes the four major sections—Introduction, Method, Results, and Discussion—of a standard experimental report in psychology. The contents of each section are outlined. For example, the manual advises:

> In writing the introduction, consider: What is the point of the study? What is the rationale or logical link between the problem and the research design? What are the theoretical implications of the study and its relationship to previous work in the area? A good introduction answers these questions in a paragraph or two and gives the reader a firm sense of what you are doing and why.

The *APA Manual* offers a definition of a "good" experimental report in terms of specific text features. Performative Assessment tasks and scoring rubrics could be developed for the criteria set out in the *APA Manual*. Instructors who teach a course emphasizing writing for the behavioral sciences could present students with an array of background information and data, ask students to write a research report using the information and data, and then assess specific text features of the introduction, methods, results, and discussion sections of the students' compositions. An instructor teaching a course in writing for engineers could do the same with a technical report. Similarly, tasks and rubrics could be developed for such discipline-specific writing assignments as the case study, the explication of a text, and the book review.

The contribution of Performative Assessment lies not so much in the particular tasks and rubrics we have presented here as in the general procedure for developing them. If the theory and practice of writing assessment are to follow changes in how we understand and teach writing, then evaluators of writing must turn to descriptive kinds of assessment. Performative Assessment is one of several possibilities. We offer another direction for descriptive assessment in Part III.

Assessing Changes
in Processes of Composing

In Part II, we set out a method of assessing writers' knowledge as it is manifested in writing performance, a method that we call "Performative Assessment." In Part III, we examine more direct ways of describing changes in composing processes.

We see the assessment of changes in writing processes as one of the most critical issues in writing assessment. We noted in the Introduction that many college writing programs have shifted to what they consider to be process-oriented curricula and instructional methods. This trend, however, brings into question prevailing methods of evaluating writing abilities and outcomes of writing courses and programs. Up to now, evaluations of writing have considered for the most part only written products. But if instruction is to focus on processes of composing as well as products, then evaluation efforts must accommodate this shift in focus. Evaluations must provide useful descriptions of the ways students compose in order to identify and assess changes in these processes that result from instruction.

Chapter 10 sets out some assumptions inherent in efforts to assess changes in composing, describes some methods that other researchers have used to investigate both knowledge of cognitive processes and control over those processes, and outlines the origins and development of the instruments we have used to investigate students' composing strategies. Chapter 11 presents methods we have developed to analyze the discursive data that our instruments elicit. Chapter 12 offers suggestions for using the instruments as teaching tools and explores directions for future research on composing processes.

Chapter 10

Can Composing Processes
Be Measured?

Any effort to assess changes in composing processes—including the present one—is met with a host of difficulties, both theoretical and methodological. Three problems are paramount. First, composing processes differ among individuals and situations. A great deal of testimony collected in studies of experts (e.g., Plimpton, 1963, 1967, 1976) and nonexperts (e.g., Faigley & Witte, 1981) indicates that different people have different ways of composing. Furthermore, common sense tells us that different situations induce different methods of composing. We don't write grocery lists the same way we write scholarly essays.

The second major difficulty is a consequence of the first. Because processes of composing vary, it is hard to define "good" composing practices. When Beach (1976) concluded that extensive revisers wrote better papers than infrequent revisers, some teachers were led to believe that revison was necessarily a "good" composing practice, one that should be encouraged among students. As we pointed out in Chapter 4, however, Beach's conclusion has not been supported by subsequent research. For instance, Bridwell (1980) found that the amount of revision had very little to do with ratings of quality.

A third difficulty is that there is no simple, unobtrusive way to assess changes in composing. A student's composing processes are "buried" in his or her mind, and attempts to infer those processes from observations of behavior or from written products cannot answer every critical question about composing. On the other hand, methods that require writers to report their processes, either during or after writing, alter the processes being investigated. The problem is not simply that experimental observation affects performance, a phenomenon commonly known as the "Hawthorne effect." The situation is much more complicated because reports of processes involve many situational variables, including those identified in rhetorical theory (e.g., the nature of the subject matter and audience) and immediate conditions (e.g., interruptions, time pressure).

Furthermore, assessment of a writer's processes becomes in itself a kind of writing instruction. The writer's attention is directed away from concerns of the final product such as avoiding errors, and it is steered toward a consciousness of the processes of developing a text. For this reason, writers who have been subjects in studies of composing often remark that they better understand how they write as a result of participating in these studies. Asking writers to be conscious of composing necessarily alters how they compose. We see no way of avoiding this confound; indeed, we see the redirecting of writers' attention toward their own processes of composing to be desirable. Nevertheless, it does complicate the problems of assessment.

In an essay that examines the theoretical and methodological foundations of the social sciences, Mishler (1979) sees the problem that we have identified extending to virtually all research in the social sciences. He argues that theoretical work and methodological approaches in the social sciences have followed too closely the model of the natural sciences. Theoretical research has attempted to formulate general laws that will apply in any situation. Experimental research has attempted to demonstrate these laws by removing the constraints of particular contexts. Mishler writes, "To test the generality of our hypotheses, we remove subjects from their natural social settings; their normal roles and social networks are left behind as they enter our experimental laboratories" (p. 2). The paradox Mishler points out is that "we all know that human action and experience are context dependent and can only be understood within their contexts" (p. 2). According to Mishler, the reason that educational research in general has produced such disappointing results is that it is tied to a theoretical model that is unsuited to its subject—human thought and action. He urges educational researchers to adopt context-sensitive methods such as those employed in phenomenology, sociolinguistics, and ethnomethodology. Mishler is not alone in his criticism. Even Cronbach, one of the chief architects of the positivist approach to educational research, admits that

> An observer collecting data in one particular situation is in a position to appraise a practice or proposition in that setting, observing effects in context. In trying to describe and account for what happened, he will give attention to whatever variables were controlled, but he will give equally careful attention to uncontrolled conditions, to personal characteristics, and to events that occurred during treatment and measurement. (1975, pp. 124–125)

In our research on composing processes, we have tried to acknowledge the many variables that affect students' writing and their reports of their composing processes. We have not tried to establish "experimental" conditions because we believe that in the investigation of writing processes, experimental studies do not always produce valid results. We have attempted to accommodate such contextual variables as student's writing histories, difficulty of writing tasks assigned, classroom instruction in composing processes, and teachers' evaluations of written products.

THE DEVELOPMENT OF COMPOSING PROCESSES

In light of the difficulties we have outlined, the problems for those who would attempt to describe how writing instruction affects students' composing processes are formidable indeed. But there is some research on the cognitive strategies involved in composing that has great potential value for assessing changes in composing processes. While nothing approaching a comprehensive theory of the development of composing processes has yet been suggested, researchers have identified certain cognitive strategies that seem to be requisite of mature writing ability. Moreover, the work of some researchers has suggested that writers' increasing awareness of these strategies may signal their having achieved greater control of composing processes.

In Part I we reviewed research suggesting that beginning writers have limited strategies for producing texts. We pointed out in Chapter 2 that by age 12, children have acquired a writing strategy that allows them to complete most school-sponsored writing tasks. Scardamalia and Bereiter (in press) call this strategy "knowledge telling." It involves translating the writing task into a topic, then telling what is known about that topic. Many times, however, the knowledge-telling strategy leads to an inappropriate response. For example, when children are asked to compare X and Y, they often translate X into a topic, tell what they know about it, do the same for Y, but then neglect to analyze the aspects of X and Y that are similar and dissimilar.

There are some academic writing situations—for instance, short-essay quizzes—for which the knowledge-telling strategy may be effective, but a problem arises when students have only the knowledge-telling strategy to rely upon. Flower and Hayes (1980a) observe that many unskilled college writers use the knowledge-telling strategy to generate text. Flower (1979) sees evidence of some college students' dependence on this strategy in their tendency to present information as they remember it rather than in an order that the reader might expect. High school and college writing teachers, moreover, claim that their students sometimes use this strategy when they cannot answer a question on an essay examination. Rather than leave the page blank, students will pick a related topic and tell what they know about it in the hope that their answer will receive at least some credit.

If the goal of writing is to demonstrate knowledge of a subject to a teacher—a goal that Britton et al. (1975) find typical of most school-sponsored writing tasks—then the knowledge-telling strategy is frequently appropriate. But if the goal of writing is to persuade an audience unfamiliar or even hostile to the writer's position or to explore the limits of a subject for a reader unfamiliar with that subject, then the knowledge-telling strategy is likely to be ineffective since it does not adjust for a rhetorical situation—the relationship of writer, subject, and audience. Flower and Hayes contend that a major difference between expert and inexperienced writers is that experts generate goals for a text from the rhetorical situation (1977, 1980a, 1981a). Novice writers, on the other hand, generate most ideas in response to the writing topic.

Another consequence of inexperienced writers' limited strategies for composing is their ineffectiveness in revising what they write. Novice adult writers often revise frequently, but their revisions are typically limited to "correcting" what they have written (Perl, 1979; Sommers, 1980). Their revisions most often involve changes in spelling, punctuation, and substitution of words. Experts, on the other hand, often rework the content of their text (Faigley & Witte, 1981; Sommers, 1980).

These studies of inexperienced writers' strategies lead us to conclude that as writers mature, changes in composing processes may be manifested not only in overt behavior, but also in the heightened awareness that accompanies the broadened repertoire of composing strategies that more experienced writers possess. Consequently, efforts to assess changes in composing should examine awareness of composing processes and the range of strategies for composing as well as the physical production processes themselves.

Some researchers refer to awareness of cognitive processes and control over these processes as *metacognition*. The term has become a label for a new area of research, an area that has many potential implications for research in composing. In an effort to define the field, Flavell (1979) explains that metacognitive knowledge "is that segment of your . . . stored world knowledge that has to do with people as cognitive creatures and with their diverse tasks, goals, actions, and experiences" and that metacognitive experiences "are any conscious cognitive or affective experiences that accompany and pertain to any intellectual enterprise" (p. 906). An example of meta-cognitive knowledge is your belief that you are better at spelling than you are at arithmetic. Flavell points out further that some metacognitive experiences are items of metacognitive knowledge that have entered one's consciousness, and he adds that metacognitive experiences can activate strategies aimed at either of two types of goals—cognitive or metacognitive. He provides an example of the interplay of knowledge, experiences, goals and actions. Suppose, he writes, that

> you sense (metacognitive experience) that you do not yet know a certain chapter in your text well enough to pass tomorrow's exam, so you read it through once more (cognitive strategy, aimed at the straightforward cognitive goal of simply improving your knowledge). . . . [You] wonder (metacognitive experience) if you understand the chapter well enough to pass tomorrow's exam, so you try to find out by asking yourself questions about it and noting how well you are able to answer them (metacognitive strategy, aimed at the metacognitive goal of assessing your knowledge, and thereby, of generating another metacognitive experience). Cognitive strategies are invoked to *make* cognitive progress, metacognitive strategies to *monitor* it. (pp.908–909)

Early metacognitive research examined memory, looking at control processes such as rehearsal of items to be memorized. Several researchers (e.g., Brown, 1978; Flavell, 1979; Flavell & Wellman, 1977; Markman, 1979) found that children who are able to monitor their memory strategies perform better on experimental memory tasks. Quickly the scope of this research expanded to other processes affected by metacognitive awareness such as reading. One area that has been recently investigated is the ability to take notes and to write summaries. Brown and Day (1983) found that children of ages 11 to 14 use a simple strategy for taking notes from a text and writing summaries of that text. They read and evaluate the text sentence by sentence. If the sentence seems important, they copy it verbatim. If it doesn't, they omit it. Expert adults, on the other hand, use very different strategies. They use a metacognitive strategy of finding or inventing a topic sentence to begin an abstract, and they look for main ideas that span paragraphs.

Metacognitive research is quite complex and, as a result, researchers are met with numerous difficulties. First, metacognition is often hard to distinguish from cognition. Second, metacognitive skills are developmental and change with s subject's maturity; consequently, any assessment of them must accommodate their being in flux. Finally, and most important for our research, any assessment of thinking skills, whether they are called cognitive or metacognitive, cannot assume that these skills are in all cases either completely present or completely absent in a subject. Flavell (1977) notes that even the best diagnostic procedures can only suggest that certain cognitive or metacognitive skills are "present sometimes and absent sometimes, depending upon the specifics of the task situation and perhaps other factors" (p. 223). As a result, a researcher who makes only one or two observations of cognitive or metacognitive skills, using simple behavioral measures, may get misleading results. A more sensible strategy, we believe, is to try to investigate these skills over an extended period of time and in a variety of settings.

In spite of these problems, what we find attractive in metacognitive research is the focus on awareness of strategies for particular tasks. Researchers studying metacognition have studied many activities, investigating such learned skills as reading, reasoning scientifically, and playing a musical instrument. From this broad perspective, we might find methodological approaches that can be applied to the study of writing since the goal of much instruction in writing classrooms—whether or not they are "process" oriented—is awareness. For example, teachers tell students to "be sure to include transitions between paragraphs" or to "think about what the reader knows." In other words, teachers often urge students to be aware of rhetorical assumptions and strategies.

Researchers studying writing have described the development of awareness in composing as a three-stage process: first, young writers have no strategies for composing extended texts; next, writers have general strategies that seem to be used in all writing situations; and finally, writers are able to adapt strategies specifically for individual writing tasks. Developing awareness in composing entails, in part, realizing that writing can involve several strategies, not just one. Skilled writers can shift and adapt strategies from one writing situation to another.

APPROACHES TO METACOGNITIVE ASSESSMENT

Since the questions posed by metacognitive research have fostered the development of new methods for investigating knowledge of cognition and control of cognition, we will briefly review six methodologies that have been employed in recent metacognitive research, and we will note, where applicable, their previous use in writing research.

Post-Hoc Interviews

With this method, widely employed by composition reseachers (e.g., Stallard, 1974; Pianko, 1977; Sommers, 1978), the investigator observes a writer composing, then questions the writer about aspects of the process immediately after he or she has finished. Although the *post-hoc* interview conforms to the research maxim of "when in doubt, ask the subject," it nonetheless includes potential problems of validity. Meichenbaum et al., (1979) point out that students' responses may present problems of interpretation:

> If a subject reports no metacognitive activity, the investigator is confronted with the difficult problem of deciding whether this indicates an absence of metacognitive activity, the operation of implicit ("unconscious") metacognitive rules, failure to comprehend questions, inability to verbally or nonverbally describe the subjective experience, or lack of motivation to offer a report. Conversely, if the student does report metacognitive operations, we must decide if he or she is reporting something he or she actually experienced, or whether he or she has "confabulated" his or her report (perhaps by inferring from his or her behavior what he or she "must have been thinking").
> (p. 6)

Thinking-Aloud Protocols

Composition research has also relied heavily for the past decade on the thinking-aloud protocol (e.g., Emig, 1971; Mischel, 1974; Perl, 1979; Flower & Hayes, 1980b). In this method, the writer is asked to verbalize everything that is going through his or her mind during the act of composing. These verbalizations are tape recorded and analyzed by the investigators. The thinking-aloud protocol offers the advantage of immediacy since writers report what they are thinking while they are writing, not afterward.

Advocates of the use of thinking-aloud protocols do admit that many aspects of composing are unavailable for reporting (Hayes & Flower, 1983). Furthermore, thinking-aloud protocols are intrusive, forcing the writer to speak and write at the same time. Black, Galambos, and Reiser (in press) find that giving verbal reports while composing distorts the writing process, causing students to write shorter and poorer quality compostions. A more important limitation for large-scale assessments is the time required to collect and analyze a thinking-aloud protocol.

Stimulated-Recall Sessions

A method of metacognitive assessment that has some of the advantages of the thinking-aloud protocol without the protocol's intrusiveness is the stimulated-recall session (Rose, 1984). Using this method, the investigator videotapes a writer at work then immediately replays the tape in the presence of the writer. Seeing the tape stimulates recall of the writer's thoughts so that the investigator can ask specific or open-ended questions about what he or she notices on the videotape. The discussion occurring between the investigator and the writer while they are viewing the videotape can be audiotaped for later transcription and analysis.

The stimulated-recall session allows the investigator to use the videotape as a prompt to encourage the writer to talk about his or her writing process. If sophisticated video equipment is available, the sesion can capture visual representations of both the emerging text and the writer's head, face, and upper body. The writer's starting, stopping, pausing, and continuing can produce commentary from the writer viewing the videotape.

Stimulated-recall sessions, however, also have problems. Rose (1984), a practitioner of the methodology, describes four of them. First, the methodology introduces an element of the unnatural, and students might be uncomfortable composing for an extended time in front of cameras. Second, stimulated-recall sessions, like *post-hoc* interviews, depend on recall and do not provide an immediate mental rendering of the composing activity. Third, stimulated-recall sessions are not as accurate as thinking-aloud protocols. Rose explains:

> During a two-minute pause, a writer might daydream for 20 seconds, mentally rehearse a sentence for 40 seconds, daydream again for 30 seconds, and think of his audience for 30 seconds. During a stimulated-recall session, the writer could remember that he was daydreaming, rehearsing a sentence, and considering his audience, but he might not recall the order of these activities and certainly could not report precisely on the time spent on each activity. If, however, the writer were speaking aloud . . . a researcher would have access to the order of mental activities and the time spent on each. (p. 24)

Fourth, stimulated-recall sessions rely heavily on the videotape of the printed page. Rose comments that any aspect of the writer's process that is manifest in the written product is more likely to stimuate recall than a mental process the writer might have engaged in but which left no tangible mark. Finally, researchers have found that the time required to conduct and analyze stimulated-recall sessions make them a very expensive data source.

Reporting-In Techniques

A fourth method of metacognitive assessment, one that closely resembles the Process Log questionnaires used in our research, is the technique of Reporting-In. Peitzman (1981) employed this approach in a study of the composing processes of three college freshmen. She used audio-tapes to record their descriptions of their composing processes while writing a first draft, a second draft, and a final draft of their compositions. Before their first draft, students were asked to describe their plans for inventing ideas on the topic. After writing part of their first draft, when they felt they wanted to "take a rest," students were asked to report on what they had done so far. Before working on their second draft, they were asked to discuss reactions they had received from their peers. During their work on the second draft, they were asked to comment on their level of satisfaction with their work up to that point. Before writing their final draft, the students were instructed to read aloud the comments that the instructor had written on their earlier drafts and to describe which ones they agreed with and which ones they disagreed with. Finally, during or after revising their final draft, the students were asked to report to the instructor their evaluation of how successfully they believed they had solved problems during their revisions.

Although we were not aware of Peitzman's work when we began developing our Process Log questionnaire three years ago, our approach is similar to hers. Like Peitzman, we ask students to "report in," by writing their Process Log, at three stages of the composing process: when they receive the assignment, when they have started writing, and after they have finished the assignment. However, our research differs from Peitzman's in focus: while her reporting-in techniques were designed to provide insights about students' revising behaviors, our Process Log questionnaires aim to elicit information about students' processes of invention, revision, collaboration, and evaluation.

Concurrent Interviews

Concurrent interviewing resembles the methodology of thinking-aloud protocols, but permits the investigator to ask more pointed questions than when collecting protocols. The work of Cameron (1977) exemplifies the methodology of concurrent interviewing. Cameron studied cognitively impulsive and reflective children playing a pattern-matching game. He identified three areas in which the impulsive children lacked the problem-solving skills to play the game: their failure to understand or remember directions, their failure to formulate rules to make moves in the game, and their violation of formulated rules while making moves. Cameron was able to learn more about why children had difficulty with the pattern-matching game by asking them specific questions while they were playing it. Researchers studying students' composing processes could employ a similar methodology by asking specific questions while students compose.

Inferring Metacognition from Task Performance

A few cognitive psychologists have attempted to assess metacognitive behavior without the benefit of self-reports, preferring instead to construct hypotheses about metacognition based on task performances. Butterfield, Wambold, and Belmont (1973), for example, trained mentally retarded subjects to rehearse sequentially the items in a short-term memory task. A huge increase in correct memory behavior led these researchers to develop hypotheses about how retarded people remember items. Meichenbaum (1977) trained normal children to teach cognitively impulsive children how to do a Matching Familiar Figures task. After performing observational analyses of this peer teaching, Meichenbaum was able to make inferences about both cognition and metacognition.

These attempts to infer metacognition from task behavior resemble many experiments performed by composition researchers who have observed such phenomena as writers' starting, stopping, pausing, moving their eyes, scratching out, and so forth. In Chapter 2 we discussed Matsuhashi's (1981) study of the pauses of four skilled high school writers. Matsuhashi assumed that "pauses during writing offer clues to cognitive planning processes during written discourse production" (p. 113). From her data she concluded that students must plan longer in writing highly abstract sentences than in writing sentences that add detail to support the abstractions.

THE PROCESS INSTRUMENTS

Research in metacognition offers some helpful directions for researchers investigating changes in composing processes. Process researchers must tap a student's "knowing about knowing"—his or her awareness of strategies for writing. In order to gain access to this information, we have developed three instruments that combine the methodologies of subject interviewing, in-process reporting, and *post-hoc* evaluation of proceses and products.

Our efforts have been guided by the assumption that the development of composing processes is extremely complex and that no one methodology or instrument can elicit all the strategies that a student may employ in writing. Flavell (1977) notes that

> there is no single, overarching process or principle sufficient to describe how all cognitive-developmental advances are made. Different sets of processes may typically be involved in different kinds of cognitive acquisitions. Different individuals may even use quite different processes to acquire the same thing. (p. 243)

Consequently, we have attempted to allow in the instruments for as much open-ended, discursive response as students wish to provide. The Process Log is essentially a composing diary in which students write at three different stages of their work on a composition. The Self-Evaluation Questionnaire is a summative evaluation that students write when they hand in a composition to their instructor. The Pre-Term and Post-Term Interviews are structured dialogues between the interviewer and the student in which general ideas about writing that are unrelated to any specific task are elicited.[1]

These three instruments were tested in various preliminary versions in several sections of freshman- and sophomore-level composition and technical writing classes at the University of Texas and were then revised into the forms presented here. The remainder of this chapter describes the instruments in detail.

The Process Log

The Process Log asks students for specific information on how they go about completing a writing assignment. It is designed so that entries are made at different times during the process of composing. Questions 1 through 3 are to be answered before students have started writing. Students complete the second section of the Process Log, Questions 4 through 6, when they have begun writing. We suggest that students answer these questions after they have completed a

---

[1]We also developed a quantitative instrument to give teachers a "quick read" of students' awareness of their writing processes. This instrument, which we call the "Process Checklist," is presented in Appendix D.

first draft and before they begin a second draft. The last two questions on the Process Log are designed to be answered after students have completed a final draft of the paper. The Process Log appears below:

Process Log

When You Get The Writing Assignment:

1. Do you know much about the topic you are about to write on? What do you know?

   Have you written a paper like this one before?

2. How are you going to get your ideas for this paper? Are you going to start writing and let the ideas develop? Will you think about it for a while? Will you make notes or an outline?

3. Are you thinking of a reader or readers for your paper other than your teacher? Who?

   Why did you choose this reader or these readers?

When You Have Started Writing: (Suggestion: Answer questions 4 through 6 after you write one of your preliminary drafts but before you write your final draft.)

4. Have your ideas about the topic changed since you started writing the paper? How?

5. Have your assumptions about what your readers know or believe to be true about the subject affected how you are writing the paper? How?

6. Have you made changes in your paper during or after writing a draft?

   What are the three most important changes you have made?

   Why did you make these changes?

After You Have Finished Writing:

7. Did you talk about the paper with anyone before or during the writing of the paper? Who? What did you talk about?

8. In the process of writing this paper, did you do anything that was different from what you have done when writing papers in the past? What was it?

The questions in the first section of the Process Log assess the writer's knowledge of subject matter and strategies for invention before the actual writing begins. Question 1 asks how much knowledge a student has about the subject matter of the paper and how much experience he or she has with this type of composition. The importance of such prior knowledge is neglected in many discussions of composing. Only a handful of scholars have investigated the relationship of subject-matter knowledge and text planning. The little research that does exist indicates a writer's level of knowledlge about a subject affects the production of text (e.g., Voss, Vesonder, & Spilich, 1980). We theorized that students' levels of experience with writing different kinds of texts would influence their ability to conceptualize goals and strategies for text production.

Question 2 concerns invention. Students are asked to consider consciously how they will go about getting ideas for their papers. We believed that this question might show whether students are beginning to experiment with new methods of generating ideas that they have learned in their writing classes.

Question 3 asks students who their audience for the paper will be and why they have chosen this audience. We constructed this question to investigate the relationships of audience with content and purpose and to allow responses that might prove helpful for teachers who have begun to emphasize the importance of writing to different types of audiences.

The questions in the middle section of the Process Log are prompted by research findings, especially those of Flower and Hayes, which suggest that expert writers are more capable of altering goals and strategies while writing than are nonexpert writers. Question 4 asks students whether their ideas about their topic have developed in any way since they began writing their papers. In other words, the question probes whether the students have decided that the presentation of their topic must be altered from their original conception of it. Question 5 asks students whether their sense of audience is having any impact on shaping the written product. The intent of this question is to discover whether students' considerations of what the audience knows about the topic are affecting their manipulation of the subject matter. Question 6 asks the student to describe and justify revisions that have been made.

The final section of the Process Log contains two questions. Question 7 asks whether the writer has talked to anyone about the paper while writing it and what effect this collaboration has had on the written text. This question might be omitted in writing classes where talking to other students about an assignment is forbidden.

Many composition classes, however, are beginning to use collaborative learning, encouraging students to talk with other students about their writing (see Beck, Hawkins & Silver, 1978; S. Bloom, 1976; Bruffee, 1973, 1978). Question 8 asks students whether they did anything different when writing this paper than when writing previous papers. This question offers the teacher a means of seeing whether the student is aware of any new writing strategies that may be developing and prompts the type of retrospective analysis of composing processes elicited by the Self-Evaluation Questionnaire.

Examples of completed Process Logs are analyzed in Chapter 11 and are presented in Appendix E.

Self-Evaluation Questionnaire

One very important skills that expert writers have is their ability to evaluate their own texts (Flower & Hayes, 1981a). We designed much of the Self-Evaluation Questionnaire with this skill in mind, assuming that writers become more specific and accurate in their reporting as they become more perceptive in evaluation. Students fill out this instrument after finishing an assigned composition.

Self-Evaluation

1. List the most successful things you did in writing this paper. List the things that a reader will think are successful.

2. List the things you were unable to do in this paper that would have made it more successful.

3. In the process of writing this paper, what aspects were easier than when you have written previous papers?

4. In the process of writing this paper, what aspects were more difficult than when you have written previous papers?

Questions 1 and 2 ask students to evaluate successful and unsuccessful aspects of their papers from both their own perspective and from the perspective they think a reader would have. Both of these questions seek to uncover students' developing awareness of their intentions and to ascertain how accurately and specifically they are able to explain these intentions.

Questions 3 and 4 ask students what aspects of writing the paper were easier and more difficult, respectively, than when they have written previous papers. We believe these two questions prompt students to think about changes that may be occurring in their composing processes, but we also acknowledge that students' responses to these questions will be highly sensitive to differences among writing tasks. We do not expect that students' responses will show steady linear growth; on the contrary, we assume that changes in composing will only be inferable over an extended period of time.

Examples of completed Self-Evaluations are analyzed in Chapter 11 and presented in Appendix F.

Pre-Term and Post-Term Interviews

Since we collected responses to the Process Log and Self-Evaluation Questionnaire in freshman- and sophomore-level writing classes, we thought it was necessary to incorporate a methodology that would prompt students to think consciously about their composing processes throughout the term of instruction. We developed the Pre-Term and Post-Term Interviews to accomplish two purposes: to stimulate conscious thinking about composing processes at the beginning of the term and to provide a chance for students to summarize their perceptions of composing at the end of the term. We asked the same five questions in both the Pre-Term Interview, which took place on the first day of class, and the Post-Term Interview, which took place on the last day of class. These five questions follow.

Pre-Term and Post-Term Interview Questions

1. What is good writing?

2. What is good writing for a college student?

3. What do good writers do when they write?

4. What kind of writing do you think you will have to do in college?

5. What kind of writing to you think you will have to do after college?

These very general questions are designed to prompt students to consider, at the beginning of the term, what their own standards for evaluating writing are, what composing processes consist of, and what applications their writing may have during and after college. We found that many beginning college students believe that good writing is a matter simply of following rules (see Rose, 1980). We also found that many college students have little idea of the types of writing their college courses and their proposed career will require.

Sample transcripts of Pre-Term and Post-Term interviews are analyzed in Chapter 11 and presented in Appendix G.

How the Process Instruments Show Changes in Students' Composing Strategies: Two Approaches

While investigating students' discursive responses on our Process Logs and Self-Evaluation Questionnaires and their responses in our Pre-Term and Post-Term interviews, we continually had to ask ourselves two important questions. First, do changes in students' responses really signal changes in their composing processes? In other words, are they really doing in their composing what their responses in their Process Logs and Self-Evaluations say they are doing? Second, confronted with this bulk of qualitative data, how can we analyze it, categorize it, and use it for purposes of assessment? This chapter presents two approaches we developed to answer these questions.

We argued in Chapter 10 that potentially valid approaches to assessing changes in composing processes are those that accommodate the many variables affecting students' writing. We employed no controls in collecting data other than those specified by the instrument and those imposed by the classroom teacher as part of a regular writing assignment. We collected no data under "experimental" conditions. Both of our methods of analysis require a kind of "close reading," an analytical methodology familiar to students of literature that has recently gained favor among some researchers in discourse. For example, Bartholomae (1980) advocates close reading to diagnose students' errors in composition and to plan programs to remediate errors. Agar and Hobbs (1982) employ a kind of close reading to analyze three levels of coherence in ethnographic interviews.

A CLOSE-READING APPROACH

Our first approach directs the teacher or researcher to use close-reading methods to consider students' responses in the context of the students' writing histories (cf. Szwed, 1981) and the instruction they have received. The teacher or researcher using this approach can generate case studies that describe changes in students' composing processes. In course and program evaluations, these case studies might provide supplemental, in-depth explanations of changes observed on other measures of performance. Case studies, for example, might help to explain *why* one instructional treatment appeared to be more successful than another.

To provide a fuller representation of how a teacher or researcher can investigate students' writing processes using this approach, we present in the following sections examples of several students' responses to the Process Log, the Self-Evaluation Questionnaire, and the Pre-Term and Post-Term Interviews, along with teachers' assessments of these responses. The examples we present here are positive ones: they show students who appear to be developing new, successful composing strategies. Our analyses, however, provided many examples of students whose composing strategies changed very little over a semester of instruction. One such case ("Pat") is described later in the chapter when we explain our second approach to analyzing the data elicited by our instruments.

We gathered data from different levels of writing classes, including technical writing classes. The students whose responses are analyzed here were enrolled in freshman- and sophomore-level writing classes at the University of Texas. The teachers provided us with their analyses throughout the term.

The Process Log: Responses and Analyses

Section One. When the student settles upon a topic, he or she answers three questions on the Process Log:

1. Do you know much about the topic you are about to write on? What do you know?

    Have you written a paper like this one before?

2. How are you going to get your ideas for this paper? Are you going to start writing and let the ideas develop? Will you think about it for a while? Will you make notes or an outline?

3. Are you thinking of a reader or readers for your paper other than your teacher? Who?

    Why did you choose this reader or these readers?

Here are two students' responses to the questions in this section, along with a summary of their teachers' analyses of the responses.

The first student was writing a paper on teenage gangs in his hometown of Boston. To the question, *Do you know much about the topic you are about to write on? What do you know?* he answered, "Yes. I lived among gangs a long time and many of my classmates joined gangs." He had written about U.S.–U.S.S.R. relations for his previous paper, a topic about which he knew very little. His teacher noticed that he chose a familiar topic for this paper—why teenagers in Boston joined gangs.

To the question, *Have you written a paper like this one before?* this student responded, "Informative, yes, but on this subject, no." He chose to write an informative rather than a persuasive paper and in an individual conference explained that he thought he had made the appropriate choice of purposes for expressing what he wanted to say.

To the question, *How are you going to get your ideas for this paper?* this student answered, "Think about it, my experiences, and write down the ideas as they come to me. I might look in a few magazines at articles dealing with gangs." This student's process of idea generation, at least in this class, had expanded from his previous paper where he had indicated that he would "think about it for awhile," then write his paper. His teacher felt he had realized that even a familiar topic calls for care in choosing and developing ideas.

Changes in this student's writing processes were also indicated by his responses to the third set of questions, *Are you thinking of a reader or readers other than your teacher? Who? Why did you choose this reader or these readers?* He had not tried to write before in the class to anyone other than the teacher. For this paper he chose "Boston policemen" because "they are the ones who need to read it. They cause a lot of the trouble because they intimidate all teenagers, even ones who don't join gangs." The teacher had urged students to write to an imagined audience that might be interested in the writer's topic and to develop ideas that were sensitive to the needs of their audience. The teacher saw evidence in the Process Log that the student was beginning to use this strategy.

The second student also chose a familiar topic to write about, a topic that had been a source of trouble for her personally. The student argued that adolescents should have an older friend outside the immediate family as a confidant, a role that neither parents nor peers could fill adequately. To the question, *Do you know much about the topic you are about to write on?* the student answered, "Yes, I have an older friend that I am close to." She answered "yes" to the question, *Have you written a paper like this one before?* adding that she "[had] written several persuasive papers."

The teacher felt that this student's answer to *How are you going to get your ideas for this paper?* indicated a change in her invention strategies. For all previous papers, this student had used only one strategy: she developed an outline, then claimed to have followed it carefully when writing her paper. For this paper, the student wrote that she would "think about them [her ideas], write them down, and look over [her] first copy, then arrange it in a clear order." The teacher concluded that she was trying an alternative strategy for developing ideas.

To the third question asking who the reader or readers would be for the paper and why they were chosen, this student responded that she chose her "family and peers . . . because they are the ones that need to be persuaded in this area." The teacher explained that this student for the first time chose an audience well-suited to her topic.

Section Two. When the students have started writing their papers, they are to answer a second set of questions:

4.   Have your ideas about the topic changed since you started writing the paper? How?

5.   Have your assumptions about what your readers know or believe to be true about the subject affected how you are writing the paper? How?

6.   Have you made changes in your paper during or after writing a draft of it?

What are the three most important changes you have made?

Why did you make these changes?

The responses of two students in a technical writing class illustrate how changes in composing can be reflected through these questions. Both students filled in this section of the Process Log after writing their first draft of a paper. One student wrote about the steam injection process used in oil recovery for an assignment requiring him to define some term or process used in his field of study.

To the questions, *Have your ideas about the topic changed since you started writing the paper? How?* he answered,

> No, but my approach to the topic did. I first started off by trying to define the term "viscosity" and relate its importance to Petroleum Engineering, but I found it difficult to express in simple words. I found that I need to use lots of other technical terms which also need defining. Thus, I finally had to abandon this idea.

Since this student's audience was supposed to be a reader with a college liberal arts education, his teacher saw that he changed his discussion to accommodate his reader. The teacher reported that over the semester this student's attention to his reader's needs—even a fictitious reader's needs—had continuously increased. This composing change was reflected, the teacher said, not only by his papers but also by his Process Logs and Self-Evaluation Questionnaires.

The student's answer to the next questions on the Process Log for this paper also reflected the changing sense of audience. The questions were: *Have your assumptions about what your readers know or believe to be true about the subject affected how you are writing the paper? How?* The student answered:

> Yes. When writing this essay, my main assumption about my reader is that he is most interested in acquiring more basic knowledge about Petroleum Engineering, especially in a field where the "big bucks" are. Otherwise, he might be bored.

The last questions to be answered while the student was writing the paper were: *Have you made changes in your paper during or after writing a draft of it? What are the three most important changes you have made? Why did you make these changes?* This student answered that he had made only one major change:

> I first started with a lengthy introduction by explaining primary and secondary recovery before I touched on steam injection. I finally decided that I might mislead my reader by defining other terms first. So I changed my introduction to start with the definition of steam injection.

He explained that he made these changes "for the sake of clarity—my reader may have been confused by the first introduction." The student's answer again reflected his increasing accommodation of audience needs. In addition, the student included an explanation of primary and secondary oil recovery in his paper at an appropriate point after his introduction. His teacher felt that the Process Log reflected an increasing ability to revise effectively by restructuring the presentation of information.

The Process Log responses for the second student are based on his work on an assignment asking him to write a letter of application and resumé for a fictitious job of his choice. To the question, *Have your ideas about the topic changed since you started writing the paper? How?* this student answered:

> Yes. First I planned to write an application for a cooking position, but then I thought that an application letter addressed to the Manager of a Hotel for such a job is unreal and would be of limited content. So I changed over to applying for the kitchen manager position.

This student's answer and self-revised writing task revealed a change in his invention strategies. In previous papers and accompanying Process Logs, the student had not shown much attention to choosing and developing his topic based on a consideration of purpose or audience.

To the question, *Have your assumptions about what your readers know or believe to be true about the subject affected how you are writing the paper? How?* this student answered:

> Yes. I imagined my old boss who is too quick to judge the character of someone from what he writes, says or the way he behaves. Thus, I tried to be accurate and precise about my background work experience, but at the same time, I tried to keep a modest attitude throughout the letter.

The final questions in this section are *Have you made changes in your paper during or after writing a draft of it? What are the three most important changes you have made? Why did you make them?* This student answered that he had made only one major change:

> I changed the way I presented my qualifications in the second paragraph [concerning job experience]. I tried to present them more accurately, more economically, yet represent as many of my qualifications as possible.

He claimed that he made these changes "to stand a better chance of getting hired." According to his teacher, the student had demonstrated an awareness that "revision" meant more than proofreading for mechanical errors.

Section Three. After the students have finished writing their papers and are ready to turn them in, they answer two questions:

7. Did you talk about the paper with anyone before or during the writing of the paper? Who? What did you talk about?

8. In the process of writing this paper, did you do anything that was different from what you have done when writing papers in the past? What was it?

The following are students' responses on this final section. One student in a freshman composition class answered that she had talked to "[the teacher] first, then friends and writing lab helpers" to get their reaction to her paper on the advantages of attending a private high school in Dallas instead of the area's public high schools. She wrote that all the talks about the paper focused on"getting my ideas clearly stated." Her paper improved noticeably over previous ones, and her teacher attributed her improvement to getting reactions from several outside readers, a practice he encouraged.

Another freshman student wrote on the topic "Should freshmen live in an apartment or dormitory?" She had talked to friends about her topic: "Because I never lived in an apartment, I talked to several friends who live in apartments to see why they preferred them over dorms." The student's teacher said that the student had drawn on outside resources for her paper, and her paper had shown much fresher arguments than usually are found in papers on this topic.

The last question on the Process Log is, *In the process of writing this paper, did you do anything that was different from what you have done when writing papers in the past? What was it?* One freshman student's answer showed that he had tried the strategy of allowing extra time for his writing—"I left the essay for one day, and then I came back and read it again and made some big changes."

A sophomore student answered the question this way:

> I didn't ask my roommate (as previously) to read my essay and tell me what he understood and compare that with what I expected the designated reader to understand. Instead, I tried to catch and clear up all confusing areas of the paper by myself.

The student's teacher said that this student's previous papers were excellent, and this paper, too, proved to be very good. The teacher judged that the student was becoming more confident in his ability to evaluate and revise since he knew he could always draw on outside help for revising his papers.

These answers to the Process Log questions were selected to show how the Process Log can show changes in students' writing processes, or, at the least, how it can show some of the writing strategies that students use.

Self-Evaluation Questionnaire: Responses and Analyses

The Self-Evaluation Questionnaire asks students to assess the text they have just produced and to reflect on what was difficult or easy about writing it. Teachers who used these questionnaires looked for students to become increasingly precise when responding to the questions about what was easy and what was difficult, as well as to display more accuracy and specificity in judging their own writing.

To interpret students' responses, teachers draw on their knowledge of class activities and the students' writing performance in the class. Below are examples of how students' responses on this questionnaire can reflect their development as writers. The examples are taken from freshman and sophomore students' responses in classes at the University of Texas, and discussion of the responses is based on their teachers' interpretations of the reports, provided in interviews during the term.

One freshman student's response to *List the most successful things you did in writing this paper* was "I gave factual examples by using some of my own experiences." To *List the things that a reader will think are successful*, this student responded, "Almost every time I talked about a point, I gave an example." The student's teacher reported that his previous two papers contained numerous statements that needed support and clarification. Although the student did not work his examples smoothly into his discussion in this paper, his teacher believed that the student had sensed the need to develop support for general claims.

Another student also felt that one of the successes in her paper was an effective use of supporting examples. To the question, *List the most successful things you did in writing this paper*, she answered, "Talked to you and went to the writing lab so I got more confidence. Also, supported *all* my statements this time." To *List the things that a reader will think are successful*, the student answered, "Supporting my statements so the audience won't be left with questions. I also tried to write tight, concise paragraphs." This student's teacher noticed her increasing awareness of the need to provide supporting evidence and her willingness to seek help with her paper from "expert writers" in addition to classmates.

The second question on the Self-Evaluation Questionnaire is *List the things you were unable to do in this paper that would have made it more successful*. One sophomore student in a technical writing class who had written a paper "defining" a wind tunnel responded, "I should have described how a test is performed in a wind tunnel. I didn't realize this until 3/4 way through my final draft, and then it was too late to change it." The student's teacher reported that she felt the student's assessment was correct; he had made an important omission in his paper. His Self-Evaluation Questionnaire showed an accurate, if belated, sense of audience needs.

Another sophomore in a technical writing class who wrote a letter of application and resumé for her assignment wrote, "I feel like I could have emphasized my qualifications for this job more in my letter of application, but I was trying to be cautious about sounding too self-centered, maybe." The teacher felt the student's answer showed a developing sense of audience awareness. At this point, however, she clearly had not developed the sense of self that she wanted to project.

To the question, *In the process of writing this paper, what aspects were easier than when you have written previous papers?* one freshman wrote simply, "A lot of things about the paper were easier because I really meant everything I said." Her teacher explained that for the first time that semester, this student wrote about a topic on which she had strong opinions ("People Must Stop Smoking"). She learned what a difference this sense of commitment could make.

To the question, *What aspects were more difficult . . .?* one freshman answered, "Making one of my paragraphs fit, I ended up writing the paper all over, but I felt the new draft was a whole lot better." Later, in an individual conference with his teacher, the student said that having to revise a whole paper so extensively was a new experience for him. His teacher judged that the student had broadened his notion of revision.

Although the Self-Evaluation Questionnaire makes use of the benefits of *post-hoc* interviewing, it also carries with it some of the limitations of the procedure. The Self-Evaluation Questionnaire allows students an opportunity to look back on their recently completed composing process and summarize how their texts match their own and their readers' expectations; moreover, it allows the students to assess any changes in their processes. Nevertheless, students are sometimes reticent when asked to respond to the questionnaire, and there is always the possibility that answers will merely be fabricated. But we have found that if students regularly use the Self-Evaluation Questionnaire, are not "punished" for answering honestly, and are given encouraging responses from their teachers, most are motivated to respond and truthfully report their perceptions of their papers.

Pre-Term and Post-Term Interviews:
Responses and Analyses

As a means of prompting students to begin thinking about their composing processes, and in this case their attitudes about writing, we conducted interviews with volunteers from three freshman writing classes. The students were interviewed on the first day of class by their teacher and during the last week of class by someone other than their teacher. The students were asked the same questions at both interviews. These interviews were recorded on audio tape and later were transcribed. Following is an account of one student's pre-term and post-term interviews.

In the pre-term interview, when the interviewer asked this student the first question, *What is good writing?* she replied, "Writing that is very formal and doesn't . . . have grammar mistakes . . ." Good writing for a college student was defined in much the same way—"no stupid errors like grammar or spelling," "more sophisticated," with "a large vocabulary." And when the interviewer asked this student what writing she would have to do in college, she replied immediately, "Formal writing." Then she paused and added that she wasn't really sure. She said that she was shocked that her class had written a theme the first class meeting with another one planned for the next day: "I mean, that's more papers than I wrote my whole junior year, it seems like!" She explained that she thought that good writers spend a lot of time on their writing, but she didn't seem to see the writing process itself as a potential source of ideas: "[Good writers] collect all their thoughts and write them down before they start writing the paper, and see what they have, and put them into categories and, uh, just kind of work with that, I guess." The last question the interviewer asked was whether the student thought she'd have to write a lot after college, to which she replied, "Not really, not in what I want to go in." She added that she was going "to do something with social work" or possibly "something in advertising . . . drawing advertising instead of . . . magazine writing."

In the post-term interview, this student showed several changes in her conceptions about writing. "Good writing" no longer meant "writing that is very formal . . ." She said instead,

I think good writing is writing so that the writer can express his feelings and ideas clearly, but in a way that the reader can understand exactly what he's trying to say . . . maybe being a little more simplified than some are led to belive. You don't really need to elaborate to make it sound sophisticated and more witty.

When the interviewer asked this student what good writers do when they write, she answered,

Um, I think they need to think about the topic a lot. I just don't think that they can just sit down and, you know, start writing their paper. They need to think about it and jot their ideas down as they come to 'em, and then go back and try to put it in some kind of order . . . so that the reader can flow through the paper.

To the question about what kind of writing she expected she would have to do in college, she responded,

Not what I first thought. It seems like it's a lot more informal than what I had to do in high school because there's a drastic change, but just mainly essay-type writing . . . you can use "I" and not have to worry about it and that sort of thing.

This student now expected that she will have to write frequently after college: "I'm sure that I'll do a lot of different kinds of writing when I get out and when I decide what I want to do."

When the interviewer asked her what kinds of writing she would have to do after college, this student's response showed her new understanding of the importance of rhetorical concerns:

You need to be able to, well, some kind of writing that's going to deal with people instead of uh, like, you wouldn't write a letter saying, "One does this and one does that." You'd write referring to a certain situation and use more informal sytle, but, um, just relating to, maybe groups of people, or just one person, instead of, you know, a teacher.

The student's teacher judged that her notions of writing were broader after a semester of writing instruction.

Uses of the Close-Reading Approach

The close-reading approach requires intensive investigation of each student's writing history, both before and during the term of instruction. Our experience has suggested that using this approach helps to create a good working relationship between student and teacher and allows both parties to see that writing assessment consists of more than a teacher judging written products. Consequently, we believe the approach has great benefits as a teaching tool. We will discuss specific classroom applications in Chapter 12.

We also see the close-reading approach as a valid research methodology, but several cautions need to be made. The close-reading approach is essentially a case-study approach, a methodology that has produced valuable insights about composing but one that is not designed to produce generalizable results. The case study approach is only as good as the researcher practicing it, and some researchers use this approach to great advantage. But consumers of such research need constantly to be on guard against hidden agendas and tacit biases about what constitutes good writing and good composing practices, a problem we described in Chapter 10 and one to which we will return in the next chapter. We urge teachers using the individualized approach of this chapter to be aware of similar preconceptions they may have themselves.

A CONTINUUM APPROACH

A main concern throughout our investigations is what students' self-reports tell us about the nature of composing processes. The approach presented in this section addresses that concern and offers a method for analyzing students' responses to our instruments that may have potential for more extensive investigations of writers' awareness. We want to emphasize, however, the exploratory nature of this approach. No researcher in any field has established without qualification that subjects really do what they say they do. Much additional research is required on this matter, and we suspect that discussion of results will inevitably begin with the qualification, "it depends."

In spite of these reservations, let us examine the persistent issue in other terms: do students' responses on instruments such as the Process Log, the Self-Evaluation Questionnaire, and the Pre/Post Term Interviews enable us to draw conclusions about their composing processes? Several researchers in cognitive psychology have argued that discursive responses such as these do enable investigators to make such discriminations and predictions (e.g., Lieberman, 1979; Meichenbaum & Butler, 1980). Meichenbaum et al. (1979) contend that "it is not only what students do in a situation, but also what they say about what they do that provides a useful basis for understanding and predicting behavior" (p. 22). Our approach, then, is to look for evidence of awareness of composing strategies as well as textual indications that these strategies have been put to work. With this theoretical premise we can investigate students' responses with the assumption that greater specificity implies a stronger sense of control over composing.

Some support for this assumption appears in the literature on writing research discussed in Part I. Flower and Hayes (1980b) characterized the differences between thinking-aloud protocols of expert and novice writers in terms of their specificity. In representing the rhetorical situation, novice writers "never moved beyond the sketchy, conventional representation of audience and assignment with which they started" (p. 26). By contrast, an expert writer produced

> a sophisticated, complex image of a reader . . . which she will have to deal with in the act of writing. No doubt it will be harder to write for such an audience than for a simple stereotype, but the final result is going to be more effective if she has indeed represented her audience accurately. (p. 26)

Flower and Hayes concluded that good writers "were clearly representing their rhetorical problem as a complex speech act," while the poor writers "often seemed tied to their topic" (p. 27).

We observed a similar continuum in responses to our self-report instruments ranging from general responses to the writing assignment to very specific efforts to characterize the rhetorical problem in terms of the relationship between writer and reader. Our problem was to find some way to differentiate particular points along this continuum. We discovered a classification scheme sensitive to such differences in a dissertation on what distinguishes effective piano-practicing skills (Gruson, 1980). On the surface, writing processes and piano-practicing skills appear fundamentally different. Gruson's investigation, however, provides us with more than just a study of various piano-practicing skills; it provides us with a taxonomy that we believe can be used to classifiy reports of metacognitive strategies in the execution of many kinds of processes.

Gruson classifies her subjects' responses to piano practicing gathered in *post-hoc* interviews into four categories: simple undifferentiated responses, which indicate no specific behaviors; concrete behavioral responses, which represent strategies that are employed in all situations of the task being investigated; general-strategy responses, which reflect specific behaviors adapted for a particular task situation; and higher-order responses, which indicate a "chunking" of the task into component subprocesses.

Gruson's categories proved useful and, in large measure, transferable to our study of composing processes. However, we did find it necessary to adapt the taxonomy to represent certain aspects of writers' composing activities. We have classified students' responses to our Process Log using the following categories.

1. *General-Intention Responses.* These responses are very general and give no indication of any knowledge of specific composing strategies. In addition, they often suggest only a student's abstract motivation to succeed in the writing task. General-intention responses often take the form of such statements as "I really worked hard on this essay," or "I really tried to do my best."

2. *General-Strategy Responses.* These responses reflect a general approach that might apply to all writing situations. They are often mechanically employed and do not take into account the specific dimensions of the writing task or previous experience with tasks of the sort that are being commented on. Our research revealed such general-strategy responses as "I went back and corrected my errors," or "I made an outline for this essay."

3. *Task-Specific-Strategy Responses.* Responses in this category represent task-specific behavioral elaborations that have been adapted to meet the demands of the particular writing situation. We found task-specific strategies in such responses as "I wrote the rough draft of this essay very quickly since I wanted to have time to change my mind on this subject," and "I know exactly how someone feels in this situation since I have been in this situation many times before."

We have not adopted Gruson's final category—dividing a task into its component subprocesses—since it was not appropriate for our research. All of our instruments assume that composing entails several subprocesses which, by their nature, are separate but related. Thus our instruments provide ready-made divisions for students to apply.

This approach, like the case-study approach, requires interpretation of students' responses. We do not pretend to overlook the many difficulties accompanying such efforts. Nevertheless, we do feel that the application of Gruson's system can provide guidelines for interpreting case studies. A brief investigation of portions of two students' responses to questions on our Process Log and Self-Evaluation Questionnaire will show how our classification system can indicate changes in composing. Both students were enrolled in a 6-week summer course in beginning freshman composition at the University of Texas.

Student 1: Jan

"Jan's" responses on our instruments suggest that she gained a greater sense of control over her composing process during her summer writing course. Near the beginning of the course, her responses consistently fell into the general-strategy category, indicating that she followed nearly the same steps for every writing task. As the term progressed, she began to employ more task-specific strategies.

Jan's growth in control of her writing processes was reflected on the Process Log questionnaires. Her responses on four successive logs to the question asking writers to describe the three most important changes they made while drafting their papers show a change from general strategies to task-specific strategies. The first assignment for which Jan filled out a Process Log called for expressive writing. She described her three most important changes: "describing more, added more interesting ideas, and changed the form." The changes were made "because the paper was not getting across to the reader correctly." We classified these as general-strategy responses. They do signal discrete behaviors, but these behaviors are not necessarily task specific.

On her second Process Log, for an informative composition where she was to describe the activities of professional modeling, Jan wrote that her three most important changes were, "I categorized my topic, put ideas in areas where they belonged, and described each topic thoroughly." She made these changes "in order to finish the paper in an organized and readable fashion." These responses, according to our system, would represent a task-specific strategy. Jan here sees this task as requiring a categorization of elements not necessarily required in every task.

Jan's third Process Log showed her taking yet another direction. The assignment in this case was a persuasive task in which she was trying to convince both her fellow students and her teachers that high school students should have to take minimal competency examinations in reading, writing, and mathematics. Her three most important changes here were task-specific strategies. She described them as follows: "(1) Directing more to the students, (2) Directing more to the teacher, (3) Making it as persuasive as possible." She wrote that she made these changes "so the paper would improve and so I could get my ideas over to the reader." Jan's responses are task-specific insofar as she realizes that persuasion requires immediate contact with the audience.

On her final Process Log during this short term of freshman composition, Jan went back to general strategies. For this assignment, she was trying to explore what she would do if her source of funds for college were cut off. She wrote that her three most important changes were "changing the topic, putting myself into the paper, and trying to change my mother's (i.e., my reader's) mind, trying to get her to help me." Although Jan's acknowledgement of a specific audience does suggest a task-specific strategy, the remainder of her response contains little that could be labeled as requisite to this specific task. Jan's Process Logs show her progressing from a dependence on general strategies to task-specific strategies then finally returning to general strategies.

An investigation of Jan's responses to our Self-Evaluation Questionnaire, which was filled out in class just before students turned in their assignments, shows a similar progression of strategies. On her first Self-Evaluation, Jan responded to the question asking her to list the most successful things she did in writing her paper as follows: "I made it a very interesting letter, one you would not put down. It included the assignment assigned and more." Our system would label this response as a general-intention strategy because of its generality and simple, motivational content. In response to the same question on her second Self-Evaluation, however, Jan replied in a different manner: "I grouped the ideas together, used the examples and the notes that we explained in class, and put them in my paper." This response can be classified as a task-specific strategy because of its sense of the need to classify and its use of specific examples generated during a class discussion. On her third Self-Evaluation, for an assignment calling for persuasive writing, Jan cited as her successes the fact that she "made it very persuasive. I enthused the reader and tried to make the reader choose my side." This response reflects task-specific strategies. Jan seems to realize that the essence of persuasion is the ability to move an audience. On her final Self-Evaluation, Jan again responded with task-specific strategies. She wrote that her successes were: "I had good ideas, I explained what I would do if I could not go to college, I persuaded my mother to reconsider helping me if her problem was solved." Here Jan's focus is on the task-specific content of the assignment. She has moved beyond "trying to make an interesting assignment" to assessing her knowledge of the subject matter.

When we assessed Jan's responses on the continuum from generality to specificity of intentions and strategies, we discovered that her Process Logs and Self-Evaluation Questionnaires revealed that she was at least better able to report her strategies for composing, and she may have become better able to adapt those strategies for specific tasks.

Student 2: Pat

Unlike Jan's responses to our self-report instruments, "Pat's" responses did not suggest any change in control over his composing processes during the term. His responses on our instruments consistently reflected general strategies and never showed much sensitivity to specific writing tasks. Pat is a good example of a writer who probably had a broader range of strategies than his self-reports indicate, but he showed little awareness of these strategies.

On his first Process Log, which described his work on an expressive assignment, Pat answered the question asking how students intend to get their ideas for the composition as follows: "By trying the new things we learned in class (Invention, answering questions, who, what, etc.). I will prepare an outline." Pat was building up a repertoire of invention strategies, but his response here is clearly a general strategy. His response does not focus on specific invention strategies that he has adapted to the task at hand. On his second Process Log, this one for an informative assignment about his hometown, Pat continued to employ general strategies: "I am going to sit down and write all the areas that I want to talk about. I will think about it for a while and I will make an outline." On the third Process Log, this one for a persuasive task aimed at convincing students and teachers that minimal competency examinations are a good idea, Pat described a task-specific strategy. He wrote that he intended to get his ideas, "First by pretending that I would have to take the test and second how I think my friends at school will feel. I plan to make a rough draft and an outline." The strategy of imagining how a person interested in this issue might respond was a first for Pat. On his final Process Log, however, Pat reverted to a general strategy. He wrote that he intended "to sit down and write a rough draft." Even though the task put the writer in the difficult sitation of trying to explore what he or she would do if funds for college were cut off, Pat wrote about no invention strategies specific to that situation.

Similarly, in his Self-Evaluations, Pat's responses were characterized by general-intention and general-strategy responses. His responses to the question that asks the writer to describe what aspects of the composition were more difficult than on previous papers show this consistency.

On his first Self-Evaluation, Pat wrote that "trying to explain the subject in a more concrete way was really kinda hard," but nowhere in his other responses did he suggest that concrete detail was more important for this assignment than for others he had written in the past. On his second Self-Evaluation, Pat wrote that "at first trying to get enough words in" was difficult, "but after a few rewrites I got plenty." This response suggests that Pat was thinking mostly about meeting the length requirement for the paper, not about any potential effects that his paper might have. On his third Self-Evaluation, for the persuasion assignment, Pat's response does indicate a task-specific strategy. He claimed that what was difficult was "deciding whether I was for or against the tests." Finally, on his last Self-Evaluation, this one for an exploratory assignment, Pat wrote that was difficult was "trying to face the fact that someday the situation might be true."

In short, Pat's responses seem characteristic of the difficulties basic writers have with gaining control of their composing processes. Generally his responses were concerned only with demands of getting the assignment written.

Uses of the Generality-Intention-Specificity Continuum

We see our use of the hierarchy adapted from Gruson as a first step in developing a method of assessing students' changes in composing based on self-report instruments. Much remains to be done to validate this approach. Our methods include no way to discover whether students actually executed the levels of behavior indicated by our instruments. We have little data to suggest that students' written products improved or deteriorated significantly over the term during which we gathered data from them. In fact, our only independently rated writing samples from Jan and Pat for which they had an extended amount of time to compose are two argumentative essays. On the pretest essay, Jan received a holistic score of 3 (of a possible 4) from two raters; on the posttest essay, which was matched in diffculty with the pretest, she received a 4 from both raters. Pat received scores of 2 and 3 on the pretest essay and scores of 2 and 1 on the posttest. Certainly the correlation between writers' awareness of composing and the quality of their products is worth further investigation.

Although our very limited sample does not enable us to generalize, we do see promise in this approach to describing changes in composing processes. To investigate whether other readers of our instruments could identify the three levels of response we posit in this chapter, we trained raters to use the taxonomy described above and asked them to classify the responses on 101 completed Process Logs. Raters were instructed to classify general-intention responses as level 1, general-strategy responses as level 2, and task-specific responses as level 3. Any yes/no responses or blank responses were coded with an X.

Two groups of completed Process Logs were rated. The 56 logs in the first group were completed while students worked on drafts of highly structured assignments in which the instructor had specified the purpose and the audience for the compositions. The 45 logs in the second group were written while students worked on drafts of unstructured assignments on a variety of topics.

Three raters coded responses on the first group of Process Logs. Interrater reliability was computed on the basis of a formula developed by Scott (1955) that is designed specifically for cases in which raters must place discursive responses into designated categories. Reliability statistics calculated using Scott's formula are lower than Pearson correlation coefficients or figures that are derived from other common methods of determining reliability because the Scott formula subtracts the likelihood of chance agreement. Interrater reliability for the first group of Process Logs was computed to be .58. Two raters coded responses on the second group. Interrater reliability for this group was .55. These figures represent a relatively high degree of interrater reliability using the Scott formula, and they suggest that the continuum approach proposed in this chapter may have potential for larger-scaled assessment of changes in students' composing processes. We will return to this prospect in the following chapter.

Using the Process Instruments for Teaching and Evaluating Writing

In Chapter 12 we discuss how our process instruments can be used as tools for assessment and teaching. We describe uses for the instruments in their present form, as well as modifications that teachers and researchers may wish to make. Finally, we offer some practical suggestions and cautions concerning the use of the instruments.

USES IN ASSESSMENT

We believe that the instruments described in Part III, especially the Process Log and the Self-Evaluation Questionnaire, can be employed both as the primary focus of an assessment of changes in composing processes and as the secondary focus of comprehensive evaluations of written products and writing processes.

The instruments could be used in diagnostic, formative, and summative evaluations. To assess students as they enter a writing program, an investigator could ask them to complete the Process Log and Self-Evaluation Questionnaire for a diagnostic essay. The investigator could assess students' levels of awareness of their composing processes by classifying their responses on the continuum described in Chapter 11. Explicit, task-specific responses to the second question on the Process Log, for example, could signal that the student already has a well-developed sense of invention strategies. Similarly, a significant number of general-intention or general-strategy responses to Question 6 concerning revision could suggest that the student has not received much instruction in strategies for revising prose.

For formative (on-going throughout a term of instruction) assessments, an investigator could follow some advice set forward by Flavell (1977). Flavell explains that in any assessment of students' cognitive strategies, the researcher must ask whether students actually have the particular strategy in question, whether students sense the context for using the strategy, and whether the diagnostic task actually demands its use. Flavell proposes that a researcher do a cognitive-training study in which students are taught the strategy in question and its proper use. In later replications of a similar task, the researcher could assess whether students have mastered the strategy based on their responses to the training efforts.

We believe a similar tactic might be applied when using the Process Log and Self-Evaluation Questionnaire in formative evaluations of students' composing processes. Researchers could work individually with students on their Process Logs and Self-Evaluation Questionnaires, helping them to be aware of and to use task-specific strategies in their writing. For example, teachers could show students how to perform certain kinds of revisions and then how to apply this knowledge to a text they have written. Assessment of Process Logs and Self-Evaluation Questionnaires for later compositions would determine whether students were aware of the adaptations in their writing processes demanded by particular writing situations. For teachers, this kind of research essentially would amount to investigating whether their instruction in the skills was successful. Independent researchers, however, could use this stategy to test whether certain writing skills are teachable and transferable.

In summative (final) evaluations, teachers or researchers could investigate the progression of students' responses on Process Logs and Self-Evaluation Questionnaires using the taxonomy proposed in the previous chapter. The summative evaluation could investigate, for example, whether students became more task-specific in their responses about planning, invention, audience analysis, and revisions during the term of instruction. The responses could be investigated in isolation; a more profitable use, however, would be to investigate them in relation to the written texts described in the self-report instruments.

USES IN TEACHING WRITING

Shortly after we developed the process instruments, we discovered that they could be extremely useful teaching aids, both in beginning writing courses and in upper-division courses requiring a substantial amount of writing, such as technical writing courses. A recent national survey of college and university writing teachers (Witte, Meyer, & Miller, 1982) found that the two most frequently cited "successful aspects" of teaching writing were conferencing and teaching revision. We found that the Process Log and the Self-Evaluation Questionnaire are helpful in conferencing and in teaching revision. Any teacher who has used conferencing and has taught revision knows that both are labor-intensive, requiring much extra time and effort from both teacher and student. For those who teach three, four, or five composition classes in a single term, these methods demand far more time than most teachers can afford. We believe that using the process instruments can make these methods more efficient.

We found that the process instruments assist in focusing conferences concerning first drafts. Students' responses can serve as starting points for discussions and also help a teacher decide where a student needs help. For example, a teacher could discover that a student has a limited awareness of invention strategies and could tailor conferences to these concerns. Moreover, the Process Logs can alert teachers who do not require individual conferences to students who need special attention. For example, a teacher may want to call in a student whose paper is weak and whose Process Log and Self-Evaluation Questionnaire suggest that the student has a limited awareness of certain composing strategies. On the other hand, a teacher might want to delay calling in a student who writes a weak paper but says on his Self-Evaluation Questionnaire: "I should have started working on it earlier instead of the night before it was due so I could have had more time to think about it and do a better job."

These instruments not only help teachers design and run conferences on writing strategies, but also help teachers make suggestions for revision on students' papers. Particularly useful in this regard are Questions 2 and 4 on the Self-Evaluation Questionnaire, which ask students what might have been unsuccessful in their compositions and what was more difficult than in previous papers. Responses to these questions can prompt specific, task-oriented suggestions that might make students more aware of their composing processes. This awareness, as we described in Chapter 10, has been identified by researchers in cognitive processes of composition as an indication of more mature, controlled writing. In addition, reflection on writing is one of the chief practices of the "epistemic" approach to teaching writing. For example, Dowst (1980) calls for teachers to give assignments which will stimulate a student's " 'reflective review' of his or her experience in addressing the writing task" (p. 77).

The process instruments can provide a starting point for class discussions of composing. Teachers can point to different composing practices of members of the class as examples of how people go about writing. They can find useful examples for discussion in students' comments about invention strategies, ways of shaping content, and revising. Not every Process Log and Self-Evaluation Questionnaire is helpful to a teacher. Some responses show a clear lack of interest (or lack of time) for completing the instruments. Nevertheless, when a teacher lets students know that the instruments are important to both the students and the teacher, and when the teacher gives students feedback on their responses and uses the instruments exclusively as a source of encouragement rather than punishment, students usually respond conscientiously. Students' careful assessment of their own writing and composing processes not only helps them to become better writers, but also provides the teacher with a wealth of information that can be used to direct in-class and out-of-class instruction.

We have suggested in Part III some methods that researchers and teachers might use to describe changes in students' processes of composing. We have discussed several of the major obstacles—both theoretical and methodological—to assessing changes in composing strategies, and we have detailed our approach to compensating for these problems in our research. In order for the process instruments to become useful tools in the classroom, researchers and teachers must keep in mind two cautions. The first is that there are no "right" and "wrong" answers to any of the questions on the Process Log and Self-Evaluation Questionnaire. What might be considered desirable answers will vary depending on the writing ability of the student and the type of writing instruction going on in the class. What the process instruments probe is awareness rather than correctness.

A second caution is that students may not give lengthy, articulate answers the first time they use the instruments. We have found that there are several means by which teachers can encourage careful, detailed responses. First, teachers should give students a clear idea of the purpose of the instruments. Second, teachers should not grade or penalize students in any way for their answers, but rather use the instruments as a means of reinforcing awareness of composing strategies. Finally, teachers should respond directly, either verbally or through occasional written remarks on students' Process Logs and Self-Evaluation Questionnaires. We have found that through such efforts teachers receive much more care and attention in students' responses. We invite teachers to change these instruments to suit their own needs by adding or deleting questions. Consultants to our research, for example, suggested that the question, "What did you do when you got into trouble while writing this essay?," might be a useful addition to the Process Log.

New Directions for Writing Assessment

In Part I we reviewed research studies that, taken together, suggest the great complexity of writers' knowledge and processes of composing. In Parts II and III, we set forth two possible approaches to writing assessment that take into account important aspects of this complexity. In Part IV we show the need for a theory of writing assessment that seeks to understand and accommodate how people learn the skills and knowledge that enable them to communicate in writing. We argue that current methods of evaluation that reduce writing abilities to a single quantitative score are inadequate responses to the complexity of writing. In our view, a sound theory of writing assessment is a necessary framework for guiding practical evaluation efforts.

Chapter 13

The Need for a Theory
of Writing Assessment

Of necessity, practice has far outrun theory in writing assessment. Practical demands for assessments of general proficiency for the purposes of placement and certification, as well as for course and program evaluation, have forced the use of procedures that are quite limited in scope. By and large, the history of writing assessment has been a series of attempts to quantify writing abilities on a single continuum. The assumption has been that intellectual abilities and writing abilities are like height and weight, reducible to a single number if the right yardstick or scale is used. Early efforts at assessment (reviewed in Wesdorp, Bauer, & Purves, 1982) required students to write essays on fixed topics. Students' essays were then rated according to previously scored essays on the same topics. Later, essays came to be rated according to judges' general impressions of overall quality, a procedure that is called holistic evaluation. Much has been written about how to obtain and measure agreement among raters in holistic evaluations. Often overlooked, however, is the fact that holistic evaluations yield nothing more than relative, impressionistic judgments that cannot give detailed information about writing abilities. Another popular method of writing assessment is the use of standardized tests of writing-related skills. Such tests measure primarily students' recognition of standard usage and their reading comprehension. These abilities are said to correlate highly with writing abilities, but they can give no direct information about writing abilities.

The principal arguments for using procedures such as holistic evaluation and standardized tests of writing-related skills are tied to the purposes for their use. Educators need tests that reduce writing abilities to a single quantifiable score to sort students when making admissions decisions and in tracking students within an institution. Both holistic evaluations and standardized tests of writing-related skills produce single quantifiable scores, and both methods are relatively inexpensive. They have found great favor among those who administer writing programs and among writing researchers whose interests are commensurate with educational management. If, however, the purpose of assessing writing abilities is not admitting or tracking students, but understanding how writing abilities develop and how instruction affects writing abilities, then the inadequacies of methods like holistic evaluation and standardized testing at once become evident. Such procedures are clearly insensitive to the complex nature of writers' knowledge that we discussed in Chapter 5.

Similarly, procedures such as holistic assessment and standardized tests are often insensitive to the ideologies that underlie writing instruction in a particular class, program, or institution. Unless the holistic task or standardized test is extremely well designed, students who have received instruction dominated by the literary view of composing, for example, would no doubt score differently than those who have received instruction under the cognitive view or the social view, even if those students are relatively equal in writing abilities. Similarly, a brief review of writing topics used in comparison-group pedagogical experiments shows that the topics generally favor students taught by the "experimental" method, the method that is under investigation.

The need for alternative methods of assessing writing became evident in the 1920's and 1930's when researchers began to analyze linguistic features in students' texts, design objective tests to measure discrete subskills such as knowledge of mechanics, and develop the first analytic scales for assessing student essays. In Chapter 7 we described the development of analytic and Primary-Trait scoring systems as attempts to obtain descriptive information about student writing, and we placed our efforts in developing Performative Assessment in this tradition. Others, such as Odell (1981), have called for the collection of more than one kind of student writing when making an assessment. Taking an even broader view, Takala, Purves, and Buckmaster (1982) have begun to investigate differences in student writing across cultures and how those differences figure into evaluation of writing abilities.

ELEMENTS OF A THEORY OF WRITING ASSESSMENT

New methods of assessing written products are one response to changing notions of writing abilities. The very complexity of writing abilities and the uses of writing, however, suggest that no single approach will be adequate. Throughout this book, especially in

Chapter 6, we have advocated the use of multiple approaches in the assessment of writing abilities. Such assessments would be descriptive rather than normative, and they would proceed from a theory of writing assessment. Aspects of writing abilities that must be included in such a theory can be abstracted from the three views of composing described in Chapter 1.

Accommodating the Literary View of Composing

A theory of writing assessment must accommodate how people use writing as a means of personal growth and development—in other words, how people use writing to "construct" their conceptions of selfhood and their place in the world. This view of composing, which we have labelled the literary view, holds close affinities to what some composition theorists have called the "epistemic" approach. Dowst (1980) outlines the three central tenets of an epistemic approach to composing:

> (1)We do not know the world immediately; rather, we *compose* our knowledge by composing language; (2) how we act depends on what we know, hence on the language with which we make sense of the world; (3) serious experimenting in composing with words is experimenting in knowing in new ways, perhaps better ways. (p. 70)

In a similar vein, Berthoff (1978) writes, "When it comes to writing, you compose statements that represent your thinking; in the process you are making meaning" (p. 80).

The literary view poses questions such as the following for a theory of assessment:

- How do writers use writing to find out what they know?
- How do writers discover new knowledge and ways of thinking by writing?
- How do writers develop a sense of self by writing?
- How do writers find their own voice?
- How does reflecting on what one has written change how one conceives of writing?
- How is creativity in writing stimulated?

Accommodating the Cognitive View of Composing

The cognitive view of composing insists that learning to write should be understood in terms of general cognitive development and reminds us of the connections between writing and the other language arts—reading, speaking, and listening. We reviewed in Chapter 2 studies that describe how children's writing strategies develop through the grades. Some researchers, notably Kroll (1981) and Wilkinson (discussed in Sternglass, 1982), have characterized writing development in terms of more general stages of cognitive growth.

Questions presented by the cognitive view include the following, among many others:

- When do writers acquire certain strategies for writing?
- How is learning to write different for children and adults?
- What are the relationships between oral and written discourse production?
- What are the relationships between writing and reading?
- When and under what circumstances do writers sense the need to survey another's perspective?
- What is the nature of a writer's cognitive "load"? In other words, how many cognitive variables can a writer manipulate at one time?
- How is learning to write associated with other kinds of cognitive development?

Accommodating the Social View of Composing

A comprehensive theory of writing assessment will also need to describe writers' abilities to demonstrate the types of knowledge and processes of composing demanded by the discourse communities they belong to or wish to belong to. The need to accommodate the social dimension of composing apparently has already come to the attention of many writing program administrators, as evidenced by the current development of writing-across-the-curriculum programs in colleges and universities. One set of writing-across-the-curriculum innovators, Maimon, Belcher, Hearn, Nodine, and O'Connor (1981) base their program for teaching writing in the arts and sciences in part on the assumption that "writing in every discipline is a form of social behavior in that discipline" (p. xii). A diagnostic assessment of the social aspects of writing would have as its goal the description of writers' awareness of the knowledge structures of a particular discourse community, as well as that community's conceptions of the purposes and conventions of writing.

Questions for a theory of assessment for the social view include:

- What constitutes a discourse community?
- What purposes does writing serve in particular discourse communities?

- What subject matters constitute the domains of writing in specific discourse communities?
- What forms do written texts characteristically take in particular communities?
- What conventionalized "ways of speaking" do writers in particular communities employ?
- How does writing convey social status?

IMPLEMENTING WRITING ASSESSMENTS

We have argued implicitly and explicitly throughout this book that efforts to assess writing abilities that do not grow out of clearly articulated theoretical assumptions are inevitably *ad hoc* responses to the need for evaluation. The methodologies we have outlined in this book are capable, we believe, of accommodating the broad theoretical perspective suggested by the three views of composing first outlined in Chapter 1.

Ethnographic methodology provides an extremely valuable means for studying writing instruction because this methodology offers a rich assortment of data-gathering techniques and because, ideally, researchers taking an ethnographic perspective make a great effort to face the community with an open mind in their attempt to understand, describe, and explain what they see. Ethnographic methods could provide evidence of the literary, cognitive, or social dimensions of composing. For example, questions concerning the literary view of composing might be explored by having writers keep composing journals. Journals might reveal whether writers use written language as a tool for thinking. Ethnographic methods might identify certain patterns of classroom interaction that help or hinder the development of cognitive strategies for writing. Similarly, ethnographic observation could investigate writing as a social act.

Schemes for text analysis, such as our Performative Assessment instruments, can assess certain text-production skills that writers employ. In addition, by assessing students' abilities to "frame" their texts for specific audiences, text analysis systems such as Performative Assessment provide insights into the social aspects of composing by probing the extent to which students are able to accommodate the knowledge and perspectives of a community of readers.

Finally, verbal reports from writers, such as our process instruments, can reveal aspects of the literary dimension of composing by assessing whether the writer's sense of self-image is reflected in the reports. They can assess writing from a cognitive view by diagnosing whether the writer has developed any new cognitive strategies or metacognitive knowledge. They can assess elements of the social dimension of writing by describing the writer's efforts to implement the conventions of a specific discourse community.

While we advocate the use of these three methodologies, we realize at the same time that those persons charged with evaluating writing programs and individual students often have limited resources. We are aware that every assessment cannot use every possible approach and methodology. These practical constraints make it even more important that teachers and evaluators consider very carefully what is involved in a particular evaluation. A starting point is to examine who wants what information for what purpose. Are administrators demanding accountability or information for placement decisions? Do teachers want diagnostic information? In short, who is being evaluated, who wants that group evaluated, and why is an evaluation desired? Answers to these questions will help to determine what information will be most useful for a given purpose and will lead to a methodology consistent with the reasons for conducting the evaluation.

If, for example, evaluators wish to observe the changes in students' writing skills resulting from a particular course, then they should consider first what changes can be anticipated given the influences that shape that course. A writer's performance is influenced by many factors besides those contained in a curriculum or an instructional approach. Factors such as the writer's social background, previous experiences with writing instruction, and perceptions of the importance of writing all influence how that student writes. An individual's attitudes and beliefs, in turn, reflect in some way the attitudes and beliefs of the society. All of these influences must be weighed before selecting a methodology for describing changes in writing skills. We will give examples to illustrate these notions.

Consider a hypothetical example of a college basic writing course. The continued funding of this course depends on evidence that the course improves students' writing abilities. In the past, efforts have been made to examine student performance at the beginning and end of the term through standardized tests and holistic evaluations of writing samples. Neither measure showed that students improved significantly as a result of instruction. Teachers of the course, however, felt that in spite of the test scores, the course had had a strong effect on students; moreover, responses of students to the course had been favorable. Perhaps the course was indeed effective, but not in ways that were measurable given the kinds of assessment procedures that were used. It may well be that the most important outcomes of the course were the changes in students' attitudes toward writing and strategies for composing. Students who in the past may have avoided writing now found it to be important enough to enroll in additional courses that require writing. Students who never would have voluntarily rewritten a paper might now be willing to attempt more than one draft. Since it is unrealistic to expect every student's written products to improve dramatically at the end of 30 or 45 hours of instruction, a more appropriate procedure might be to interview students concerning their attitudes toward writing at the beginning of the term and at some delayed interval after the course is completed. In addition, students' self-reports of writing processes collected during the course of the term might show these shifting attitudes.

At the level of a writing program or a national assessment of writing abilities, theoretical issues should be fully explored before evaluations are attempted. Suppose, for example, that students in a writing program receive instruction from teachers who vary in specialization and experience from tenured full professors of literature to teaching assistants in graduate programs in composition. Suppose additionally that composition classroom teaching techniques in this program range from reading and imitating the expository essays of published writers to hearing lectures on style from the professor, to peer tutoring and collaborative writing among students. How could any holistic assessment or standardized test hope to assess the influences of the wide variation in instruction employed in such a program? It may be appropriate and necessary in such a case to use each of the methodologies we have described in a detailed comprehensive evaluation. Such issues are even more important for national assessments of writing abilities since these assessments often provide normative data and models for smaller-scale evaluations.

Finally, and we think most importantly, theory-based notions of assessment are critical to the writing teacher who must decide how best to teach individual students. Many teachers are successful in fostering writing abilities almost by instinct. Nevertheless, the successful curricula and instructional methods of these teachers need to be articulated in terms of a theory so that other teachers can know when and how to employ them. Without understanding how writing develops and how writing is used, teachers deal with a misleading surface record of students' performance rather than an understanding of writing abilities. Our motivation throughout the three years of conducting the research reported in this book was to produce something of practical value for individual classroom teachers. We first conceived of this contribution in terms of tangible, useable products. We now think, however, that if we have indeed contributed anything, it is in pointing new directions for teachers and researchers to understand the contexts, ideologies, and uses of writing. It is our hope that from this understanding can come sounder, more informative, and more useful assessments of writing abilities.

Appendices

Descriptive Statistics for
Performative Assessment Instruments

The statistics reported here are for all instruments administered as pretests and are based on the scoring of two indepenent raters. Except for the second Deduction task (Taxes), all figures are based on regular freshman English classes. Some upper division students are included for the second Deduction task.

Table A.1. Descriptive Statistics for Performative Assessment Instruments

| Task | Mean | s.d. | s.e. | Confidence Interval | |
				Lower 95%	Upper 95%
Classification[a]					
Benefits	13.38	3.96	.86	11.53	18.10
Dangers	15.90	2.38	.75	14.10	21.50
Induction					
TVs	16.00	3.96	.85	13.15	18.84
Teachers	15.33	4.30	1.43	10.22	20.55
Deduction					
Scholastic					
Dishonesty	15.47	3.56	.65	13.62	17.31
Taxes	18.94	5.89	1.43	15.91	21.97
Constructing-a-Hypothesis					
Coal	24.38	4.05	1.01	21.40	27.36
Motorcycles	21.06	3.26	.81	17.96	24.18
Addressing-a-Specific Audience					
Water					
Project	20.50	4.62	1.16	17.54	23.47
Snoqualmie					
Forest	19.31	4.06	1.01	16.37	22.25

[a]The Classification scoring rubric contains only three scoring categories, whereas all other instruments contain four. The scoring ranges, then, from 6–24 for the Classification tasks and 8–32 for all others.

Sample Induction Essays

Example 1

With all of the data and information I was given about each of the four television sets I made my recommendations as follows. First I chose the Cosmoscreen because of the better than average picture and the average repair record. Although the Astrovision set had the best picture I chose it to be second because it had a below average repair record. I chose the Diamond set third because it had an average picture, better than average service and a good quality cabinet. Last, I chose the Star because the cabinet was below average. The prices of these sets range from $100.00 to $285 depending upon the quality and design of the set.

This essay was rated as follows by two independent raters:

	Rater 1	Rater 2
Category A	1	1
Category B	1	2
Category C	2	2
Category D	2	2
Totals	6	7

Example 2

Recommending television sets is a hard job because of the factors to be considered. These factors include picture quality, the condition of the cabinet, repair record, and the price.

The first brand of televisions to be considered is Star. The picture quality of Star televisions is average, and the repair record is better than average. The cabinet is of very poor quality. Even for the price of $100, the Star television is not a good buy, because of poor quality and the poor condition of the cabinet.

Astrovision televisions cost $210. For $210, the set provides the best picture quality and an average cabinet, but the repair record is poor. The poor repair record might mean the price of the set would increase.

The next brand name is Diamond. Diamond television sets cost $180. These sets have average picture quality, the best cabinets, and a better than average repair record. The Diamond television sets are a good deal, but most people buy television sets for picture quality.

Finally, the television set I recommend is Cosmoscreen. The picture quality and cabinet are better than average, and the repair record is average. The price of $285 is steep, but the other qualities make up for the price.

This essay received the following ratings:

	Rater 1	Rater 2
Category A	2	2
Category B	2	3
Category C	3	2
Category D	3	3
Totals	10	10

Example 3

This month in *Consumer Rates* we are going to rate the four best black and white televisions. The four televisions we came up with are: Astrovision, Diamond, Star, and Cosmoscreen. These televisions will be judged on picture quality, cabinet, repair record, and price.

Picture quality is a factor you look for in buying a television set, because your eyes need to focus on a clear screen. The Astrovision is top rate in picture quality. Its cabinet is average. Although the quality of the picture is the best, the repair record is high. The total price of this set is $210, only $30 more dollars than the Diamond set.

The Diamond set costs $110. The cabinet setting seems to agree with most buyers' taste, but the quality of the screen is fair. This particular television set has a small record of repair work, unlike that of the Cosmoscreen.

The Cosmoscreen is the most expensive. This T.V. set sells for $285. The cabinet is better than average; it's one of the more contemporary. It has a good quality picture, even though the repair work is only fair.

The Star television set is the least expensive T.V. set. If you're unable to afford a television but you're in desperate need of one, this would be your best recommendation. The cabinet is simple and plain. The quality of the picture isn't the best, but this is a good television set. The record of repairs is below average, and customers never seem to complain about this set.

For all T.V. watchers I would recommend the Diamond set. It has the best qualities and sells at a reasonable price for everyone's pocket book.

This essay was rated as follows:

	Rater 1	Rater 2
Category A	4	4
Category B	2	3
Category C	3	3
Category D	3	4
Totals	12	14

Sample Audience Essays

Example 1

Letter 1

Dear Mr. Abercrombie:

I have received your letter concerning the opening of several of the Cascade Crest trails to motorcyclists. I do appreciate your concern, but I am sorry to hear that our decision does not meet with your approval. Perhaps I should explain in greater detail our position here at the Snoqualmie National Forest.

For years, motorcyclists have been banned from the many trails leading into the Cascade Crest area. All 52 trails have been limited to hikers, and I must admit that the forest area has not been taken advantage of. That is, many of the trails are not attempted by hikers because of the distance involved, the lack of public facilities in the more remote areas, and the difficult terrain.

In an effort to accommodate the most people, we decided to open some of the trails, ones more suitable for cycling, to motorcyclists. Twenty-five trails are open to anyone, including those who wish to use motorcycles, while 27 trails are strictly for hikers' use.

There are miles and miles of forest trails still available to those who wish to "get away from machines." If you are interested in holding a hikers convention in our area, I am sure you will enjoy the trails just as you have in the past. Please contact me if I can be of any assistance to you in your search for a location.

Sincerely,

Letter 2

Dear Mr. Rutherford:

I received your letter concerning our decision to open part of the Cascade Crest trails to motorcyclists, and I do appreciate your concern. However, I had hoped that the opening of 25 of our 52 trails to bikers would be met with approval, as a compromise was our best alternative.

You will find that the 25 trails now available to cyclists are best suited for such a sport; the trails will provide you with hours of demanding, exciting biking over miles of beautiful terrain. The Snoqualmie National Forest is for *everyone* to enjoy, and I sincerely hope that you and other bikers will find fun and adventure in our forest, with facilities located throughout.

If I can be of some service to you, please let me know. Until then, I look forward to your next visit to Cascade Crest.

Sincerely

These two letters (considered as a single piece of discourse) were rated by two independent raters as follows:

	Rater 1	Rater 2
Category A	4	4
Category B	3	3
Category C	4	4
Category D	4	4
Totals	15	15

Example 2

Letter 1

Dear Mr. Abercrombie,

I'm sorry you are dissatisfied with our decision to open some of the hiking trails in Snoqualmie National Forest to bikers. I wish to discuss a few points that, perhaps, will help you better understand this decision.

First of all Snoqualmie National Forest is just that—a national forest. Since the national forests are all financed by the Federal and state governments, all of our operating money is derived from taxes. Considering that all citizens pay taxes do you think it would be fair to let only one group or the other use the forest? We think not. As a result we have divided the forest into two areas. One is only for hikers and the other for bikers. It only seems fair to let each group enjoy the forest in the way they wish to.

Another reason for our decision has to do with the fact that it would not reduce the number of trails available to hikers. All of the trails are open to hikers, whereas only the 25 specified trails are open to bikers. Hikers have as many trails to hike on as before. Doesn't this seem like a fair compromise? I hope that you will earnestly consider what I have to say. I hope that the hikers and bikers can peacefully share and fully enjoy the beauty, serenity, and recreation our forest has to offer. I also hope that under this light you will seriously reconsider your position on having the Hiker's Convention in the Cascade Crest area. Regardless of this, I would like to thank you for showing a sincere interest in our beautiful forest.

Cordially,
District Ranger
Snoqualmie National Forest

Letter 2

Dear Mr. Rutherford,

In response to your letter concerning the trails in Snoqualmie National Forest, I would like to make two points. First of all, we are in no way "letting only one kind of people enjoy the forest." In contrast we have gone to great effort to see that both the hikers and bikers can enjoy what our forest has to offer, without disturbing each other. This was our purpose in dividing the forest into two sections so that each group had trails that were designated for certain uses.

Second of all, we realize that motorcyclists are no more responsible for pollution, be it noise or trash, than hikers. This is precisely why we have opted to let both groups use the forest. I must point out, though, that it would be hard for hikers to enjoy the forest if motorcycles were always riding by. Furthermore, we are concerned about the possible danger of cyclists and hikers using the same crowded trail. Our plan separates the groups to some degree, enhancing the safety of each group.

In closing, I would like to thank you, Mr. Rutherford, for expressing a sincere interest in our beautiful forest. I hope that in the future all types can enjoy without conflict the beauty and recreation our forest has to offer.

Cordially,
District Ranger,
Snoqualmie National Forest

These letters were rated as follows:

	Rater 1	Rater 2
Category A	3	3
Category B	3	3
Category C	4	4
Category D	2	2
Totals	12	12

Example 3

Letter 1

Dennis Abercrombie, President
Western Washington Hiking Association

Dear Sir:

My decision to open the trails was made to give the bikers and the hikers a chance to use the trails in the Cascade Crest area.

I can see that you are seriously concerned about the commonwealth of the town but I think that the depression of the lumbering industry is irrelevant.

I think that the decision to let the bikers use 25 of the trails was a good decision. It was claimed that the bikes created too much air and noise pollution. I understand that. But I also understand that the bikers aren't the only ones that create air pollution and that they should have the opportunity to use the area just as the hikers should.

I'm sorry if I'm putting your convention in grave jeopardy but I am afraid that my decision will remain the same.

Sincerely,
District Ranger
Snoqualmie National Forest
U.S. Forest Service

Letter 2

A.K. Rutherford
President of Seattle Dirt Bikers

Sir:

The decision to open 25 trails for dirt bikers showed no discrimination. I think the decision was a good one.

I must admit that dirt bikers do make a lot of noise and do create a lot of havoc. When I made my decision I had other people to consider also. Some people use the forest as a type of get away for the weekend and the loud noises created by the bikers would be neither pleasant to them nor the animals.

The trails that are open now are in a place where they won't disturb visitors as much as they would if all 52 were open.

As you stated in your letter, "a limited access to the trails is better than no access at all."

Sincerely,
District Ranger
Snoqualmie National Forest
U.S. Forest Service

These letters received the following ratings:

	Rater 1	Rater 2
Category A	1	2
Category B	2	2
Category C	1	2
Category D	1	1
Totals	5	7

The Process Checklist

We developed the Process Checklist to enable teachers and evaluators to obtain a "quick read" on the level of students' confidence about their composing skills. We did not try to construct a comprehensive instrument. Rather, we limited the focus to those concerns we found to be the most important indications of students' confidence on the Process Log and Self-Evaluation Questionnaire. The questions were intended to measure perceptions of success in invention, sustaining the text, evaluating the text, and revising. The Process Checklist appears below.

Process Checklist

Directions: Please indicate the extent to which you agree or disagree with each of the following statements. Respond to each statement by circling one of the following: (1) strongly agree, (2) agree, (3) undecided, (4) disagree, or (5) strongly disagree.

		SA	A	U	D	SD
1.	When I wrote this paper, I knew how to get the ideas.	1	2	3	4	5
2.	When I wrote this paper, I knew how to adapt it for my reader.	1	2	3	4	5
3.	When I wrote this paper, I wasn't sure how to organize it.	1	2	3	4	5
4.	It was easy to for me to get started writing this paper.	1	2	3	4	5
5.	Once I began writing, I had trouble keeping the paper going.	1	2	3	4	5
6.	I knew if changes needed to be made in this paper.	1	2	3	4	5
7.	I wasn't able to make the changes that I needed to make.	1	2	3	4	5
8.	I don't think this paper is as effective as it should be.	1	2	3	4	5

	SA	A	U	D	SD
9. It was easy for me to judge whether this paper is effective.	1	2	3	4	5
10. I don't know if my reader will understand what I am trying to say in this paper.	1	2	3	4	5

Over the course of the 1982–1983 school year, we gathered 112 responses to the Process Checklist from students enrolled in regular freshman composition classes at the University of Texas at Austin. Students responded to the questionnaire when they handed in out-of-class assignments. We collected a sizeable number of responses not so much to obtain data on mean scores for each of the questions, but more in order to determine which aspects of the writing process were being tapped by the questionnaire. We used factor analysis to identify these underlying process dimensions, or factor structures. Essentially, factor analysis uses the correlations among a set of variables—in this case questions—to determine which of them are closely related to one another. Once groupings of related variables are identified on a statistical basis, however, it remains for the researcher to determine what cognitive domain or skill is reflected by this grouping.

A two-factor solution proved to be most satisfying for the Process Checklist. Table D.1 shows factor loadings for the questions that loaded significantly on one or more of the two factors.

Table D.1. Factor Loadings on Process Questionnaire

	Factor 1	Factor 2
Question 1		.88074
Question 4		.40447
Question 5	.49734	.43655
Question 7	.69611	
Question 8	.73398	
Question 10	.72576	

As Table D.1 shows, two factors emerge from an analysis of the Process Questionnaire data. The first factor is made up of questions 5, 7, 8, and 10. Factor 2 consists of Questions 1, 4, and 5. (Question 5 loads about equally on factors 1 and 2, so we are including it on both factors.) Questions 7, 8, and 10 involve students' judgments about their ability to evaluate their own work-in-progress and to revise accordingly. Factor 1, then, identifies a dimension of the writing process concerned with self-evaluation and revision.

Questions 1 and 4, on the other hand, involve students' judgments of their ability to generate material for their written work. Factor 2, then, appears to tap that aspect of composing commonly termed invention. Question 5 indeed appears to bridge Factors 1 and 2 since it involves both an appraisal of the text produced so far and the invention of material to keep the text going.

These results provide some evidence that it is possible to devise quantitative instruments to assess certain aspects of composing processes. More extensive testing might demonstrate the possibility of tapping other dimensions of writing processes that our brief instrument has not fully explored.

Process Logs and Rating Commentary

Following are two completed Process Logs. After each response are given the ratings on the Generality–Intention–Specificity continuum described in Chapter 4 and an explanation of why these ratings were assigned to the response.

Example 1

When You Get the Writing Assignment:

1. Do you know much about the topic you are about to write on? What do you know?

Yes, I do. I know the basic steps of photography and also some very precise details. I have done some very in-depth research of many aspects of photography.

Our raters categorized this response as level 3, a task-specific response since it addressed directly the subject of the composition.

Have you written a paper like this one before?

No.

"Yes" or "no" responses for all questions on the Process Logs were coded as "X" because they cannot be analyzed.

2. How are you going to get your ideas for this paper? Are you going to start writing and let the ideas develop? Will you think about it for a while? Will you make notes or an outline?

I will do some further research of very detailed aspects of photography. I will start by listing the basic steps I use in producing a photograph and also things I do to produce a well-done shot.

Our raters agreed that this was also a level 3, task-specific response since the writer proposes invention strategies tied specifically to the subject of the composition.

3. Are you thinking of a reader or readers for your paper other than your teacher? Who?

Yes, the person I am applying to for a job.

Raters classified this response as level 3, task-specific, since it reflects the actual purpose of the composition.

Why did you choose this reader or these readers?

The assignment states to imagine I am writing a letter of application to the photography department as a teacher or tutor. Therefore, I will write to the supervisor of the photography department.

Our raters called this a level 3, task-specific response, since it reflects requirements of the writing task.

When You Have Started Writing:

4. Have your ideas about the topic changed since you started writing the paper? How?

No.

This response receives an "X" for a yes/no response.

5. Have your assumptions about what your readers know or believe to be true about the subject affected how you are writing the paper? How?

I assumed the reader had little knowledge about photography and I tried to give all the necessary information.

Our raters assigned this response to level 3, task-specific responses since the writer did consider the level of knowledge of the specific audience.

6. Have you made changes in your paper during or after writing a draft of it?

Yes.

Again, this response was an "X" on all Process Logs.

What are the three most important changes you have made?

Punctuating and adding more detail and explanation.

Our raters called this a level 2, general-strategy response, since nothing indicates that these changes were influenced by the specific writing task at hand.

Why did you make these changes?

It helped the reader understand the paper better.

Our raters classified this as a level 1, general-intention response, since it contains little more than an abstract motivation to succeed on the task.

After You Have Finished Writing:

7. Did you talk about the paper with anyone before or during the writing of the paper? Who? What did you talk about?

Yes, I spoke with a professional photographer about how I should present the material.

The raters agreed that this was a level 3, task-specific response, since the writer had consulted with someone who could assist with the writing task at hand.

8. In the process of writing this paper, did you do anything that was different from what you have done when writing papers in the past? What was it?

I concentrated more heavily on writing better transitions.

Our raters classified this as a level 2, general-strategy response, since it does not suggest that the writer developed any new strategies specifically for the writing task at hand.

Example 2

When You Get the Writing Assignment:

1. Do you know much about the topic you are about to write on? What do you know?

Yes, I know of events connected to incidents like this.

Two raters called this a level 3, task-specific response, since it does suggest that the writer has in mind some task-specific ideas. However, one rater classified it as level 1, general-intention, since it implied no strategy for manipulating the specific subject matter.

Have you written a paper like this one before?

No.

Again, this question always received an "X".

2. How are you going to get your ideas for this paper? Are you going to start writing and let your ideas develop? Will you think about it for a while? Will you make notes or an outline?

I will think about it for a while then write down all my facts.

The raters agreed that this was a level 2, general-strategy response. It suggests no task-specific invention strategies.

3. Are you thinking of a reader or readers for your paper other than your teacher? Who?

Yes, a group of intelligent people.

Our raters called this a level 2, general-strategy response. It suggests nothing about directing the paper to a specifically interested or appropriate audience.

Why did you choose this reader or these readers?

Because I am comfortable writing for this class of people.

Again, this response was classified as level 2, general-strategy, since it reflects no specific choice of an appropriate audience for the composition.

When You Have Started Writing:

4. Have your ideas about the topic changed since you started writing the paper? How?

Yes, I feel better than I did about the subject.

The raters agreed that this was a level 1, general-intention response, since it reflects no composing strategy and shows only the writer's altered feelings.

5. Have your assumptions about what your readers know or believe to be true about the subject affected how you are writing the paper? How?

Yes, I have to gear the paper for what they believe is true in the subject.

Our raters called this a level 2, general-strategy response, since it suggests no composing strategy specifically adapted for this writing task.

6. Have you made changes in your paper during or after writing a draft of it?

Yes.

Again, this response was an "X" on all Process Logs.

What are the three most important changes you have made?

I changed my wording and sentence fragments. I made it all more diversified.

Our raters called this a level 2, general-strategy response. It suggests no changes influenced by the specific task at hand.

Why did you make these changes?

I was wrong in some of the grammar usage. I made it more profound.

Our raters classified this as a level 2, general-strategy response, since it reflects no need to change the composition mandated by the specific task.

After You Have Finished Writing:

7. Did you talk about the paper with anyone before or during the writing of the paper. Who? What did you talk about.

Yes, the teacher. He helped me with grammatical usage.

The raters called this a level 2, general-strategy response, since the consultation was not task-specific.

8. In the process of writing this paper, did you do anything that was different from what you have done when writing papers in the past? What was it?

Yes, it was all "my" self expression.

Two of our raters called this a level 3, task-specific response, since it does suggest that for the first time the writer realizes that self-expression may be appropriate in writing compositions. However, a third rater called it a level 1, general-intention response, since it states no actual new composing strategy.

Self-Evaluation Questionnaires

Following are two completed Self-Evaluation questionnaires.

Example 1

1. List the most successful things you did in writing this paper.

I put down my personal experiences with the topic. It was easy to explain to the reader. I hope that the introductory quote gave the reader a sense of being right there.

List the things that a reader will think are successful.

The introduction, the explanation of the paper itself.

2. List the things you were unable to do in this paper that would have made it more successful.

Go into a little more detail on weights, but that may have confused the reader some.

3. In the process of writing this paper, what aspects were easier than when you have written previous papers?

The fact that it was a personal experience, it just kind of flowed—very easy to write.

4. In the process of writing this paper, what aspects were more difficult than when you have written previous papers?

The concluding paragraph—it was hard not to repeat myself. It took me longer to write it than it should have.

Example 2

1. List the most successful things you did in writing this paper.

(a) Listed the ideas that I was going to discuss in the paper.
(b) Listed specific changes.

List the things that a reader will think are successful.

They will like how I listed the psychological changes. I had a separate paragraph for each idea.

2. List the things you were unable to do in this paper that would have made it more successful.

(a) Gone into a few more details about going off to college.
(b) Gotten more opinions from people about how they felt the first time.

3. In the process of writing this paper, what aspects were easier than when you have written previous papers?

Nothing really because I knew exactly what I felt and some others did about going away the first time. With ideas, I could just begin my paper. No research had to be done.

4. In the process of writing this paper, what aspects were more difficult than when you have written previous papers.

The difficult thing was expressing the psychological changes in people.

Sample Interviews

Student A: Preterm Interview

Interviewer: I'm going to ask you some questions about writing. And there are no correct or incorrect answers, so don't worry about trying to . . . if you can't think of an answer don't worry about that; just give me your honest opinion, and just relax and enjoy yourself.
What is good writing?

Student: Uh, what is good writing? Uh, Ok, uh, something that you can read and enjoy. Understand. Uh, I think, just anything that you feel comfortable with, writing that you . . . I think the only way that I would enjoy writing is when I write something down and I enjoy writing it, and if it makes sense to the teacher hopefully because I've had trouble before with past teachers before asked for quite a bit, very, uh, grammar and content both and it was, very hard for me and like my last teacher which was an advanced teacher, she expected a lot from her students, but my final last grade was a very good paper I was very pleased to get out of there because I wrote a paper that I enjoyed and it, and I just took into consideration what she taught me and I wrote a good paper, which took a lot of time finally, but I finally got to write a paper and . . . So . . .

Interviewer: Well, what is good writing for a college student, do you think?

Student: Well, uh, you, grammar is all a part of it. I mean, that should be already. That should just come naturally, which I've had trouble with, spelling, I'm a terrible speller. . . . Just something that interests everyone. Uh, you know, what you ask for. Uh, something hopefully the teacher will ask for things that will interest the students so that they won't, you know, feel that every assignment that they get is just some busy work type of writing thing just to get a grade on, something that we can go out and enjoy to do, so that when we spend the time on it, we can, you know, uh, really learn a lot and just feel good about the paper we write.

Interviewer: Yeah, good, well, what do good writers do when they write?

Student: Well they think, just, open their mind up and just think, let all ideas flow to them and just, uh, try to write them down as fast as you can so that they make sense, and uh, just basically just being able to enjoy the paper, I think, just enjoying what you write, and writing about it, you know, interesting topics, because I love to write it's just depending on the assignment that I get sometimes it's hard. I love creative writing it just depends on the subjects I get or if I, you know, if I just out in the open think up anything. I get a little stuck but I can usually think up something and enjoy writing about it. You know.

Interviewer: Well, what writing will you have to do in college do you think?

Student: I think, uh. Maybe going out and researching certain topics, uh, maybe, uh, criticism on people, uh, hopefully some creative writing assignments, just picking up anything being very imaginative, and just learning how to basically write a good paper, uh, for when you get out later on so at least we'll know how to write other things for whatever career we have.

Interviewer: Do you expect to have to write a lot after college?

Student: I think so. I want to go in pre-law right now, I plan, whatever I do with that I'm sure there'll be a lot of English involved with that and writing and you know, just any type of writing for, uh, to, even to people, uh, just writing on information that you've learned, uh, something that you need to base a subject, some subject matter that you have to present somwhere just, uh, you know, for speeches. Things like that.

Interviewer: Good. Great. Thank you. That's all.

Student A: Postterm Inverview

Interviewer: What is good writing?

Student: Um, good writing is learning how to speak, tell, OK, talk about the main point you're talking about, support your subject, state everything clearly, and state it clearly to the audience you're talking to, and uh, depending on who you're talking to it's different situations depending on how much they know about the subject you're talking about and um, just stating facts clearly and uh, supporting your point of your paper and just getting everything across clearly so that you're proving what you're writing about.

Interviewer: Um-hum. What do good writers do when they write?

Student: Uh, well. Do you mean in the process, what we got there?

Interviewer: Uh huh, yeah.

Student: Uh, well what I do is, I think a lot about what I'm writing about, then what I think about in my head, I think about how I can organize it, how I can, uh, make it clear to the reader, on, you know, certain supporting things that I can talk about, and examples then I write down a format, an outline, then I try writing about it, writing up my whole paper, making a rough draft and getting a lot of people to proofread it and discuss it with other people, so, and then I just, finally make a final copy and hopefully that'll be right.

Interviewer: OK. What kinds of writing do you expect to have to do in college?

Student: Uh, well right now I know . . . we're learning how to do research papers, persuasive papers, and just basic essays to learn how to write essays for when we get out of college. For many of our careers there are a lot of writing expectations and uh, basically learn how to write essays in other classes not dealing with English, history, government, uh, let me think, science . . .

Interviewer: How about writing after college? What kind of things do you expect to have to write after college?

Student: Well, I'm going into law, hopefully, and I know there's going to be a lot of reports and things that I have to discuss, cases and things, and writing business letters to other business partners, consultants, uh, you have to write a lot of reports and you know, just some, people, clients, and other jobs like science, altogether a lot of writing, that's the best way to . . . letters to just business associates, as I said.

Interviewer: OK.

Student B: Preterm Interview

Interviewer: I'm going to ask you some questions about writing. There are no correct or incorrect answers so don't, so if you feel unsure about some answer, just relax and give me your honest opinion. What is good writing?

Student: Good writing? What I like to write about, or what I think is good?

Interviewer: What you think is good.

Student: Uh, stuff that's interesting. Writing about things that I enjoy and that I would like.

Interviewer: Uh huh. Anything else?

Student: I don't know, well, like where you learn stuff . . . just about all.

Interviewer: What is good writing for a college student?

Student: Probably about the same, I mean, you should look for the same things, enjoyment, and . . .

Interviewer: OK. What do you think good writers do when they write?

Student: What they do? Uh, try and get a message to people, try and get something across, like a feeling, the way they feel about something or just describing, stuff like that.

Interviewer: Well, what writing will you have to do while you're in college?

Student: I, uh, my sister's . . . from what she's told me what she's had to do in like, to write about, look at a picture and write a story about it and, uh, a lot of things about the family she's had to do in her writing. So I don't know what I'm expecting, probably lots of everything.

Interviewer: Do you expect you'll have to write a lot after college?

Student: Um, I don't know. I haven't, I don't really have a major so I'm not sure exactly what field or exactly what I'm going into, and uh, it depends what kind of job and stuff I get into.

Interviewer: That's all.

Student B: Postterm Interview

Interviewer: What is good writing?

Student: Um, writing, when you write about something that, whatever feeling you have, whatever you're trying to accomplish, you get that feeling across to the readers, the people who are reading it, so that they understand, you know, they get the same feeling that you do when you're trying to write it.

Interviewer: OK. Is there more to good writing?

Student: Um . . .

Interviewer: OK. What do good writers do when they write?

Student: They just . . . whatever they're writing about, just to make it clear, make it understandable, make it so people don't have to wonder what they're trying to say and what they're doing, they just . . . I don't know.

Interviewer: Uh huh. What kinds of writing do you expect to have to do in college?

Student: Um, uh, research, essays, compositions, just about everything.

Interviewer: What does that, what does that entail? Is there, is there more than that?

Student: I don't know. I'm all, I expect just that stuff, just, you know, research papers and just regular papers.

Interviewer: How about after college? What kind of writing will you have to do after college, when you get out of school?

Student: Um, it, well I guess in every profession there's a
                    lot of writing that has to be done more than I re-
                    alized, but um, I'm thinking about maybe going
                    into law, so I know I'll be having, there's a lot of
                    writing, writing cases and stuff.
Interviewer: Is that it? OK!

References

Agar, M., & Hobbs, J. R. (1982). Interpreting discourse: Coherence and analysis of ethnographic interviews. *Discourse Processes, 5,* 1–32.

Akinnaso, F. N. (1982). On the differences between spoken and written language. *Language and Speech, 25, Part 2,* 97–125.

Alatis, J. E., & Tucker, J. R. (Eds.). (1979). *Language in public life.* Washington, DC: Georgetown University Press.

Alred, G. J., Reep, D. C., & Limaye, M. R. (1981). *Business and technical writing: An annotated bibliography of books, 1880–1980.* Metuchen, NJ: Scarecrow.

American Psychological Association. (1974). *Standards for educational and psychological tests.* Washington, DC: American Psychological Association.

Anderson, J. R., & Bower, G. H. (1973). *Human associative memory.* Washington, DC: Winston.

Anderson, P. V. (1980, December). Research into the amount, importance, and kinds of writing performed on the job by graduates of seven university departments that send students to technical writing courses. Paper presented at the Annual Meeting of the Modern Language Association, Houston, TX.

Anderson, R. C. (1978). Schema-directed processes in language comprehension. *In* A. Lesgold, J. Pelligreno, S. Fokkema, & R. Glaser (Ed.), *Cognitive psychology and instruction.* New York: Plenum.

Applebee, A. N. (1978). *The child's concept of story: Ages two to seventeen.* Chicago, IL: University of Chicago Press.

Applebee, A. N. (1981). *Writing in the secondary school.* Urbana, IL: NCTE.

Arbur, R. (1977). The student–teacher conference. *College Composition and Communication, 28,* 338–342.

Aristotle. (1954). *The rhetoric and poetics of Aristotle.* (W. R. Roberts, trans.). New York: Random House.

Arnold, L. V. (1963). *Effects of frequency of writing and intensity of teacher evaluation upon performance in written composition of tenth-grade students.* Doctoral dissertation, Florida State University.

Arthur, B. (1980). Gauging the boundaries of second language competence: A study of learner judgments. *Language learning, 30,* 177–194.

Atlas, M. (1979). *Addressing an audience: A study of expert–novice differences in writing.* (Document Design Project Technical Report No. 3.) Pittsburgh, PA: Carnegie-Mellon University.

Atwell, M. (1981). *The evolution of text: The interrelationship of reading and writing in the composing process.* Doctoral dissertation, Indiana University.

Austin, J. (1962). *How to do things with words.* Oxford, England: Clarendon.

Bach, E., & Harms, R. T. (Eds.). (1968). *Universals in linguistic theory.* New York: Holt, Rinehart, & Winston.

Bach, K., & Harnish, R. M. (1979). *Linguistic communication and speech acts*. Cambridge, MA: M.I.T. Press.

Bain, A. (1866). *English composition and rhetoric*. New York: D. Appleton.

Barritt, L., & Kroll, B. (1978). Some implications of cognitive-developmental psychology for research in composing. In C. R. Cooper & L. Odell (Ed.), *Research on composing: Points of departure*. Urbana, IL: NCTE.

Barthes, R. (1968). *Elements of semiology*. (A. Lavers & C. Smith, trans.). New York: Hill and Wang.

Bartholomae, D. (1980). The study of error. *College Composition and Communication, 31*, 253–269.

Bartlett, E. J. (1982). Learning to revise: Some component processes. In M. Nystrand (Ed.), *What writers know: The language, process, and structure of written discourse*. New York: Academic Press.

Bartlett, F. (1932). *Remembering*. Cambridge, England: Cambridge University Press.

Basso, K. H. (1974). The ethnography of writing. In R. Bauman & J. Sherzer (Ed.), *Explorations in the ethnography of speaking*. London: Cambridge University Press.

Bata, E. J. (1972). *A study of the relative effectiveness of marking techniques on junior college freshmen English composition*. Doctoral dissertation, University of Maryland.

Bazerman, C. (1981). What written knowledge does: Three examples of academic discourse. *Philosophy of the Social Sciences, 11*, 361–387.

Bazerman, C. (1983). Scientific writing as a social act: A review of the literature of the sociology of science. In P. V. Anderson, R. J. Brockman, & C. Miller (Ed.), *New essays in technical writing and communication: Research, theory, and practice*. Farmingdale, NY: Baywood.

Bazerman, C. (in press). The writing of scientific nonfiction: Contexts, choices, and constraints. *Pre/Text*.

Beach, R. (1976). Self-evaluation strategies of extensive revisers and non-revisers. *College Composition and Communication, 27*, 160–164.

Beach, R. (1979). The effects of between-draft teacher evaluation versus student self-evaluation on high school students' revising of rough drafts. *Research in the Teaching of English, 13*, 111–119.

Bean, J. C. (1983). Computerized word-processing as an aid to revision. *College Composition and Communication, 34*, 146–148.

Beaugrande, R. de (1980). *Text, discourse, and process: Toward a multidisciplinary science of texts*. Norwood, NJ: Ablex.

Beaugrande, R. de (1982). Psychology and composition: Past, present, future. In M. Nystrand (Ed.), *What writers know: The language, process, and structure of written discourse*. New York: Academic Press.

Beaugrande, R. de (1984). *Text production: Toward a science of composition*. Norwood, NJ: Ablex.

Beaugrande, R. de, & Dressler, W. (1981). *Introduction to text linguistics*. London: Longman.

Beck, P., Hawkins, T., & Silver, M. (1978). Training and using peer tutors. *College English, 40*, 432–449.

Becker, A. (1965). A tagmemic approach to paragraph analysis. *College Composition and Communication, 16*, 237–248.

Bell, D. (1981). The social framework of the information society. In T. Forester (Ed.), *The microelectronics revolution*. Cambridge, MA: MIT Press.

Bell, D. (1982). *The social sciences since the Second World War*. New Brunswick, NJ: Transaction Books.

Bereiter, C. & Scardamalia, M. (1982). From conversation to composition: The role of instruction in a developmental process. *In* R. Glaser (Ed.), *Advances in instructional psychology (Volume 2)*. Hillsdale, NJ: Lawrence Erlbaum.

Bereiter, C., & Scardamalia, M. (1983). Levels of inquiry in writing research. *In* P. Mosenthal, L. Tamor, & S. Walmsley (Ed.), *Research on writing: Principles and methods*. New York: Longman.

Berkenkotter, C. (1981). Understanding a writer's awareness of audience. *College Composition and Communication, 32*, 388–399.

Berkenkotter, C., & Murray, D. (1983). Decisions and revisions: The planning strategies of a publishing writer, and response of a laboratory rat—or, being protocoled. *College Composition and Communication, 34*, 156–172.

Berlin, J. A. (1982). Contemporary composition: The major pedagogical theories. *College English, 44*, 765–777.

Bernstein, B. (1971). *Class, codes, and control*. London: Routledge and Kegan Paul.

Berthoff, A. E. (1978). *Forming/thinking/writing: The composing imagination*. Rochelle Park, NJ: Hayden.

Bissex, G. L. (1980). *GYNS AT WORK: A child learns to write and read*. New York: Harvard University Press.

Bitzer, L. (1968). The rhetorical situation. *Philosophy and Rhetoric, 1*, 1–14.

Bizzell, P. (1982). Cognition, convention, and certainty: What we need to know about writing. *Pre/Text, 3*, 213–243.

Black, J., Galambos, J., & Reiser, B. (in press). Coordinating discovery and verification research. *In* D. Kieras & M. Just (Ed.), *New methods in the study of immediate processes in comprehension*. Hillsdale, NJ: Lawrence Erlbaum.

Black, J., Wilkes-Gibbs, E., & Gibbs, R. (1982). What writers need to know that they don't know they need to know. *In* M. Nystrand (Ed.), *What writers know: The language, process, and structure of written discourse*. New York: Academic Press.

Bloom, B. S., (Ed.). (1956). *Taxonomy of educational objectives, Handbook I: Cognitive domain*. New York: David McKay.

Bloom, S. (1976). *Peer and cross-age tutoring in the schools*. Washington, DC: National Institute of Education.

Bloomfield, L. (1933). *Language*. New York: Henry Holt.

Booth, W. C. (1963). The rhetorical stance. *College Composition and Communication, 14*, 139–145.

Bracewell, R. J., Frederiksen, C. H., & Frederiksen, J. D. (1982). Cognitive processes in composing and comprehending discourse. *Educational Psychologist, 17*, 146–164.

Braddock, R. (1974). The frequency and placement of topic sentences in expository prose. *Research in the Teaching of English, 8*, 287–304.

Braddock, R., Lloyd-Jones, R., & Schoer, L. (1963). *Research in written composition*. Champaign, IL: NCTE.

Bradley, V. N. (1982). Improving students' writing with microcomputers. *Language Arts, 59*, 732–743.

Bransford, J., & Franks, J. (1971). The abstraction of linguistic ideas. *Cognitive Psychology, 2*, 331–350.

Breland, H. M., & Gaynor, J. L. (1979). A comparison of direct and indirect assessments of writing skill. *Journal of Educational Measurement, 16*, 119–128.

Brewer, W. F. (1980). Literary theory, rhetoric, and stylistics: Implications for psychology. *In* R. J. Spiro, B. C. Bruce & W. F. Brewer (Ed.), *Theoretical issues in reading comprehension: Perspectives from cognitive psychology, linguistics, artifical intelligence, and education*. Hillsdale, NJ: Lawrence Erlbaum.

Bridwell, L. S. (1980). Revising strategies in twelfth grade students' transactional writing. *Research in the Teaching of English, 14*, 197–222.

Bridwell, L., Nancarrow, P., & Ross, D. (1984). The writing process and the writing machine: Current research on word processors relevant to the teaching of composition. *In* R. Beach & L. Bridwell (Ed.), *New directions in composition research.* New York: Guilford.

Britton, J. (1978). The composing processes and the functions of writing. *In* C. R. Cooper & L. Odell (Ed.), *Research on composing: Points of departure.* Urbana, IL: NCTE.

Britton, J. (1982). Spectator role and the beginnings of writing. *In* M. Nystrand (Ed.), *What writers know: The language, process, and structure of written discourse.* New York: Academic Press.

Britton, J., Burgess, T., Martin, N., McLeod, A., & Rosen, H. (1975). *The development of writing abilities (11–18).* London: Macmillan.

Brown, A. L. (1978). Knowing when, where, and how to remember. *In* R. Glaser (Ed.), *Advances in instructional psychology (Volume 1).* Hillsdale, NJ: Lawrence Erlbaum.

Brown, A. L., & Day, J. D. (1983). Macrorules for summarizing texts: The development of expertise. *Journal of Verbal Learning and Verbal Behavior, 22,* 1–14.

Bruffee, K. (1973). Collaborative learning: Some practical models. *College English, 34,* 634–643.

Bruffee, K. (1978). The Brooklyn plan: Attaining intellectual growth through peer-group tutoring. *Liberal Education, 64,* 447–468.

Bruner, J. S. & Garton, A. (Eds.). (1978). *Human growth and development.* Oxford, England: Clarendon.

Burke, K. (1969). *A grammar of motives.* Berkeley, CA: University of California Press.

Burns, H. (1979). *Stimulating rhetorical invention in English composition through computer-assisted instruction.* Doctoral dissertation, University of Texas at Austin.

Burtis, P., Bereiter, C., Scardamalia, M., & Tetroe, J. (1983). The development of planning in writing. *In* C. Wells & B. Kroll (Ed.), *Exploration of children's development in writing.* Chichester, England: John Wiley & Sons.

Butterfield, E., Wambold, C., & Belmont, J. (1973). On the theory and practice of improving short-term memory. *American Journal of Mental Deficiency, 77,* 654–669.

Butterworth, B. (1980). *Language production: Speech and talk.* New York: Academic Press.

Buxton, E. W. (1958). *An experiment to test the effects of writing frequency and guided practice upon students' skill in written expression.* Doctoral dissertation, Stanford University, CA.

Caccamise, D. J. (1981). *Cognitive processes in writing: Idea generation and integration.* Doctoral dissertation, University of Colorado.

Calkins, L. M. (1979). Andrea learns to make writing hard. *Language Arts, 56,* 569–576.

Calkins, L. M. (1980). Children learn the writer's craft. *Language Arts, 57,* 207–213.

Cameron, R. (1977). *Conceptual tempo and children's problem solving behavior: A developmental task analysis.* Doctoral dissertation, University of Waterloo, Ontario, Canada.

Campbell, D. T., & Stanley, J. C. (1963). *Experimental and quasi-experimental designs for research.* Chicago, IL: Rand McNally.

Campbell, L. J., & Holland, V. M. (1982). Understanding the language of public documents because readability formulas don't. *In* R. J. Di Pietro (Ed.), *Linguistics and the professions.* Norwood, NJ: Albex.

Chafe, W. L. (Ed.). (1980). *The pear stories: Cognitive, cultural, and linguistic aspects of narrative production.* Norwood, NJ: Ablex.

Chafe, W. L. (1982). Integration and involvement in speaking, writing, and oral literature. *In* D. Tannen (Ed.), *Spoken and written language: Exploring orality and literacy*. Norwood, NJ: Ablex.

Chomsky, N. (1957). *Syntactic structures*. The Hague, Netherlands: Mouton.

Chomsky, N. (1965). *Aspects of the theory of syntax*. Cambridge, MA: M.I.T. Press.

Christensen, F. (1965). A generative rhetroic of the paragraph. *College Composition and Communication, 16,* 144–156.

Christensen, F. (1967). *Notes toward a new rhetoric*. New York: Harper & Row.

Christensen, F. (1968a). *The Christensen rhetoric program*. New York: Harper & Row.

Christensen, F. (1968b). The problem of defining a mature style. *English Journal, 57,* 572–579.

Christensen, F., & Christensen, B. (1976). *A new rhetoric*. New York: Harper & Row.

Cicero. (1942). *De Inventione*. (H. M. Hubbell, trans.). Cambridge, MA: Loeb Classical Library.

Cicero. (1959). *De Oratore*. (E. W. Sutton & H. Rackham, trans.). Cambridge, MA: Harvard University Press.

Cicourel, A. V. (1980). Three models of discourse analysis: The role of social structure. *Discourse Processes, 3,* 101–132.

Clark, C., Florio, S., Elmore, J., Martin, J., & Maxwell, R. (1983). Understanding writing instruction: Issues of theory and method. *In* P. Mosenthal, L. Tamor, & S. Walmsley (Ed.), *Research on writing: Principles and methods*. New York: Longman.

Clark, H. (1977). Inferences in comprehension. *In* D. LaBerge & S. J. Samuels (Ed.), *Basic processes in reading: Perception and comprehension*. Hillsdale, NJ: Lawrence Erlbaum.

Clark, H. & Clark, E. (1977). *Psychology and language: An introduction to psycholinguistics*. New York: Harcourt Brace Jovanovich.

Clark, H., & Haviland, S. E. (1977). Comprehension and the given-new contract. *In* R. O. Freedle (Ed.), *Discourse production and comprehension*. Norwood, NJ: Ablex.

Clifford, J. (1981). Composing in stages: The effects of a collaborative pedagogy. *Research in the Teaching of English, 15,* 37–53.

Cohen, J. (1977). *Statistical power analysis for the behavioral sciences*. (Rev. Ed.) New York: Academic Press.

Coles, W. E. (1978). *The plural I: The teaching of writing*. New York: Holt, Rinehart & Winston.

Collier, R. M. (1983). The word processor and revision strategies. *College Composition and Communication, 34,* 149–155.

Conklin, H. C. (1968). Ethnography. *In* D. Sills (Ed.), *International encyclopedia of the social sciences*. London: Macmillan.

Cooper, C. R. (1977). Holistic evaluation of writing. *In* C. R. Cooper & L. Odell (Ed.), *Evaluating writing: Describing, measuring, judging*. Urbana, IL: NCTE.

Cooper, C. R., & Odell, L. (Eds.). (1978). *Research on composing: Points of departure*. Urbana, IL: NCTE.

Corbett, E. P. J. (1971). *Classical rhetoric for the modern student*. (2nd ed.). New York: Oxford University Press.

Cronbach, L. J. (1975). Beyond the two disciplines of scientific psychology. *American Psychologist, 30,* 116–127.

Crothers, E. J. (1978). Inference and coherence. *Discourse Processes, 1,* 51–71.

Crothers, E. J. (1979). *Paragraph structure inference*. Norwood, NJ: Ablex.

Crowley, S. (1977). Components of the composing process. *College Composition and Communication, 28,* 166–169.

Daiker, D., Kerek, A., & Morenberg, M. (1978). Sentence combining and syntactic maturity in freshman English. *College Composition and Communication, 29,* 36–41.

Daiute, C. (1981). Psycholinguistic foundations of the writing process. *Research in the Teaching of English, 15,* 5–22.

Daiute, C. (1983). The computer as stylus and audience. *College Composition and Communication, 34,* 134–145.

Daly, J., & Hexamer, A. (1983). Statistical power in research in English education. *Research in the Teaching of English, 17,* 157–164.

Daly, J., & Miller, M. (1975). The empirical development of an instrument to measure writing apprehension. *Research in the Teaching of English, 9,* 242–249.

Daly, J., & Shamo, W. (1976). Writing apprehension and occupational choice. *Journal of Occupational Psychology, 49,* 55–56.

Daly, J., & Shamo, W. (1978). Academic decisions as a function of writing apprehension. *Research in the Teaching of English, 12,* 119–126.

Daneš, F. (1964). A three-level approach to syntax. *Travaux linguistiques de Prague, 1,* 225–240.

Daneš, F. (1970). One instance of Prague School methodology: Functional analysis of utterance of text. In P. L. Garvin (Ed.), *Method and Theory in Linguistics.* The Hague, Netherlands: Mouton.

Daneš, F. (Ed.). (1974). *Papers on functional sentence perspective.* Prague, Czechoslovakia: Academia.

D'Angelo, F. J. (1974). A generative rhetoric of the essay. *College Composition and Communication, 25,* 388–396.

D'Angelo, F. J. (1975). *A conceptual theory of rhetoric.* Cambridge, MA: Winthrop.

D'Angelo, F. (1979). Paradigms as structural counterparts of *topoi.* In D. McQuade (Ed.), *Linguistics, stylistics, and the teaching of composition.* Akron, OH: L&S Books.

D'Angelo, F. J. (1981). *Topoi,* paradigms and psychological schemata. In M. Marcuse & S. Kleimann (Ed.), *Proceedings of the inaugural conference of the University of Maryland Junior Writing Program.* College Park, MD: University of Maryland.

Davenport, G. (1982). From indifference to attention. *New York Times Book Review,* (April 4), 30.

Davis, R. M. (1977). How important is technical writing? A survey of the opinions of successful engineers. *The Technical Writing Teacher, 4,* 83–88.

Delia, J. G., & Clark, R. A. (1977). Cognitive complexity, social perception, and the development of listener-adapted communication in six-, eight-, ten-, and twelve-year-old boys. *Communication Monographs, 44,* 326–345.

Della-Piana, G. (1978). Research strategies for the study of revision processes in writing poetry. In C. R. Cooper & L. Odell (Ed.), *Research on composing: Points of departure.* Urbana, IL: NCTE.

DeVito, J. A. (1966). The encoding of speech and writing. *The Speech Teacher, 15,* 55–60.

DeVito, J. A. (1967). Levels of abstraction in spoken and written language. *Journal of Communication, 17,* 354–361.

Dewey, J. ([1899]. 1915). *The school and society.* (2nd ed.). Chicago, IL: University of Chicago Press.

Diederich, P. (1964). Problems and possibilities of research in the teaching of written composition. In D. H., Russell, E. J. Farrell, & M. J. Early (Ed.), *Research design and the teaching of English: Proceedings of the San Francisco conference.* Champaign, IL: National Council of Teachers of English.

Diederich, P. (1966). How to measure growth in writing ability. In R. Gorrell (Ed.), *Rhetoric and school programs.* Champaign, IL: National Council of Teachers of English.

Diederich, P., French, J., & Carlton, S. (1961). *Factors in judgments of writing ability.* (Research Bulletin RB–61–15). Princeton, NJ: Educational Testing Service.

Dijk, T. A. van. (1977). *Text and context.* London: Longman.

Dijk, T. A. van. (1980). *Macrostructures: An interdisciplinary study of global structures in discourse, interaction, and cognition.* Hillsdale, NJ: Lawrence Erlbaum.

Dillon, G. L. (1981). *Constructing texts: Elements of a theory of composition and style.* Bloomington, IN: Indiana University Press.

Di Pietro, R. J. (Ed.). (1981). *Linguistics and the professions.* Norwood, NJ: Ablex.

Dowst, K. (1980). The epistemic approach. *In* T. R. Donovan & B. W. McClelland (Ed.), *Eight approaches to teaching composition.* Urbana, IL: NCTE.

Dressler, W. U. (Ed.). (1978). *Current trends in textlinguistics.* Berlin, Germany: de Gruyter.

Drieman, G. H. J. (1962). Differences between written and spoken language. *Acta Psychologica, 20,* 36–57; 78–100.

Eco, U. (1976). *A theory of semiotics.* Bloomington, IN: Indiana University Press.

Eco, U. (1979). *The role of the reader.* Bloomington, IN: Indiana University Press.

Ehninger, D. W. (1968). On systems of rhetoric. *Philosophy and Rhetoric, 1,* 131–144.

Eisenstein, E. L. (1979). *The printing press as an agent of change.* New York: Cambridge University Press.

Elbow, P. (1973). *Writing without teachers.* New York: Oxford University Press.

Emig, J. (1964). The uses of the unconscious in composing. *College Composition and Communication, 15,* 6–11.

Emig, J. A. (1971). *The composing processes of twelfth graders.* (NCTE Research Report, No. 13.) Urbana, IL: NCTE.

Ericsson, K. A., & Simon, H. A. (1980). Verbal reports as data. *Psychological Review, 87,* 215–251.

Faigley, L. (1979a). Another look at sentences. *Freshman English News, 7,* 18–21.

Faigley, L. (1979b). The influence of generative rhetoric on the syntactic fluency and writing effectiveness of college freshmen. *Research in the Teaching of English, 13,* 197–206.

Faigley, L. (1979c). Problems of analyzing maturity in college and adult writing. *In* D. Daiker, A. Kerek, & M. Morenberg (Ed.), *Sentence combining and the teaching of writing.* Akron, OH: L&S Books.

Faigley, L. (1980). Names in search of a concept: Maturity, fluency, complexity, and growth in written syntax. *College Composition and Communication, 31,* 291–300.

Faigley, L., Daly, J., & Witte, S. (1981). The role of writing apprehension in writing performance and competence. *Journal of Educational Research, 75,* 16–21.

Faigley, L., & Miller, T. (1982). What we learn from writing on the job. *College English, 44,* 557–569.

Faigley, L., & Witte, S. (1981). Analyzing revision. *College Composition and Communication, 32,* 400–414.

Faigley, L., & Witte, S. (1984). Measuring the effect of revisions on text structure. *In* R. Beach & L. Bridwell (Ed.), *New direction in composition research.* New York: Guilford.

Faigley, L., & Witte, S. (1983). Topical focus in technical writing. *In* P. V. Anderson, R. J. Brockmann, & C. Miller (Ed.), *New essays in technical writing and communication: Research, theory, and practice.* Farmingdale, NY: Baywood.

Faure, E., Herra, F., Kaddoura, A., Lopes, H., Petrovsky, A., Rahnema, M., & Ward, F. (1972). *Learning to be: The world of education today and tomorrow.* Paris: UNESCO.

Fay, D. (1981). Substitutions and splices: A study of sentence blends. *Linguistics, 19,* 717–749.

Felker, D., & Rose, A. (1981). *The evaluation of a public document: The case of FCC's marine radio rules for recreational boaters*. (Document Design Project Technical Report No. 11.) Washington, DC: American Institutes for Research.

Fergus, P. M. (1973). *Spelling improvement: A program for self-instruction*. New York: McGraw-Hill.

Flavell, J. H. (1968). *The development of role-taking and communication skills in children*. New York: John Wiley & Sons.

Flavell, J. H. (1974). The development of inferences about others. *In* T. Mischel (Ed.), *Understanding other persons*. Oxford, England: Blackwell.

Flavell, J. H. (1977). *Cognitive development*. Englewood Cliffs, NJ: Prentice-Hall.

Flavell, J. H. (1979). Metacognition and cognitive monitoring. *American Psychologist, 34*, 906–911.

Flavell, J. H., & Wellman, H. (1977). Metamemory. *In* R. V. Kail & J. W. Hagen (Ed.), *Perspectives on the development of memory and cognition*. Hillsdale, NJ: Lawrence Erlbaum.

Florio, S., & Clark, C. (1982). The functions of writing in an elementary classroom. *Research in the Teaching of English, 16*, 115–130.

Flower, L. (1979). Writer-based prose: A cognitive basis for problems in writing. *College English, 41*, 19–37.

Flower, L. (1981). *Problem-solving strategies for writing*. New York: Harcourt Brace Jovanovich.

Flower, L., & Hayes, J. R. (1977). Problem-solving strategies and the writing process. *College English, 39*, 449–461.

Flower, L., & Hayes, J. R. (1980a). The cognition of discovery: Defining a rhetorical problem. *College Composition and Communication, 31*, 21–32.

Flower, L., & Hayes, J. R. (1980b). The dynamics of composing: Making plans and juggling constraints. *In* L. Gregg & E. Steinberg (Ed.), *Cognitive processes in writing: An interdisciplinary approach*. Hillsdale, NJ: Lawrence Erlbaum.

Flower, L., & Hayes, J. R. (1981a). A cognitive process theory of writing. *College Composition and Communication, 32*, 365–387.

Flower, L., & Hayes, J. R. (1981b). Plans that guide the composing process. *In* C. H. Frederiksen & J. F. Dominic (Ed.), *Writing: The nature, development, and teaching of written communication; Volume 2, Writing: Process, development and communication*. Hillsdale, NJ: Lawrence Erlbaum.

Flower, L., & Hayes, J. R. (1981c). The pregnant pause: An inquiry into the nature of planning. *Research in the Teaching of English, 15*, 229–244.

Fodor, J. A., Bever, T. G., & Garrett, M. F. (1974). *The psychology of language*. New York: McGraw-Hill.

Ford, M. (1982). Sentence planning units: Implications for the speaker's representation of meaningful relations underlying sentences. *In* J. Bresnan (Ed.), *The mental representation of grammatical relations*. Cambridge, MA: M.I.T. Press.

Foucault, M. (1972). *The archaeology of knowledge*. (A. M. S. Smith, trans.). New York: Pantheon Books.

Frederiksen, C. H. (1977). Semantic processing units in understanding text. *In* R. Freedle (Ed.), *Discourse production and comprehension*. Norwood, NJ: Ablex.

Freedman, S. W. (1979). An analysis of readers' responses to essays. *Journal of Educational Psychology, 71*, 328–338.

Freedman, S. W. (1981). Evaluation in the writing conference: An interactive process. *In* M. C. Hairston & C. L. Selfe (Ed.), *Selected papers from the 1981 Texas Writing Research Conference*. Austin, TX: University of Texas at Austin.

Frith, U. (Ed.). (1980). *Cognitive processes in spelling*. London: Academic.

Fromkin, V. A. (Ed.). (1973). *Speech errors as linguistic evidence.* The Hague, Netherlands: Mouton.

Fulkerson, R. (1978). Some cautions about pedagogical research. *College English, 40,* 463–466.

Garrett, M. F. (1975). The analysis of sentence production. *In* G. Bower (Ed.), *Advances in learning theory and motivation, 9.* New York: Academic Press.

Gee, T. (1972). Students' responses to teacher comments. *Research in the Teaching of English, 6,* 212–221.

Geertz, C. (Ed.). (1973). *The interpretation of cultures.* New York: Basic Books.

Gere, A. R. (1982). Insights from the blind: Composing without revising. *In* R. A. Sudol (Ed.), *Revising: New essays for teachers of writing.* Urbana, IL: ERIC/NCTE.

Gibson, J. W., Gruner, C. R., Kibler, R. J., & Kelly, F. J. (1966). A quantitative examination of differences and similarities in written and spoken messages. *Speech Monographs, 33,* 444–451.

Giuliano, V. (1982). The mechanization of office work. *Scientific American, 247,* 149–164.

Godshalk, F. I., Swineford, F., & Coffman, W. E. (1966). *The measurement of writing ability.* New York: College Entrance Examination Board.

Goldman-Eisler, F. (1961). Hesitation and information in speech. *In* C. Cherry (Ed.), *Information theory.* Washington, DC: Butterworths.

Goody, J. (Ed.). (1968). *Literacy in traditional societies.* Cambridge, England: Cambridge University Press.

Goody, J. (1977). *The domestication of the savage mind.* Cambridge, England: Cambridge University Press.

Goody, J. (1980). Thought and writing. *In* E. Gellner (Ed.), *Soviet and western anthropology.* London: Gerald Duckworth.

Goody, J. & Watt, I. P. (1963). The consequences of literacy. *Comparative Studies in Society and History, 5,* 304–345.

Gottschall, E. M. (1981). *Graphic communication '80s.* Englewood Cliffs, NJ: Prentice-Hall.

Gould, J. D. (1980). Experiments on composing letters: Some facts, some myths, some observations. *In* L. W. Gregg & E. R. Steinberg (Ed.)., *Cognitive processes in writing.* Hillsdale, NJ: Lawrence Erlbaum.

Grady, M. (1971). A conceptual rhetoric of the composition. *College Composition and Communication, 22,* 348–354.

Grant, W. V., & Eiden, L. J. (1982). *Digest of educational statistics, 1982.* Washington, DC: National Center for Educational Statistics.

Graves, D. H. (1975). An examination of the writing processes of seven-year-old children. *Research in the Teaching of English, 9,* 227–241.

Graves, D. H. (1979). What children show us about revision. *Language Arts, 56,* 312–319.

Graves, R. L. (1978). Levels of skill in the composing process. *College Composition and Communication, 29,* 227–232.

Green, G. M. (1982). Linguistics and the pragmatics of language use. *Poetics, 11,* 45–76.

Greenberg, J. (Ed.). (1963). *Universals of language.* Cambridge, MA: M.I.T. Press.

Grice, P. (1975). Logic and conversation. *In* P. Cole & J. Morgan (Ed.), *Syntax and semantics III: Speech acts.* New York: Academic Press.

Grimes, J. (1975). *The thread of discourse.* The Hague, Netherlands: Mouton.

Groot, A. de. (1965). *Thought and choice in chess.* The Hague, Netherlands: Mouton

Gruner, C. R., Kibler, R. J., & Gibson, J. W. (1967). A quantitative analysis of selected characteristics of oral and written vocabularies. *Journal of Communication, 17*, 152–158.

Gruson, L. (1980). *Piano practicing skills: What distinguishes competence?* Doctoral dissertation, University of Waterloo, Ontario, Canada.

Gumperz, J. J. (1971). *Language in social groups.* Stanford, CA: Stanford University Press.

Gumperz, J. J. (1982a). *Discourse strategies.* Cambridge, England: Cambridge University Press.

Gumperz, J. J. (Ed.). (1982b). *Language and social identity.* Cambridge, England: Cambridge University Press.

Gumperz, J. J., & Cook-Gumperz, J. (1982). Introduction: Language and the communication of social identity. In J. J. Gumperz (Ed.), *Language and social identity.* Cambridge, England: Cambridge University Press.

Gundlach, R. A. (1981). On the nature and development of children's writing. In C. H. Frederiksen & J. F. Dominic (Ed.), *Writing: The nature, development, and teaching of written communication; Volume 2, Writing: Process, development and communication.* Hillsdale, NJ: Lawrence Erlbaum.

Hairston, M. C. (1978). *A contemporary rhetoric.* (2nd ed.). Boston, MA: Houghton Mifflin.

Hairston, M. C. (1982). The winds of change: Thomas Kuhn and the revolution in the teaching of writing. *College Composition and Communication, 33*, 76–88.

Halliday, M. A. K. (1978). *Language as a social semiotic.* Baltimore, MD: University Park Press.

Halliday, M. A. K., & Hasan, R. (1976). *Cohesion in English.* London: Longman.

Halpern, J., & Liggett, S. (1984). *Computers and composing: How the new technologies are changing writing.* Carbondale, IL: Southern Illinois University Press.

Hammarberg, B. (1974). The insufficiency of error analysis. *IRAL, 12*, 185–192.

Hansen, B. (1978). Rewriting is a waste of time. *College English, 39*, 956–960.

Hanson, N. R. (1958). *Patterns of discovery.* Cambridge, England: Cambridge University Press.

Harris, W. (1977). Teacher response to student writing: A study of the response patterns of high school English teachers to determine the basis for teacher judgment of student writing. *Research in the Teaching of English, 11*, 175–185.

Harris, Z. S. (1952). Discourse analysis: A sample text. *Language, 28*, 1–30; 474–494.

Hartley, J. (Ed.) (1980). *The psychology of written communication.* New York: Nichols.

Havelock, E. A. (1963). *Preface to Plato.* Cambridge, MA: Belknap Press of Harvard University Press.

Havelock, E. A. (1976). *Origins of Western literacy.* Toronto, Ontario, Canada: Ontario Institute of Education.

Havelock, E. A. (1981). *The literate revolution in Greece and its cultural consequences.* Princeton, NJ: Princeton University Press.

Hayes, J. R., & Flower, L. (1980). Identifying the organization of writing processes. In L. Gregg & E. Steinberg (Ed.), *Cognitive processes in writing: An interdisciplinary approach.* Hillsdale, NJ: Lawrence Erlbaum.

Hayes, J. R., & Flower, L. (1983). Uncovering cognitive processes in writing: An introduction to protocol analysis. In P. Mosenthal, L. Tamor, & S. Walmsley (Ed.), *Research on writing: Principles and methods.* New York: Longman.

Hayes-Roth, B., & Hayes-Roth, F. (1979). A cognitive model of planning. *Cognitive Science, 3*, 275–310.

Heath, S. B. (1980). The functions and uses of literacy. *Journal of Communication, 30*, 123–133.

Heath, S. B. (1981). Toward an ethnohistory of writing in American education. *In* M. F. Whiteman (Ed.), *Writing: The nature, development, and teaching of written communication; Volume 1, Variation in writing: Functional and linguistic-cultural differences.* Hillsdale, NJ: Lawrence Erlbaum.

Heath, S. B. (1982). Protean shapes in literary events: Ever-shifting oral and literate traditions. *In* D. Tannen (Ed.), *Spoken and written language: Exploring orality and literacy.* Norwood, NJ: Ablex.

Hildick, W. (1965). *Word for Word: The rewriting of fiction.* London: Faber & Faber.

Hillocks, G. (1975). *Observing and writing.* Urbana, IL: ERIC/RLS.

Hillocks, G. (1979). The effects of observational activities on student writing. *Research in the Teaching of English, 13,* 23–35.

Hillocks, G. (1982a). Inquiry and the composing process: Theory and research. *College English, 44,* 659–673.

Hillocks, G. (1982b). The interaction of instruction, teacher comment, and revision in teaching the composing process. *Research in the Teaching of English, 16,* 261–278.

Hirsch, E. D. (1977). *The philosophy of composition.* Chicago, IL: University of Chicago Press.

Hoggart, R. (1957). *The uses of literacy.* New York: Oxford University Press.

Howell, W. S. (1971). *Eighteenth-century British logic and rhetoric.* Princeton, NJ: Princeton University Press.

Hull, G., Arnowitz, D., & Smith, W. (1981, November). Interrupting visual feedback in writing. Paper presented at a postconvention workshop at the Annual Meeting of the National Council of Teachers of English, Boston, MA.

Humes, A. (1980). *A method for evaluating writing samples.* Technical Note 2–80/02. Los Alamitos, CA: SWRL Educational Research and Development. (ERIC No. ED 193 631.)

Hunt, K. W. (1965). *Grammatical structures written at three grade levels.* (NCTE Research Report, No. 3.) Champaign, IL: NCTE.

Hunt, K. W. (1970). *Syntactic maturity in schoolchildren and adults.* (Monographs of the Society for Research in Child Development, No. 134.) Chicago, IL: University of Chicago Press.

Hunt, K. W. (1977). Early blooming and late blooming syntactic structures. *In* C. Cooper & L. Odell (Ed.), *Evaluating writing: Describing, measuring, judging.* Urbana, IL: NCTE.

Hymes, D. ([1964]. 1972). Introduction: Toward ethnographies of communication. *In* P. Giglioli (Ed.), *Language and social context.* Baltimore, MD: Penguin.

Hymes, D. (1974). *Foundations in sociolinguistics: An ethnographic approach.* Philadelphia, PA: University of Pennsylvania Press.

Hymes, D. (1980). What is ethnography? *In* D. Hymes (Ed.), *Language in education: Ethnolinguistic essays.* Arlington, VA: Center for Applied Linguistics.

Hymes, D. (1982). Ethnolinguistic study of classroom discourse. Final report. (ERIC No. ED 217 710.)

Hymes, D., & others. (1981). Ethnographic monitoring of children's acquisition of reading/language arts skills in and out of the classroom. Vols. 1, 2, & 3. (ERIC No. ED 208 096.)

Iser, W. (1978). *The act of reading: A theory of aesthetic response.* Baltimore, MD: Johns Hopkins University Press.

Jakobson, R. (1960). Linguistics and poetics. *In* T. Sebeok (Ed.), *Style in language.* Cambridge, MA: M.I.T. Press.

Johannessen, L., Kahn, E., & Walter, C. (1982). *Designing and sequencing prewriting activities*. Urbana, IL: National Council of Teachers of English.

Johnson, S. T. (1969). Some tentative strictures on generative rhetoric. *College English, 31,* 155–165.

Kamler, B. (1980). One child, one teacher, one classroom: The story of one piece of writing. *Language Arts, 57,* 680–693.

Kantor, K. J., Kirby, D. R., & Goetz, J. P. (1981). Research in context: Ethnographic studies in English education. *Research in the Teaching of English, 15,* 293–309.

Karrfalt, D. (1968). The generation of paragraphs and larger units. *College Composition and Communication, 19,* 211–217.

Kerek, A. (1981). The combining process. *In* M. C. Hairston & C. L. Selfe (Ed.), *Selected papers from the 1981 Texas Writing Research Conference.* Austin, TX: University of Texas at Austin.

Kerek, A., Daiker, D., & Morenberg, M. (1979). The effects of intensive sentence combining on the writing ability of college freshmen. *In* D. McQuade (Ed.), *Linguistics, stylistics, and the teaching of composition.* Akron, OH: L&S Books.

Kerek, A., Daiker, D., & Morenberg, M. (1980). Sentence combining and college composition. *Perceptual and Motor Skills: Monograph Supplement, 51,* 1059–1157.

Kinneavy, J. L. (1971). *A theory of discourse.* Englewood Cliffs, NJ: Prentice-Hall.

Kinneavy, J. L. (1979). Sentence combining in a comprehensive language framework. *In* D. Daiker, A. Kerek, & M. Morenberg (Ed.), *Sentence combining and the teaching of writing.* Akron, OH: L&S Books.

Kinneavy, J. L. (1982). Syllabus for English 306. Mimeograph, Department of English, University of Texas at Austin.

Kinneavy, J. L., Cope, J. Q., & Campbell, J. W. (1976). *Writing—basic modes of organization.* Dubuque, IA: Kendall/Hunt.

Kintsch, W. (1974). *The representation of meaning in memory.* Hillsdale, NJ: Lawrence Erlbaum.

Kintsch, W., & Dijk, T. A. van. (1978). Toward a model of text comprehension and production. *Psychological Review, 85,* 363–394.

Kirkpatrick, E. A. (1891). Number of words in ordinary vocabulary. *Science, 18,* 107–108.

Klaus, C., Lloyd-Jones, R., Brown, R., Littlefair, W., Mullis, I., Miller, D., & Verity, D. (1979). *Composing childhood experience: An approach to writing and learning in the elementary grades.* St. Louis, MO: CEMREL.

Kline, C. R. & Memering, W. D. (1977). Formal fragments: The English minor sentence. *Research in the Teaching of English, 11,* 97–110.

Knoblauch, C., & Brannon, L. (1981). Teacher commentary on student writing: The state of the art. *Freshman English News, 10,* 1–4.

Kress, G. (1982). *Learning to write.* London: Routledge and Kegan Paul.

Kroll, B. M. (1978). Cognitive egocentrism and the problem of audience awareness in written discourse. *Research in the Teaching of English, 12,* 269–281.

Kroll, B. M. (1981). Developmental relationships between speaking and writing. *In* B. M. Kroll & R. J. Vann (Ed.), *Exploring speaking—writing relationships.* Urbana, IL: NCTE.

Kroll, B. M. & Schafer, J. C. (1978). Error analysis and the teaching of composition. *College Composition and Communication, 29,* 242–248.

Kuhn, T. (1977). *The essential tension: Selected studies in scientific tradition and change.* Chicago, IL: University of Chicago Press.

Labov, W. (1966). *The social stratification of English in New York City.* Arlington, VA: Center for Applied Linguistics.

Labov, W. (1973). *Language in the inner city.* Philadelphia, PA: University of Pennsylvania Press.

LaBrandt, L. (1933). A study of certain language developments in children in grades four to twelve, inclusive. *Genetic Psychology Monographs, 14,* 387–489.

Larson, R. L. (1971). Toward a linear rhetoric of the essay. *College Composition and Communication, 22,* 140–146.

Larson, R. L. (1976). Structure and form in nonfiction prose. In G. Tate (Ed.), *Teaching composition: Ten bibliographical essays.* Forth Worth, TX: Texas Christian University.

Lautamatti, L. (1978). Observations on the development of the topic in simplified discourse. In V. Kohonen & N. E. Enkvist (Ed.), *Text linguistics, cognitive learning and langauge teaching.* Turku, Finland: University of Turku.

Leonard, S. A. (1923). How English teachers correct papers. *English Journal, 12,* 517–532.

Leont'ev, A. A. (1977). Some new trends in Soviet psycholinguistics. In J. V. Wertsch (Ed.), *Recent trends in Soviet psycholinguistics.* White Plains, NY: M. E. Sharpe.

Lieberman, D. (1979). Behaviorism and the mind. A (limited) call for a return to introspection. *American Psychologist, 34,* 319–333.

Lloyd-Jones, R. (1977). Primary trait scoring. In C. R. Cooper, & L. Odell (Ed.), *Evaluating writing: Describing, measuring, judging.* Urbana, IL: NCTE.

Loban, W. (1976). *Language development: Kindergarten through grade twelve.* (NCTE Research Report No. 18.) Urbana, IL: NCTE.

Lockridge, K. A. (1974). *Literacy in colonial New England.* New York: Norton.

Longacre, R. E. (1976). *An anatomy of speech notions.* Lisse, Netherlands: Peter de Ridder.

Lunsford, A. (1978). What we know—and don't know—about remedial writing. *College Composition and Communication, 29,* 47–52.

Lunsford, A. (1979). Cognitive development and the basic writer. *College English, 41,* 38–46.

Luria, A. R. (1981). *Language and cognition.* J. V. Wertsch (Ed.), New York: John Wiley & Sons.

Lybert, E. K., & Cummings, D. W. (1969). Rhetorical syntax, economy, and the theme-rheme distinction. *Language and Style, 2,* 244–256.

MacNeilage, P., & Ladefoged, P. (1978). The production of speech and language. In E. C. Carterette & H. Friedman (Ed.), *Handbook of perception.* New York: Academic.

Macrorie, K. (1980). *Telling writing.* (3rd ed.). Rochelle Park, NJ: Hayden.

Maimon, E. P. & Nodine, B. F. (1978). Measuring syntactic growth: Errors and expectations in sentence-combining practice with college freshmen. *Research in the Teaching of English, 12,* 233–244.

Maimon, E. P., Belcher, G. L., Hearn, G. W., Nodine, B. F., & O'Connor, F. W. (1981). *Writing in the arts and sciences.* Cambridge, MA: Winthrop.

Mandler, J. M. & Johnson, N. S. (1977). Remembrance of things parsed: Story structure and recall. *Cognitive Psychology, 9,* 111–151.

Markman, E. M. (1979). Realizing that you don't understand: Elementary school children's awareness of inconsistencies. *Child Development, 50,* 643–655.

Matalene, C. B. (1982). Objective testing: Politics, problems, possibilities. *College English, 44,* 368–381.

Matsuhashi, A. (1981). Pausing and planning: The tempo of written discourse production. *Research in the Teaching of English, 15,* 113–134.

Matsuhashi, A. (1982). Explorations in the real-time production of written discourse. In M. Nystrand (Ed.), *What writers know: The language, process, and structure of written discourse.* New York: Academic Press.

McDonald, D. (1983). Natural language generation as a computational problem: An introduction. *In* W. Klein & W. J. M. Levelt (Ed.), *Crossing the boundaries in linguistics: Studies presented to Manfred Bierwisch.* Dordrecht, Netherlands: Reidel.

McDonald, N., Frase, L., Gingrich, P., & Kennan, S. (1982). The Writer's Workbench: Computer aids for text analysis. *IEEE Transactions on Communications. Special issue on communication in the automated office,* 105–110.

McLuhan, M. (1962). *The Gutenberg galaxy.* Toronto, Ontario, Canada: University of Toronto Press.

Meichenbaum, D. (1977). *Cognitive-behavior modification: An integrative approach.* New York: Plenum.

Meichenbaum, D., Burland, S., Gruson, L., & Cameron, R. (1979, October). Metacognitive assessment. Paper presented at the Conference on the Growth of Insight, Wisconsin Research and Development Center.

Meichenbaum, D., & Butler, L. (1980). Cognitive ethology: Assessing the streams of cognition and emotion. *In* K. Blankstein, P. Pliner, & J. Polivy (Ed.), *Advances in the study of communication and affect: Assessment and modification of emotional behavior.* New York: Plenum.

Mellon, J. C. (1969). *Transformational sentence-combining: A method for enhancing the development of syntactic fluency in English composition.* NCTE Research Report No. 10. Champaign, IL: NCTE.

Mellon, J. C. (1979). Issues in the theory and practice of sentence combining: A twenty year perspective. *In* D. Daiker, A. Kerek, & M. Morenberg (Ed.), *Sentence combining and the teaching of writing.* Akron, OH: L&S Books.

Meyer, B. J. F. (1975). *The organization of prose and its effect upon memory.* Amsterdam, Netherlands: North Holland.

Meyer, B. J. F. (1979). Organizational patterns in prose and their use in reading. *In* M. L. Kamil, & A. J. Moe (Ed.), *Reading research: Studies and applications.* Clemson, SC: National Reading Conference, Inc.

Meyer, B. J. F. (1981). Following the author's top-level structure. *In* R. J. Tierney, P. Anders & J. Mitchell (Ed.), *Understanding readers' understanding.* Hillsdale, NJ: Lawrence Erlbaum.

Meyer, B. J. F. & Freedle, R. O. (1979). *The effects of different discourse types on recall.* (Prose Learning Series #6). Tempe, AZ: Arizona State University, Department of Educational Psychology.

Meyer, B. J. F., & Rice, G. E. (1982). The interaction of reader strategies and the organization of text. *Text, 2,* 155–192.

Milic, L. T. (1965). Theories of style and their implications for the teaching of composition. *College Composition and Communication, 16,* 66–69, 126.

Miller, G. A. (1967). *The psychology of communication.* New York: Basic Books.

Miller, G., Galanter, E., & Pribram, K. (1960). *Plans and the structure of behavior.* New York: Holt, Rinehart, & Winston.

Mills, H. (1974). *Commanding sentences: A charted course in basic writing skills.* Glenview, IL: Scott, Foresman.

Minsky, M. A. (1975). A framework for representing knowledge. *In* P. Winston, (Ed.), *The psychology of computer vision.* New York: McGraw-Hill.

Mischel, T. (1974). A case study of a twelfth-grade writer. *Research in the Teaching of English, 8,* 303–314.

Mishler, E. G. (1979). Meaning in context: Is there any other kind? *Harvard Educational Review, 49,* 1–19.

Moffett, J. W. (1968). *Teaching the universe of discourse.* Boston, MA: Houghton Mifflin.

Morenberg, M., Daiker, D., & Kerek, A. (1978). Sentence combining at the college level: An experimental study. *Research in the Teaching of English, 12,* 245–256.

Morgan, J. L. & Sellner, M. B. (1980). Discourse and linguistic theory. In R. J. Spiro, B. C. Bruce, & W. F. Brewer (Ed.), Theoretical issues in reading comprehension. Hillsdale, NJ: Lawrence Erlbaum.

Morris, C. (1946). Signs, language, and behavior. New York: George Braziller.

Mosenthal, P. (1983). On defining writing and classroom writing competence. In P. Mosenthal, L. Tamor, & S. Walmsley (Ed.), Research on writing: Principles and methods. New York: Longman.

Mullis, I. (1980). The primary trait system for scoring writing tasks. Mimeographed manuscript, Educational Commission of the States.

Murray, D. M. (1978). Internal revision: A process of discovery. In C. R. Cooper & L. Odell (Ed.), Research on composing: Points of departure. Urbana, IL: NCTE.

Murray, D. M. (1980). Writing as process: How writing finds its own meaning. In T. Donovan & B. McClelland (Ed.), Eight approaches to teaching composition. Urbana, IL: NCTE.

Myers, M. (1983). Prototype theory and holistic scoring. Notes from the National Testing Network in Writing, 2, 15, 20.

National Assessment of Educational Progress. (1976). Expressive writing: Results from the Second National Assessment of Writing. (Report No. 05-W-02.) Denver, CO: National Assessment of Educational Progress.

National Assessment of Educational Progress. (1977). Write/rewrite: An assessment of revision skills. (Writing Report No. 05-W-04). Denver, CO: NAEP.

National Assessment of Educational Progress. (1980). Writing achievement, 1969-79: Results from the Third National Writing Assessment. (Volume III, Report No. 10-W-03.) Denver: National Assessment of Educational Progress.

Newell, A. (1980). Reasoning, problem solving, and decision processes: The problemspace as a fundamental category. In R. S. Nickerson (Ed.), Attention and performance VIII. Hillsdale, NJ: Lawrence Erlbaum.

Newell, A., & Simon, H. (1972). Human problem solving. Englewood Cliffs, NJ: Prentice-Hall.

Nold, E. (1979). Revising: Toward a theory. (ERIC No. ED 172 212.)

Nold, E. W. (1981). Revising. In C. H. Frederiksen & J. F. Dominic (Ed.), Writing: The nature, development, and teaching of written communication; Volume 2, Writing: Process, development and communication. Hillsdale, NJ: Lawrence Erlbaum.

Nold, E. W. & Freedman, S. W. (1977). An analysis of readers' responses to essays. Research in the Teaching of English, 11, 164-174.

Nystrand, M. (1982a). An analysis of errors in written communication. In M. Nystrand (Ed.), What writers know: The language, process, and structure of written discourse. New York: Academic Press.

Nystrand, M. (1982b). Rhetoric's 'audience' and lingustics' 'speech community': Implications for understanding writing, reading, and text. In M. Nystrand (Ed.), What writers know: The language, process, and structure of written discourse. New York: Academic Press.

Nystrand, M. (in preparation). Written discourse as social interaction. New York: Academic Press.

Ochs, E. (1979a). Planned and unplanned discourse. In T. Givon (Ed.), Syntax and semantics, Vol. 12: Discourse and syntax. New York: Academic.

Ochs, E. (1979b). Social foundations of language. In R. Freedle (Ed.), New directions in discourse processing. Norwood, NJ: Ablex.

Odell, L. (1974). Measuring the effect of instruction in pre-writing. Research in the Teaching of English, 8, 228-240.

Odell, L. (1977). Measuring changes in intellectual processes as one dimension of growth in writing. In C. R. Cooper, & L. Odell (Ed.), Evaluating writing: Describ-

ing, measuring, judging. Urbana, IL: NCTE.

Odell, L. (1980). Teaching writing by teaching the process of discovery: An inter-disciplinary enterprise. *In* L. W. Gregg & E. R. Steinberg (Ed.), *Cognitive processes in writing.* Hillsdale, NJ: Lawrence Erlbaum.

Odell, L. (1981). Defining and assessing competence in writing. *In* C. R. Cooper (Ed.), *The nature and measurement of competency in English.* Urbana, IL: NCTE.

Odell, L., & Cooper, C. (1980). Procedures for evaluating writing: Assumptions and needed research. *College English, 42,* 35–43.

Odell, L., & Goswami, D. (1982). Writing in a non-academic setting. *Research in the Teaching of English, 16,* 201–223.

O'Donnell, R. C. (1974). Syntactic differences between speech and writing. *American Speech, 49,* 102–110.

O'Donnell, R. C., Griffin, W. J., & Norris, R. C. (1967). *Syntax of kindergarten and elementary school children: A transformational analysis.* (NCTE Research Report, No. 8.) Champaign, IL: NCTE.

O'Hare, F. (1973). *Sentence combining: Improving student writing without formal grammar instruction.* (NCTE Research Report, No. 15.) Urbana, IL: NCTE.

Ohmann, R. (1976). *English in America: A radical view of the profession.* New York: Oxford University Press.

Ohmann, R. (1982). Reflections on class and language. *College English, 44,* 1–17.

Olson, D. R. (1977). From utterance to text: The bias of language in speech and writing. *Harvard Educational Review, 47,* 257–281.

Olson, D. R. (1980). Some social aspects of meaning in oral and written language. *In* D. R. Olson (Ed.), *The social foundations of language and thought: Essays in honor of Jerome S. Bruner.* New York: Norton.

Olson, G., Mack, R., & Duffy, S. (1981). Cognitive aspects of genre. *Poetics, 10,* 283–315.

Ong, W. J. (1975). The writer's audience is always a fiction. *PMLA, 90,* 9–21.

Oppheim, A. L. (1977). *Ancient Mesopotamia: Portrait of a dead civilization.* Chicago, IL: University of Chicago Press.

Palkova, Z., & Palek, B. (1978). Functional sentence perspective and textlinguistics. *In* W. Dressler (Ed.), *Current trends in textlinguistics.* Berlin: de Gruyter.

Park, D. B. (1982). The meanings of audience. *College English, 44,* 247–257.

Patrick, C. (1937). Creative thought in artists. *Journal of Psychology, 4,* 35–73.

Pattison, R. (1982). *On literacy: The politics of the word from Homer to the Age of Rock.* New York: Oxford University Press.

Peitzman, F. C. (1981). *The composing processes of three college freshmen: Focus on revision.* Doctoral dissertation, New York University.

Penrose, J. M. (1976). A survey of the perceived importance of business communication and other business-related abilities. *Journal of Business Communication, 13,* 17–24.

Perelman, Ch. ([1977]. 1982). *The realm of rhetoric.* (W. Kluback, trans.). Notre Dame, IN: University of Notre Dame Press.

Perelman, Ch., & Olbrechts-Tyteca, L. ([1958]. 1969). *The new rhetoric: A treatise on argumentation.* (J. Wilkinson & P. Weaver, trans.). Notre Dame, IN: University of Notre Dame Press.

Perkins, D. N. (1981). *The mind's best work.* Cambridge, MA: Harvard University Press.

Perl, S. (1978). *Five writers writing: Case studies of the composing processes of unskilled college writers.* Doctoral dissertation, New York University.

Perl, S. (1979). The composing processes of unskilled college writers. *Research in the Teaching of English, 13,* 317–336.

Perl, S. (1980). Understanding composing. *College Composition and Communication, 31*, 363–369.

Piaget, J. ([1926]. 1955). *The language and thought of the child.* (M. Gabain, trans.). New York: Modern Library.

Pianko, S. (1977). *The composing acts of college freshman writers: A description.* Doctoral dissertation, Rutgers University, NJ.

Pianko, S. (1979a). A description of the composing processes of college freshmen writers. *Research in the Teaching of English, 13*, 5–22.

Pianko, S. (1979b). Reflection: A critical component of the composing process. *College Composition and Communication, 30*, 275–278.

Pike, K. L. (1954). *Language in relation to a unified theory of the structure of human behavior, Part 1.* Glendale, CA: Summer Institute of Linguistics.

Pitkin, W. (1977a). Hierarchies and the discourse hierarchy. *College English, 38*, 648–659.

Pitkin, W. (1977b). X/Y: Some basic strategies of discourse. *College English, 38*, 660–672.

Plato. (1919). *Euthyphro, Apology, Crito, Phaedo, Phaedrus.* (H. N. Fowler, trans.). London: William Heinemann.

Plato. (1961). *Ion.* In E. Hamilton & H. Cairns (Ed.), *The collected dialogues of Plato.* (L. Cooper, trans.). Princeton, NJ: Princeton University Press.

Plimpton, G. (Ed.). (1963). *Writers at work: The 'Paris Review' interviews (2nd series).* New York: Viking Press.

Plimpton, G. (Ed.). (1967). *Writers at work: The 'Paris Review' interviews (3rd series).* New York: Viking Press.

Plimpton, G. (Ed.). (1976). *Writers at work: The 'Paris Review' interviews (4th series).* New York: Viking Press.

Polanyi, M. (1958). *Personal knowledge: Towards a post-critical philosophy.* Chicago, IL: University of Chicago Press.

Popham, W. J. (1981). *Modern educational measurement.* Englewood Cliffs, NJ: Prentice-Hall.

Popper, K. (1963). *Conjectures and refutations: The growth of scientific knowledge.* New York: Harper & Row.

Prince, E. F. (1981). Toward a taxonomy of given-new information. *In* P. Cole (Ed.), *Radical pragmatics.* New York: Academic Press.

Quintilian. (1920–1922). *Institutio oratoria.* 4 vols. (H. E. Butler, trans.). London: Loeb Classical Library.

Rader, M. (1982). Context in written language: The case of imaginative fiction. *In* D. Tannen (Ed.), *Spoken and written language: Exploring orality and literacy.* Norwood, NJ: Ablex.

Rader, M. H., & Wunsch, A. P. (1980). A survey of communication practices of business school graduates by job category and undergraduate major. *Journal of Business Communication, 17*, 33–41.

Read, C. (1980). Creative spelling by young children. *In* T. Shopen & J. M. Williams (Ed.), *Standards and dialects in English.* Cambridge, England: Winthrop.

Read, C. (1981). Writing is not the inverse of reading for young children. *In* C. H. Frederiksen & J. F. Dominic (Ed.), *Writing: The nature, development, and teaching of written communication; Volume 2, Writing: Process, development and communication.* Hillsdale, NJ: Lawrence Erlbaum.

Reddy, M. (1979). The conduit metaphor. *In* A. Ortony (Ed.), *Metaphor and thought.* Cambridge, England: Cambridge University Press.

Redish, J. C. (1981). *The language of bureaucracy.* (Document Design Project Technical Report No. 15.) Washington, DC: American Institutes for Research.

Reigstad, T. (1980). *Conferencing practices of professional writers: Ten case studies.* Doctoral dissertation, State University of New York at Buffalo.

Reither, J. (1981). Some ideas of Michael Polanyi and some implications for teaching writing. *Pre/Text, 2,* 33–43.

Rodgers, P. (1966). A discourse-centered rhetoric of the paragraph. *College Composition and Communication, 17,* 2–11.

Rohman, D. G. (1965). Pre-writing: The stage of discovery in the writing process. *College Composition and Communication, 16,* 106–112.

Rohman, D. G., & Wlecke, A. O. (1964). *Pre-writing: The construction and application of models for concept formation in writing.* U.S. Office of Education Cooperative Research Project, No. 2174. East Lansing, MI: Michigan State University.

Rommetveit, R. (1974). *On message structure.* New York: John Wiley & Sons.

Rose, M. (1980). Rigid rules, inflexible plans, and the stifling of language: A cognitivist analysis of writer's block. *College Composition and Communication, 31,* 389–401.

Rose, M. (1984). *Writer's block: The cognitive dimension.* Carbondale, IL: Southern Illinois University Press.

Rosenberg, S. (1977). Semantic constraints on sentence production: An experimental approach. *In* S. Rosenberg (Ed.), *Sentence production.* Hillsdale, NJ: Lawrence Erlbaum.

Rubin, A. (1982). The computer confronts language arts: Cans and shoulds for education. *In* A. C. Wilkinson (Ed.), *Classroom computers and cognitive science.* New York: Academic Press.

Rumelhart, D. E. (1975). Notes on a schema for stories. *In* D. G. Bobrow & A. M. Collins (Ed.), *Representation and understanding: Studies in cognitive science.* New York: Academic Press.

Rumelhart, D. E. & Ortony, A. (1977). The representation of knowledge in memory. *In* R. C. Anderson, R. J. Spiro, & W. E. Montague (Ed.), *Schooling and the acquisition of knowledge.* Hillsdale, NJ: Lawrence Erlbaum.

Ryle, G. (1949). *The concept of mind.* New York: Barnes & Noble.

Saussure, F. de. (1959). *Course in modern linguistics.* (W. Baskin, trans.). New York: Philosophical Library.

Sawkins, M. W. (1971). *The oral responses of selected fifth-grade children to questions concerning their writing expression.* Doctoral dissertation, State University of New York at Buffalo.

Scardamalia, M. (1981). How children cope with the cognitive demands of writing. *In* C. H. Frederiksen & J. F. Dominic (Ed.), *Writing: The nature, development, and teaching of written communication; Volume 2, Writing: Process, development and communication.* Hillsdale, NJ: Lawrence Erlbaum.

Scardamalia, M., & Bereiter, C. (1983a). Child as co-investigator: Helping children gain insight into their own mental processsses. *In* S. Paris, G. Olson, & H. Stevenson (Ed.), *Learning and motivation in the classroom.* Hillsdale, NJ: Lawrence Erlbaum.

Scardamalia, M. & Bereiter, C. (1983b). The development of evaluative, diagnostic, and remedial capabilities in children's composing. *In* M. Martlew (Ed.), *The psychology of written language: A developmental approach.* London: John Wiley & Sons.

Scardamalia, M., & Bereiter, C. (in press). Written composition. *In* M. Wittrock (Ed.), *Handbook of research on teaching.* (3rd ed.). New York: Macmillan.

Scardamalia, M., Bereiter, C., & Goelman, H. (1982). The role of production factors in writing ability. *In* M. Nystrand (Ed.), *What writers know: The language, process, and structure of written discourse.* New York: Academic Press.

Scardamalia, M., Bereiter, C., & McDonald, J. (1977). Role taking in written communication investigated by manipulating anticipatory knowledge. (ERIC No. ED 151 792.)

Schank, R. C. (1975). *Conceptual information processing.* New York: American Elsevier.

Schank, R. C., & Abelson, R. P. (1977). *Scripts, plans, goals, and understanding: An inquiry into human knowledge structures.* Hillsdale, NJ: Lawrence Erlbaum.

Schiller, F. von. ([1795]. 1966). *Naive and sentimental poetry and On the sublime.* (J. A. Elias, trans.). New York: Frederick Ungar.

Schmandt-Besserat, D. (1977). *An archiac recording system and the origin of writing.* Syro-Mesopotamian Studies, Vol. 1. Malibu, CA: Undena.

Scott, W. A. (1955). Reliability of content analysis: The case of nominal scale coding. *Public Opinion Quarterly, 19,* 321–325.

Scribner, S., & Cole, M. (1981a). *The psychology of literacy.* Cambridge, MA: Harvard University Press.

Scribner, S., & Cole, M. (1981b). Unpackaging literacy. *In* M. F. Whiteman (Ed.), *Writing: The nature, development, and teaching of written communication; Volume 1, Variation in writing: Functional and linguistic-cultural differences.* Hillsdale, NJ: Lawrence Erlbaum.

Searle, D., & Dillon, D. (1980). The message of marking: Teacher written responses to student writing at intermediate grade levels' responses to teacher comments. *Research in the Teaching of English, 14,* 233–242.

Searle, J. (1969). *Speech acts.* London: Cambridge University Press.

Selfe, C. L. (1981). *The composing processes of four high and low writing apprehensives: A modified case study.* Doctoral dissertation, University of Texas at Austin.

Selzer, J. (1983). The composing processes of an engineer. *College Composition and Communication, 34,* 178–187.

Shaughnessy, M. (1977). *Errors and expectations: A guide for the teacher of basic writing.* New York: Oxford University Press.

Shuy, R. W. (1981). Toward a developmental theory of writing. *In* C. H. Frederiksen & J. F. Dominic (Ed.), *Writing: The nature, development, and teaching of written communication; Volume 2, Writing: Process, development and communication.* Hillsdale, NJ: Lawrence Erlbaum.

Shuy, R. W., & Larkin, D. L. (1978). Linguistic consideration in the simplification/ clarification of insurance policy language. *Discourse Processes, 1,* 305–321.

Shweder, R. A. (1982). On savages and other children. *American Anthropologist, 84,* 354–366.

Simon, H. A. (1977). What computers mean for man and society. *Science* (18 March), *195,* 1087–1094, 1186–1191.

Sinclair, J. & Coulthard, R. (1975). *Towards an analysis of discourse: The English used by teachers and pupils.* London: Oxford University Press.

Smith, E. L. (1982). *Writer-reader interactiveness in four genres of scientific English.* Doctoral dissertation, University of Michigan.

Smith, F. (1982). *Writing and the writer.* New York: Holt, Rinehart & Winston.

Smith, J. P. (1982). Writing in a remedial reading program: A case study. *Language Arts, 59,* 245–253.

Sommers, N. I. (1978). *Revision in the composing process: A case study of experienced writers and student writers.* Doctoral dissertation, Boston University.

Sommers, N. I. (1980). Revision strategies of student writers and experienced adult writers. *College Composition and Communication, 31,* 378–388.

Sommers, N. I. (1982). Responding to student writing. *College Composition and Communication, 33,* 148–156.

Sowers, S. (1979). A six-year-old's writing process: The first half of first grade. *Language Arts, 56,* 829–835.

Spindler, G. (Ed.). (1982). *Doing the ethnography of schooling: Educational anthropology in action.* New York: Holt, Rinehart & Winston.

Stallard, C. K. (1974). An analysis of the writing behavior of good student writers. *Research in the Teaching of English, 8,* 206–218.

Stein, N. L., & Trabasso, T. (1982). What's in a story: An approach to comprehension and instruction. In R. Glaser (Ed.), *Advances in instructional psychology.* Hillsdale, NJ: Lawrence Erlbaum.

Steinmann, M. (1982). Speech-act theory and writing. In M. Nystrand (Ed.), *What writers know: The language, process, and structure of written discourse.* New York: Academic Press.

Sternberg, R. J. (1977). *Intelligence, information processing, and analogical reasoning: The componential analysis of human abilities.* Hillsdale, NJ: Lawrence Erlbaum.

Sternglass, M. (1982). Applications of the Wilkinson model of writing maturity to college writing. *College Composition and Communication, 33,* 167–175.

Stevens, A. (1973). *The effects of positive and negative evaluation on the written composition of low performing high school students.* Doctoral dissertation, Boston University.

Stiggins, R. J. (1982). A comparison of direct and indirect writing assessment methods. *Research in the Teaching of English, 16,* 101–114.

Stine, D., & Skarzenski, D. (1979). Priorities for the business communication classroom: A survey of business and academe. *Journal of Business Communication, 16,* 15–30.

Stormzand, M. J., & O'Shea, M. V. (1924). *How much English grammar.* Baltimore, MD: Warwick and York.

Strassman, P. A. (1981, June). Information systems and literacy. Paper presented at the Conference on Literacy in the 1980's, Ann Arbor, MI.

Stubbs, M. (1980). *Language and literacy: The sociolinguistics of reading and writing.* London: Routledge & Kegan Paul.

Swaney, J., Janik, C., Bond, S., & Hayes, J. R. (1981). *Editing for comprehension: Improving the process through reading protocols.* (Document Design Project Technical Report No. 14.) Pittsburgh, PA: Carnegie-Mellon University.

Swarts, H., Flower, L., & Hayes, J. R. (1984). Designing protocol studies of the writing process: An introduction. In R. Beach & L. Bridwell (Ed.), *New directions in composition research.* New York: Guilford.

Szwed, J. F. (1981). The ethnography of literacy. In M. F. Whiteman (Ed.), *Writing: The nature, development, and teaching of written communication; Volume 1, Variation in writing: Functional and linguistic-cultural differences.* Hillsdale, NJ: Lawrence Erlbaum.

Takala, S., Purves, A. C., & Buckmaster, A. (1982). On the interrelationships between language, perception, thought and culture and their relevance to the assessment of written composition. *Evaluation in Education, 5,* 317–342.

Tannen, D. (1981). The myth of orality and literacy. In W. Frawley (Ed.), *Linguistics and literacy.* New York: Plenum Press.

Tannen, D. (1982a). Oral and literate strategies in spoken and written narratives. *Language, 58,* 1–21.

Tannen, D. (Ed.). (1982b). *Spoken and written language: Exploring orality and literacy.* Norwood, NJ: Ablex.

Taylor, W., & Hoedt, K. (1966). The effect of praise upon the quality and quantity of creative writing. *Journal of Educational Research, 60,* 80–83.

Thorndyke, P. W. (1977). Cognitive structures in comprehension and memory of narrative discourse. *Cognitive Psychology, 9*, 77–110.

Tibbetts, A. M. (1970). On the practical uses of a grammatical system: A note on Christensen and Johnson. *College English, 31*, 870–878.

Toulmin, S. (1958). *The uses of argument.* Cambridge, England: Cambridge University Press.

Vachek, J. (1973). *Written language: General problems and problems of English.* The Hague, Netherlands: Mouton.

Vachek, J. (Ed.). (1975). *A functional analysis of present-day English on a general linguistic basis.* Prague, Czechoslovakia: Academia.

Vande Kopple, W. (1982). Functional sentence perspective, composition, and reading. *College Composition and Communication, 33*, 50–63.

Voss, J., Vesonder, G., & Spilich, G. (1980). Text generation and recall by high-knowledge and low-knowledge individuals. *Journal of Verbal Learning and Verbal Behavior, 19*, 651–667.

Vygotsky, L. S. ([1934]. 1962). *Thought and language.* (E. Hanfmann & G. Vakar, trans.). Cambridge, MA: M.I.T. Press.

Walker, R. L. (1970). The common writer: A case for parallel structure. *College Composition and Communication, 21*, 373–379.

Wallas, G. (1926). *The art of thought.* New York: Harcourt, Brace.

Walsche, R. D. (Ed.). (1981). *Donald Graves in Australia.* Rozelle, N.S.W., Australia: Primary English Teaching Association.

Wesdorp, H., Bauer, B. A., & Purves, A. C. (1982). Toward a conceptualization of the scoring of written composition. *Evaluation in Education, 5*, 299–315.

Whiteman, M. F. (1981). Dialect influence in writing. In M. F. Whiteman (Ed.), *Writing: The nature, development, and teaching of written communication; Volume 1, Variation in writing: Functional and linguistic-cultural differences.* Hillsdale, NJ: Lawrence Erlbaum.

Widdowson, H. G. (1978). *Teaching language as communication.* New York: Oxford University Press.

Wiener, N. (1948). *Cybernetics: or control and communication in the animal and the machine.* New York: John Wiley & Sons.

Willard, C. A. (1982). Argument fields. In J. R. Cox & C. A. Willard (Ed.), *Advances in argumentation theory and research.* Carbondale, IL: Southern Illinois University Press.

Williams. J. M. (1979). Defining complexity. *College English, 40*, 595–609.

Williams, J. M. (1981). The phenomenology of error. *College Composition and Communication, 32*, 152–168.

Winston, P. (1977). *Artificial intelligence.* Reading, MA: Addison-Wesley.

Winterowd, W. R. (1970). The grammar of coherence. *College English, 31*, 828–835.

Winterowd, W. R. (1976). Linguistics and composition. In G. Tate (Ed.), *Teaching composition: Ten bibliographical essays.* Fort Worth, TX: Texas Christian University Press.

Witte, S. (1983). Topical structure and revision: An exploratory study. *College Composition and Communication, 34*, 313–341.

Witte, S., & Faigley, L. (1981). Coherence, cohesion, and writing quality. *College Composition and Communication, 32*, 189–204.

Witte, S., & Faigley, L. (1983). *Evaluating College Writing Programs.* Carbondale, IL: Southern Illinois University Press.

Witte, S., Meyer, P., & Miller, T. (1982). *A national survey of college teachers of writing.* (Writing Program Assessment Project, Technical Report No. 4.) Austin, TX: University of Texas. (ERIC No. ED 219 779.)

Wolk, A. (1970). The relative importance of the final free modifier: A quantitative analysis. *Research in the Teaching of English, 4*, 59–68.

Woodruff, E., Bereiter, C., & Scardamalia, M. (1981–1982). On the road to computer assisted compositions. *Journal of Educational Technology Systems, 10*, 133–148.

Woods, W. (1970). Transition network grammars for natural language analysis. *Communications of the Association for Computing Machinery, 13*, 591–606.

Young, R. (1978). Paradigms and problems: Needed research in rhetorical invention. *In* C. R. Cooper & L. Odell (Ed.), *Research on composing: Points of departure.* Urbana, IL: NCTE.

Young, R., Becker, A., & Pike, K. (1970). *Rhetoric, discovery, and change.* New York: Harcourt, Brace.

Young, R., & Koen, F. (1973). *The tagmemic discovery procedure: An evaluation of its uses in the teaching of rhetoric.* Ann Arbor, MI: University of Michigan. (ERIC No. ED 084 517.)

Zebroski, J. T. (1981). Soviet psycholinguistics: Implications for the teaching of writing. *In* W. Frawley (Ed.), *Linguistics and literacy.* New York: Plenum Press.

Ziv, N. (1981). *The effect of teacher and peer comments on the writing of four college freshmen.* Doctoral dissertation, New York University.

Author Index

Italics indicate bibliographic citations

A

Abelson, R.P., 98, *261*
Agar, M., 98, 179, *243*
Akinnaso, F.N., 72, 73, *243*
Alatis, J.E., 86, *243*
Alred, G.J., x, *243*
Anderson, J.R., 29, *243*
Anderson, P.V., 78, *243*
Anderson, R.C., 16, 86, *243*
Applebee, A.N., 30, 40, *243*
Arbur, R., 64, *243*
Aristotle, 15–16, 30, 39, 82, 144, *243*
Arnold, L.V., 62, *243*
Arnowitz, D., 32, *253*
Arthur, B., 59, *243*
Atlas, M., 35, *243*
Atwell, M., 32, *243*
Austin, J., 45, 71, *243*

B

Bach, E., 19, 71, *243*
Bach, K., 71, *244*
Bain, A., 30, *244*
Barritt, L., 6, 82, *244*
Barthes, R., 12, *244*
Bartholomae, D., 49, 179, *244*
Bartlett, E.J., 59, *244*
Bartlett, F., 86, *244*
Basso, K.H., 94, *244*
Bata, E.J., 62, *244*
Bauer, B.A., 205, *263*
Bazerman, C., 12, 57, 88, *244*
Beach, R., 57, 62, 163, *244*
Bean, J.C., 58, *244*
Beaugrande, R. de, 8–10, 43, 44, 70, 79, 80, *244*
Beck, P., 40, 176, *244*

Becker, A., 17, 38, 39, 73, 96, *244*, *264*
Belcher, G.L., 208, *255*
Bell, D., 6, 78, *244*
Belmont, J., 172, *246*
Bereiter, C., 24, 26, 28, 29, 31, 36–41, 46, 47, 58, 64, 65, 67, 165, *244*, *245*, *246*, *260*, *261*, *264*
Berkenkotter, C., 37, 41, 60, 65, *245*
Berlin, J.A., 15, *245*
Bernstein, B., 13, *245*
Berthoff, A.E., 207, *245*
Bever, T.G., 44, *250*
Bissex, G.L., 69, *245*
Bitzer, L., 33, 79, *245*
Bizzell, P., 11, 17, *245*
Black, J., 71, *245*
Bloom, B.S., 107, *245*
Bloom, S., 176, *245*
Bloomfield, L., 18, 68, *245*
Bond, S., 66, *262*
Booth, W.C., 33, *245*
Bower, G.H., 29, *243*
Bracewell, R.J., 30, *245*
Braddock, R., 3, 4, 74, *245*
Bradley, V.N., 64, *245*
Brannon, L., 62, *254*
Bransford, J., 44, *245*
Breland, H.M., 103, *245*
Brewer, W.F., 74, *245*
Bridwell, L.S., 6, 54, 56, 58, 163, *245*, *246*
Britton, J., 31, 33, 35, 68, 78, 166, *246*
Brown, A.L., 167, *246*
Brown, R., 105, 107, 157, 167, *254*
Bruffee, K., 40, *246*
Bruner, J.S., 71, *246*
Buckmaster, A., 206, *262*
Burgess, T., 31, 33, 35, 78, *246*

Subject Index